Leading in
High Grwth
ASIA

# Leading in High Growth ASIA

Managing Relationship for Teamwork and Change

editors

## Dean Tjosvold
Lingnan University, Hong Kong

## Kwok Leung
City University of Hong Kong

**World Scientific**

NEW JERSEY • LONDON • SINGAPORE • BEIJING • SHANGHAI • HONG KONG • TAIPEI • CHENNAI

*Published by*

World Scientific Publishing Co. Pte. Ltd.

5 Toh Tuck Link, Singapore 596224

*USA office:* 27 Warren Street, Suite 401–402, Hackensack, NJ 07601

*UK office:* 57 Shelton Street, Covent Garden, London WC2H 9HE

**British Library Cataloguing-in-Publication Data**
A catalogue record for this book is available from the British Library.

HD
57.7
.L4375S
2004

**LEADING IN HIGH GROWTH ASIA: MANAGING RELATIONSHIP FOR
TEAMWORK AND CHANGE**

ISBN 981-238-869-9

Printed in Singapore by World Scientific Printers (S) Pte Ltd

Dedication:
To present and future leaders who work with and for Asia

# Contents

*Chapter 1*

# The Leadership Challenge in High Growth Asia: Developing Relationships[1]

Dean Tjosvold
Department of Management, Lingnan University, Hong Kong

and

Kwok Leung
Department of Management, City University of Hong Kong

*The clever combatant looks to the effects of combined energy and does not require too much from individuals. He takes individual talent into account and uses each man according to his capabilities.*

Sun Tzu, military philosopher, 4th Century BC

*Do you trust enough to be trusted?*

Lao Tzu, Taoist philosopher, 6th Century BC

[1] This work has been supported by the Research Grants Council of the Hong Kong Special Administrative Region, China, (Project No: LU3013/01H) to the first author.

The 21$^{st}$ Century may be the Pacific Century but it is already clear that the road forward is circuitous and bumpy. Organizations and economies celebrated in the business press one year, struggle a few years later. Firms cannot be put on autopilot to forge ahead, especially in the high growth countries of Asia with their complex interdependencies and diversity. In particular, the dynamic countries of the Chinese mainland and Taiwan, Southeast Asia, Australia and New Zealand need dynamic, visionary leaders to manage and thrive on change.

Fortunately, the region can draw upon not only its own people and ideas but also people and insights from the West. Companies around the world have contributed their human talents and technological know-how to the rapid development of China, Southeast Asia, Australia, and New Zealand. The region is a meeting ground for East and West and has the potential to capitalize on diverse perspectives to develop competitive, world-class organizations that excel in employee commitment and customer satisfaction.

This book gives voice to countries seldom heard in the management literature dominated as it is by the West. The chapters provide insights into the nature of effective leadership in various Asian cultural contexts and what it takes to be a successful leader in the high-growth countries of Asia Pacific. Managers, human resource specialists, and researchers can enrich their learning by listening to the people of these countries discuss their ideas and experiences. The chapters on leadership in specific countries are useful for those who now work there or may soon do so. But people from around the world can use these chapters to reflect on their own experiences, enrich their understanding, and create new approaches to leadership.

Leading Chinese people is not the same as leading Westerners nor is it the same as leading Thai people. A leadership strategy effective in one culture can be counter-productive in another. With persistent workforce immigration flows, leaders increasingly encounter cultural differences within domestic organizations in Europe and Asia as well as in such traditionally diverse countries as Australia and Canada. This book's chapters help to show how leadership knowledge can be applied in cross-cultural settings.

This introduction develops a foundation for using the book's chapters. It first defines leadership and discusses the Asian and Western common understanding that developing relationships is key to effective leadership. The Introduction then argues how discussions with colleagues can help leaders learn and apply the chapters' ideas. It concludes with a summary of the book's purposes.

## Understanding Effective Leadership

Managers around the world need ideas and support to meet the many challenges of leading. Leadership is a performing art that requires actions and strategies as well as convictions and ideas. Leadership occurs in conjunction with followers: One who leads alone is not a leader. Developing leadership research that recognizes these realities, yet provides understanding and guidance for managers has proved difficult.

Leadership has traditionally been considered in terms of influence and moving a group toward its goals. Roger Stogdill (1974), a pioneer in leadership research, defined leadership as influencing the activities of an organized group toward setting and achieving goals. Leadership involves actions that engage group members to direct and coordinate their work.

In his comprehensive review, Bernard Bass (1990) defined leadership as interaction between two or more group members that structures or restructures the situation and alters the perceptions and expectations of members. Leaders are agents of change. They modify the motivation and competence of group members so that the group is more able to reach future goals.

Leaders are especially potent and constructive. They use their power and persuasion to exert a positive impact on group success. For leaders to have a constructive impact, followers must be open and responsive to their leaders but that in turn requires that leaders be open and responsive. Leadership involves interdependence and requires coordination between managers and employees.

Whereas workers and professionals are focused on getting their tasks completed, leaders have a broad, long-term responsibility to strengthen the organization. They want the organization not just to get things done in the short-term but to develop its capabilities so that it succeeds in the long-term.

As developers of the organization, leaders align organizational goals and motivate individuals and groups to work together. Leaders are recognizing that quality relationships are the most enduring competitive advantage (Barney, 2001). Through these relationships, an organization's information flows, communication occurs, and problems are identified and solved. Spirited teamwork develops new products, reduces costs, improves quality, finds new customers, and sets ethical standards.

Leaders help organizations manage and make use of change, rather than be pawns unable to influence their destiny. But they realize that they cannot do that alone. They must work with and through people so that everyone is working together to understand threats and exploit opportunities.

Nowhere is the need for leadership to manage change more true than in the rapidly growing, highly diverse Asia Pacific region. As the book's chapters attest, Asians can turn to their traditional values of relationships to develop their modern leadership abilities.

## Asian Perspective on Relationships

Asian researchers have long argued that relationships are critical for leadership and for doing business in Asia (Hui, Law, & Chen, 1999; Tung, 1991). Bhanthumnavin and Bhanthumnavin's chapter reviews a traditional Thai saying, "a crowded environment is livable, but an uneasy relationship is unbearable". *Guanxi* and collectivism values are reinforcing ideas to understand relationships in Asia.

*Guanxi* is a close, personal relationship based upon particularistic ties (Hwang, 1987; Leung, Koch, & Lu, 2002). Leaders and employees may develop *guanxi* based in part because their families are from the same village. They are considered part of the in-group whereas those from other villages are the out-group. But the relationship has to be personal between the two individuals; just having the same background is typically insufficient. *Guanxi* should help develop trust and contribute to leader effectiveness.

Consistent with the idea of *guanxi*, researchers have proposed that Asians are collectivists who value a socially defined self. They give priority to in-group goals and accept that social norms should determine behavior (Kim, Triandis, Kagitcibasi, Choi, & Yoon, 1994). In contrast, individualists value a personal self, give priority to personal goals, and believe that their individual attitudes should determine their behavior. Asian people have been found to see themselves as part of a larger whole and place high priority on their in-groups (Triandis, 1990; Tung, 1991).

Collectivist values have been hypothesized to affect behavior, including leadership (Morris, Williams, Leung, Larrick, Mendoza, Bhatnagar, Li, Kondo, Luo, & Hu, 1998; Leung, 1997). Studies have shown that employees with high quality relationships with leaders perform their own jobs well and are willing to contribute as good citizens to the organization (Hui, Law, & Chen, 1999). Personal relationships in particular are thought to contribute to effective leadership. Employees who indicated that their relationship was collectivist with their managers rated their own commitment high and were effective organizational citizens as rated by their manager (Tjosvold, Yu, & Liu, 2001).

## Emerging Western Perspective on Relationships

The traditional emphasis on relationships in Asia is a modern perspective in the West. Researchers and practitioners in the West increasingly argue that the nature of relationships among people very much affects the leadership as well as such key organizational processes as decision-making and teamwork (Gersick, Bartunek, & Dutton, 2000; Kramer & Messick, 1995). As Tom Peters advised, "Read more novels and fewer business books: relationships really are all there is."

George Graen and his colleagues have developed an impressive empirical base that the individual relationship between managers and employees has a critical impact on leader effectiveness (Brower, Schoorman, & Tan, 2000; Graen & Uhl-Bien, 1995). Early studies had direct Asian influences (Wakabayashi & Graen, 1984; Wakabayashi, Graen, & Uhl-Bien, 1990).

Emerging Western research on transformational leadership also emphasizes the importance of leaders developing effective relationships with and among employees (Bass, 1997; Chen & Fahr, 2001). High quality leader relationships appear to be useful because they foster interaction that helps employees feel committed and motivated to contribute to the organization. Argyris and Schon (1978, 1996) have argued that open, mutually supportive interaction is the foundation for leader effectiveness.

## Leader as Head

In addition to emphasizing the importance of relationships throughout the organization, Asian managers and researchers have argued that leaders and employees have a special kind of relationship. Organizations are "families" that should be tightly knitted and managed by the "father" (Cheng, 1995; Farh &

Cheng, 2000; Redding, 1999). As the father should be a strong leader in a family business, managers are expected to act as the "head of household" in private companies (Westwood, 1997). Based on the collectivist, harmonious, and social order values of Asia, paternalistic leadership is culturally endorsed. In contrast, the individualistic, freedom-oriented West endorses open, participative leadership. Paternalistic leaders explain and teach employees but maintain some social distance from them. They strengthen their authority, expect employee obedience, and minimize conflict among employees.

But Asian paternalistic leaders are not simply autocratic as often assumed in the West. The values of *guanxi* and collectivism support a strong element of benevolence in the Asian view of leadership. Asian leaders develop personal relationships with employees and are expected to care for their employees. Their employees are to accept their direction but, in return, leaders are obligated to understand and to provide for employee needs. Asian leaders feel a moral obligation for their employees' well being. Chinese employees described those managers who ascribed to the traditional idea of leadership as head as very supportive and effective (Tjosvold, Wong & Liu, 2002). Traditional Asian leadership values involve encouragement and relationship building, not coercion.

Asian paternalistic leadership also differs from the Western idea of autocratic leadership in its emphasis on discussion between leaders and employees. Whereas autocratic leaders are closed, Asian leaders are expected to share and discuss their ideas—dialogue is the ideal. Personal relationships and taking care of employees requires leaders to listen to employee ideas and concerns. Although public debate may be difficult, private discussions are commonly used to show concern and caring, to deal with issues, and to maintain relationships and harmony (Farh & Cheng, 2000).

Paternalistic leadership also differs from the West's concept of autocracy in its orientation toward power. Theorists have proposed that, in Asia, power and authority are associated with a moral obligation to use that capacity to protect and further the interests of the less powerful (Pye, 1985; Spencer-Oatey, 1997). Power should not be primarily a tool for suppression and domination.

These Asian views help to understand limitations in Western thinking about authority and power. Asian researchers emphasize that authority is not established just because a manager has a superior position. Leaders must earn authority, especially its moral aspects, by demonstrating a commitment and an openness to employees.

Western researchers like David McClelland (1975) have also challenged the traditional belief that power, as it involves suppression and domination, invariably corrupts. Rosabeth Kanter (1979) proposed that power is often a highly productive force in organizational life. Power can promote participation, not just frustrate employee involvement: The more powerful managers assist and support their subordinates, the less powerful resist employee influence. Powerful managers have the confidence as well as ability to aid their employees and influence them collaboratively.

Coleman and Voronov (2003) found that managers who viewed power as expandable so that both the leader and the follower could enhance their power involved employees in decision making and developed constructive relationships. Experiments in North America and in China suggest that when power is considered expandable and cooperative, rather than limited and competitive, it is used to provide support and resources, not to coerce and limit the less powerful (Tjosvold, Coleman, & Sun, 2003).

Asian research and experience have helped us understand that strengthening relationships is key to effective leadership, and that leaders must be savvy and skilled to develop their authority and apply their power constructively (Tjosvold & Wong, in press). The following chapters provide guidance, suggestions, and examples of how leaders can develop their relationships so that people can work together to manage change. But learning leadership is not easy. The next section suggests a practical way for readers to increase their learning from the chapters.

## Teamwork for Becoming a Leader

Although the debate regarding whether leaders are born or made will continue to rage for many more years, we know that no one is born with the complex skills of leading. Leading must be learned not just over weeks, but over years, even a lifetime.

Appreciating the value of relationships does not give managers the abilities to help and teach others to work together. Developing high quality, productive relationships has become more difficult. People must cross many borders and barriers in today's diverse organizations. Specialists from different departments, organizations, countries, and cultural backgrounds are increasingly asked to collaborate. In geographically dispersed companies, professionals are expected to collaborate through telephone, fax, and the internet, with only occasional face-to-face meetings. They have few opportunities for informal interactions where they can feel a part of the organization, find out the latest developments, and make serendipitous contributions.

Experience is not enough to become a leader. Some people learn a great deal from facing challenging situations, others learn very little, and some may even learn the wrong lesson. Ideas help leaders analyze situations, determine what should be done, and develop plans. Experience itself does not teach; using ideas to make use of opportunities and reflecting on experience does.

We now know that people understand ideas and learn from their experiences much more effectively together than alone. Mentors and colleagues model important values and useful procedures and provide the emotional support to incorporate new ideas. Several people can use their various perspectives to create plans appropriate and effective for a given situation. It is easier to accept negative feedback if other people are able to help us use it to improve our abilities for the future. Leaders debate ideas and explore issues with colleagues, get feedback and suggestions, and gather support to take risks.

To become a leader, managers must challenge outworn ideas of their role as taskmasters and views of organizations as composed of independent individuals. They need valid models for how to lead and build successful organizations. They must also put their values and ideas to work in credible, effective ways. The ideas and experiences outlined in the chapters in this book can help leaders develop a clear focus on their mission to develop relationships and learn various approaches to make their teams synergistic and vibrant, especially if they discuss the chapters with their colleagues and other leaders.

## The Book's Purposes

Research-based and action-oriented, the present book aims at providing both a conceptual understanding of leadership and suggests how leaders can be developed in high growth Asian countries. The chapters examine leadership in these countries and describe the various assumptions, expectations, and values people around Asia Pacific have about how they lead and work with others.

The authors of the chapters drew upon a wide range of disciplines to document the leadership and organizational beliefs of people in their country. In addition to cross-cultural and other behavioral studies, they relied on literature and history to identify how people in their country think about themselves and their neighbors. Authors explicated the stereotypes of themselves and other countries, not arguing that this is the way that people in their country always lead, but that this is how they expect themselves and others to lead and work as a team.

This book contributes to effective international management. The chapters help partners, managers, and employees appreciate the variety by which Pacific Rim people work together and the expectations they have for their leaders. The chapters reduce the shock that Westerners working in the region may have when they face different leadership approaches and assumptions, and reduce the temptation to conclude that Asians are unwilling and unable to lead or to be led. We hope readers will become more open-minded and flexible in their approaches in working with the peoples of Asia Pacific.

The editing of this book represents a cross-cultural joint venture. Kwok Leung is from Hong Kong with his doctoral training in the United States whereas Dean Tjosvold is an American who has taught for years and conducted research in Canada and China. We want this book to aid better cultural understanding of leading in Asia Pacific and to contribute to the continued prosperity of the region.

Leadership requires an intellectual understanding, but it is also a complex performing art. Every leader and every employee has his or her own style, aspirations, and values. Each leadership setting is unique with its own requirements and opportunities. Cross-cultural leadership highlights the demands on managers and employees to adapt to each other. Research has documented the importance of the Asian value of two-way relationships, where leaders and employees are sensitive and open to each other and there is a need for leaders to earn their authority and to use their power constructively. Managers lead with employees and together they increase their odds of creating a better future for themselves and their organization.

# References

Arygris, C. & Schon, D. A. (1978). *Organizational learning: A theory of action perspective*. Reading, MA: Addison-Wesley.

Arygris, C. & Schon, D. A. (1996). *Organizational learning II: Theory, method, and practice*. Reading, MA: Addison-Wesley.

Bass, B. M. (1990). *Bass and Stogdill's handbook of leadership*. (3rd edition). New York: The Free Press.

Bass, B. M. (1997). "Does the transactional-transformational leadership paradigm transcend organizational and national boundaries?" *American Psychologist*, **52**, 130-139.

Brower, H. H., Schoorman, F. D. & Tan, H. H. (2000). "A model of relational leadership: The integration of trust and leader-member exchange." *Leadership Quarterly*, **11**, 227-250.

Chen, X. P. & Fahr, J. L. (2001). "Transformational and transaction leader behaviors in Chinese organizations: Differential effects in the People's Republic of China and Taiwan." In W. H. Mobley & M. W. McCall, Jr. (eds.) *Advances in Global Leadership* Vol. II (pp. 101-126), Oxford: Elsevier Science.

Coleman, P. & Voronov, (2003). "Power in groups and organizations." In M. A. West, D. Tjosvold,, & K. S. Smith (Eds.) *International Handbook of Organizational Teamwork and Cooperative Working*. Chichester, UK: John Wiley & Sons,  pp. 229-254.

Delugua, R. J. (1998). "Leader-member exchange quality and effectiveness ratings." *Group & Organization Management*, **23**, 189-216.

Farh, J. L. & Cheng, B. S. (2000). "A culture analysis of paternalistic leadership in Chinese organization." In A. S. Tsui and J. T. Li (Eds.), *Management and Organizations in China*. London: Macmillan.

Gersick, C. J. G., Bartunek, J.M. & Dutton, J. E. (2000). "Learning from academia: The importance of relationships in professional life." *Academy of Management Journal*, **43**, 1026-1045.

Graen, G. B., & Uhl-Bien, M. (1995).   "Relationship-based approach to leadership: Development of leader-member exchange (LMX) theory of leadership over 25 years: Applying a multi-level multi-domain perspective." *Leadership Quarterly*, **6**, 219-247.

Hui, C. Law, K. S. & Chen, Z.X. (1999). "A structural equation model of the effects of negative affectivity, leader-member exchange, and perceived job mobility on in-role and extra-role performance: A Chinese case." *Organizational Behavior and Human Decision Processes*, **77**, 3-21.

Hwang, K.K. (1987). "Face and favor: the Chinese power game." *American Journal of Sociology*, **92**, 944-974.

Kanter, R. M. (1977). *Men and women of the corporation.* New York: Basic Books.

Kanter, R. M. (1979). "Power failure in management circuits." *Harvard Business Review*, 65-75.

Kim, U., Triandis, H. C., Kagitcibasi, C. Choi, S. & Yoon, G. (1994). *Individualism and collectivism: Theory, method and applications.* Newbury Park, CA: Sage

Kramer, R. M. & Messick, D. M. (1995). *Negotiation as a social process.* Thousand Oaks, CA: Sage Publications.

Leung, K. (1997). "Negotiation and reward allocations across cultures." In P. C. Earley & M. Erez (Eds.) *New perspectives on international industrial/organizational psychology.* (pp.640-675) San Francisco: Jossey-Bass.

Leung, K., Koch, T. P., & Lu, L. (in press). "A dualistic model of harmony and its implications for conflict management in Asia." *Asia Pacific Journal of Management.*

McClelland, D. C. (1975). *Power: The inner experience.* New York: Irvington Publishers, Inc.

Morris, M. W., Williams, K. Y., Leung, K., Larrick, R., Mendoza, M. T., Bhatnagar, D., Li, J., Kondo, M., Luo, J. L., & Hu. J. C. (1998). "Conflict management style: Accounting for cross-national differences." *Journal of International Business Studies*, **29**, 729-748.

Pye, L. W. (1985). *Asian power and politics: The cultural dimensions of authority.* Cambridge: MA: Harvard University Press.

Schriesheim, C. A., Neider, L. L., & Scandura, T. A. (1998) "Delegation and leader-member exchange: Main effects, moderators, and measurement issues." *Academy of Management Journal*, **41**, 298-318.

Spencer-Oatey, H. (1997). "Unequal relationships in high and low power distance societies: A comparative study of tutor-student role relations in Britain and China." *Journal of Cross-Cultural Psychology*, **28**, 284-302.

Stogdill, R. M. (1974). *Handbook of Leadership: A Survey of Literature.* New York: Free Press.

Tjosvold, D. & Wong, S. H. (in press). "Leadership Research in Asia: Developing Relationships" In K. Leung and S. White (Eds.). *Handbook of Asian Management*, Kluwer Academic Publishers: The Netherlands.

Tjosvold, D., Wong, M. L. & Liu, C. H. (2002, June). "Collectivist Values and Open-Mindedness for Chinese Employees Trust of their Japanese Leaders." Paper, *Academy of International Business.* San Juan, Puerto Rico.

Triandis, H, C. (1995). *Individualism and collectivism.* Boulder, CO: Westview Press.

Triandis, H. C. (1990). "Cross-cultural studies of individualism and collectivism." In J. Berman (Ed.) *Nebraska Symposium on Motivation, 1989.* (pp. 41-133) Lincoln, Nebraska: University of Nebraska Press.

Tung, R. (1991). "Handshakes across the sea: Cross-cultural negotiating for business success." *Organizational Dynamics,* **14,** 30-40.

Wakabayashi, M. and Graen, G. (1984). "The Japanese career progress study: A 7-year follow-up." *Journal of Applied Psychology,* **69,** 603-614.

Wakabayashi, M., Graen, G., and Uhl-Bien, M. (1990). "Generalizability of the hidden investment hypothesis among Japanese line managers in five leading Japanese corporation," *Human Relations,* 43(11), 1099-1115.

Westwood, R. (1997). "Harmony and patriarchy: The cultural basis for 'paternalistic headship' among the Overseas Chinese." *Organization Studies,* **18,** 445-480.

*Chapter 2*

# Understanding Leadership in Diverse Cultures:

# Implications of Project GLOBE for Leading

# International Ventures

Vipin Gupta
The Wharton School

and

Robert J. House
The Wharton School

## New Challenges for Leading in a Global World

People of the Asia Pacific, indeed, in all regions, live in an increasingly interconnected world. There has been an explosion of cross-border trade, investments, migrations, travel, and communications since the end of the Cold War and the growth of Internet over the last decade. The leading firms in many industrial and emerging markets now boast of strategic relationships with investors, factories, employees, entrepreneurs, suppliers, and customers of multiple nationalities. Many more firms, investors, factories, employees, entrepreneurs, suppliers, and customers, around the world are seeking to benefit from the forces of globalization.  The culture of the societies is an important factor guiding the entry, organization, and growth of the organizations.  Further, differences in the cultures of the societies play an important role in foreign direct investments and in the global network of the multinational corporations.  A systematic and in-depth understanding of the societal cultures is essential for the effectiveness of national, as well as international, organizational initiatives.

Cultures represent systematic approaches, heuristics, and solutions to threats, problems, and challenges faced universally. Each society develops its own set of practices and values to address issues, such as the relationship of individuals to with groups, distribution of power and resources among members of groups, and choice of priorities among different goals. As the firms in each society interact with the global environment, they must find ways to balance and integrate diverse cultural approaches they encounter in different societies.  They must also decide whether principles, practices, and strategies that make sense in one cultural context are equally relevant for another. As they build organizations that span the globe, they must consider a diverse set of cultural variables that shape the attitudes and motivations of their varied constituencies.

In a classic work, Perlmutter (1969) underscored the costs of mentoring geocentric managers, who were historically trained through living and working in several nations.  Perlmutter noted, "It would be a mistake to underestimate the human stresses which a geocentric career creates... The economic rewards, the challenge of new countries, the personal and professional development that comes from working in a variety of countries and cultures are surely incentives, but companies have not solved by any means the human costs of international mobility to executives and their families." Since the 1970s, a substantial and reliable body of knowledge has accumulated to help improve managers' familiarity with other cultures. The first systematic organization of cultural knowledge occurred under the Human Relations Area Files project initiated by Murdock (1972). As part of that project, a vast amount of literature on each society and ethnic group was pulled together in a central database. Subsequently, over the 1980s and 1990s, two major studies – Hofstede (1980) and Trompenaars (1993) - were published that offered comparable cross-cultural data on selected cultural dimensions.

The GLOBE (Global Leadership and Organizational Behavior Effectiveness) research program is intended to further sharpen and refine the cultural knowledge for supporting the development of cultural management as a disciplined training methodology. GLOBE is a team of 150 investigators who have been working together for the last ten years, and have collected data on cultural values and practices and leadership attributes from 18,000 managers in 62 societies.

**Table 1 Cluster-wise GLOBE Society Sample**

| **Anglo Cultures** | **Latin Europe** | **Nordic Europe** | **Germanic Europe** |
|---|---|---|---|
| Australia | France | Denmark | Austria |
| Canada | Israel | Finland | Germany (Former EAST) |
| England | Italy | Sweden | Germany (Former WEST) |
| Ireland | Portugal | | Netherlands |
| New Zealand | Spain | | Switzerland |
| South Africa (White Sample) | Switzerland (French speaking) | | |
| USA | | | |
| **Eastern Europe** | **Latin America** | **Sub-Saharan Africa** | **Middle East** |
| Albania | Argentina | Namibia | Egypt |
| Georgia | Bolivia | Nigeria | Kuwait |
| Greece | Brazil | South Africa (Black Sample) | Morocco |
| Hungary | Colombia | Zambia | Qatar |
| Kazakhstan | Costa Rica | Zimbabwe | Turkey |
| Poland | Ecuador | | |
| Russia | El Salvador | | |
| Slovenia | Guatemala | | |
| | Mexico | | |
| | **Venezuela** | | |
| **Southern Asia** | **Confucian Asia** | | |
| India | China | | |
| Indonesia | Hong Kong | | |
| Iran | Japan | | |
| Malaysia | Singapore | | |
| Philippines | South Korea | | |
| Thailand | Taiwan | | |

As shown in Table 1, the 62 societies in the GLOBE sample represent ten major geographical regions of the world: (1) Anglo, (2) Latin America, (3) Latin Europe (4) Nordic Europe, (5) Germanic Europe, (6) Eastern Europe, (7) Confucian Asia, (8) Southern Asia, (9) Middle East, and (10) Sub-Saharan

Africa. The participating managers are employed in the food, financial services, and telecom sectors. These sectors offer a diverse and contrasting mix of external organizational environments, organizational sizes, and dominant organizational technology.

GLOBE is a rigorous research effort intended to clarify the universal meanings of each cultural dimension, and to highlight the techniques for leveraging cultural differentials in terms of the interpretations of various cultural dimensions and orientations. Javidan & House (2001) draw several lessons to sharpen cultural acumen for the global manager using the findings of Project GLOBE.

In this chapter, we will present the strategic significance of GLOBE's cultural dimensions, and will explain how to leverage cross-cultural differentials. A set of nine cultural dimensions are used to develop a systematic and integrated understanding about the culture of each society: (1) Performance Orientation, (2) Assertiveness Orientation, (3) Future Orientation, (4) Humane Orientation, (5) Institutional Collectivism, (6) In-group Collectivism, (7) Gender Egalitarianism, (8) Power Distance, and (9) Uncertainty Avoidance. These are aspects of a society's culture that distinguish one society from another.

*Intellectual Roots of GLOBE Constructs*: GLOBE constructs were theoretically derived, and empirically validated. Performance Orientation was derived from McClelland's (1961) work on the need for achievement. Hofstede's (1980) construct of Masculinity was used as a basis to develop the two distinct dimensions: Assertiveness Orientation and Gender Egalitarianism. Assertiveness Orientation is rooted in the interpersonal communication literature (Sarros & Woodman, 1993). Gender Egalitarianism is similar to the United Nations Development Program's (UNDP) concept of Gender Empowerment. Future Orientation is derived from Kluckhohn and Strodtbeck's (1961) Past, Present, and Future Orientation dimension, and from Hofstede's (2001) Long Term Orientation, which focuses on the temporal mode of the society. Humane Orientation has its roots in Kluckhohn and Strodtbeck's (1961) work, "Human Nature is Good versus Human Nature is Bad dimension". Institutional Collectivism captures (inversely) the same construct as Hofstede's Individualism. Family Collectivism measures pride in, and loyalty to, the family, and is derived from the Triandis et. al. (1988) work on in-groups. Power Distance and Uncertainty Avoidance are based on Hofstede's (1980) work.

*Validation of the GLOBE Cultural Constructs*: GLOBE measured each cultural construct in two ways: cultural practices focused on how things are (referred to as "As Is" construct), and cultural values focused on how things should be (referred to as "Should Be" construct). The items used to measure both practices and values were identical, but the respondents were asked to evaluate them both in "As Is" as well as "Should Be" terms.

Statistical validation of the GLOBE cultural constructs is available from Hanges and Dickson (2004). First, separate factor analyses of each of the cultural scales indicated uni-dimensionality of each cultural scale. Second, average rw g(J) for cultural practices was 0.85 and for cultural values was 0.80, showing that aggregation of the individual responses to the society level is appropriate. Third, intra-class correlation coefficients [ICC(1)] averaged 0.25 for cultural practices scales and 0.27 for cultural values scales, indicating statistically significant within-culture agreement and between-culture differences. Fourth, the cultural scales exhibited low to moderate correlations with each other, suggesting their distinctiveness. Fifth, multilevel confirmatory factor analysis provided an average CFI of 0.89 for the cultural practices scales, and an average CFI of 0.95 for cultural values scales, both indicating an adequate fit. Sixth, the average Cronbach alpha for the cultural practices scales was 0.77, and for the cultural values scales was 0.75. Seventh, the average inter-rater reliability measured by ICC(2) was 0.93 for the cultural practices scales, and 0.95 for the cultural values scales. Finally, the scales were free from response bias: cultural scales showed a low average correlation of 0.35 with the response-bias factor measured as the difference between means and standard deviations in responses of respondents from different societies.

In addition, construct validation of the GLOBE cultural scales is available in Gupta, Sully and House (2004). Gupta et. al. report strong correlation between the GLOBE cultural practices scales and the secondary data obtained from World Bank and other published sources. Further, they develop a set of

## Table 2 Groupings of GLOBE Clusters by Scores on the Societal Cultural Practice Dimensions

| Cultural Dimension | High Score Clusters | Mid Score Clusters | Low Score Clusters |
|---|---|---|---|
| Performance Orientation | Confucian Asia<br>Germanic Europe<br>Anglo<br>Southern Asia | Sub-Saharan Africa<br>Latin Europe<br>Nordic Europe<br>Middle East | Latin America<br>Eastern Europe |
| Assertiveness Orientation | Germanic Europe<br>Eastern Europe | Sub-Saharan Africa<br>Latin America<br>Anglo<br>Middle East<br>Confucian Asia<br>Latin Europe | Southern Asia<br>Nordic Europe |
| Future Orientation | Germanic Europe<br>Nordic Europe<br>Confucian Asia | Anglo<br>Southern Asia<br>Sub-Saharan Africa | Latin Europe<br>Middle East<br>Latin America<br>Eastern Europe |
| Humane Orientation | Southern Asia<br>Sub-Saharan Africa | Middle East<br>Anglo<br>Nordic Europe<br>Latin America<br>Confucian Asia | Eastern Europe<br>Latin Europe<br>Germanic Europe |
| Institutional Collectivism | Nordic Europe<br>Confucian Asia | Anglo<br>Southern Asia<br>Sub-Saharan Africa<br>Middle East | Eastern Europe<br>Germanic Europe<br>Latin Europe<br>Latin America |
| Family Collectivism | Southern Asia<br>Middle East<br>Eastern Europe<br>Latin America<br>Confucian Asia | Sub-Saharan Africa<br>Latin Europe | Anglo<br>Germanic Europe<br>Nordic Europe |
| Gender Egalitarianism | Eastern Europe<br>Nordic Europe | Latin America<br>Anglo<br>Latin Europe<br>Sub-Saharan Africa<br>Southern Asia<br>Confucian Asia | Germanic Europe<br>Middle East |
| Power Distance | Southern Asia | Latin America<br>Eastern Europe<br>Sub-Saharan Africa<br>Middle East<br>Latin Europe<br>Confucian Asia<br>Anglo<br>Germanic Europe | Nordic Europe |
| Uncertainty Avoidance | Nordic Europe<br>Germanic Europe | Confucian Asia<br>Anglo<br>Sub-Saharan Africa<br>Latin Europe<br>Southern Asia | Middle East<br>Latin America<br>Eastern Europe |

unobtrusive measures using content analysis of the descriptive material on the culture of each society included in the GLOBE sample, which are strongly correlated with the questionnaire-based GLOBE societal cultural practice scales. They also develop "outcropping measures" for validating GLOBE cultural value scales using data from the World Value Surveys (Inglehart, 1997), and demonstrate strong correlations between each of the cultural value scales and the outcropping measures. Their findings confirm both convergent as well as discriminant validity of the GLOBE constructs.

Table 2 shows groupings of the ten GLOBE cultural clusters by their scores on the nine cultural practice dimensions. Conceptual rationale for the groupings is available in Gupta and Hanges (2004).

As shown in Table 2 and as explained in Gupta and Hanges (2004), the Anglo cluster is distinguished by its high performance orientation, but low in-group collectivism, which typifies its market model. The Latin America cluster has high in-group collectivism, but low performance orientation, low future orientation, low institutional collectivism, and low uncertainty avoidance, which typify its clannish model. Latin Europe has low future orientation, low humane orientation, and low institutional collectivism, which typify its administrative bureaucracy model. Nordic Europe has low assertiveness, low in-group collectivism, and low power distance, but high future orientation, high gender egalitarianism, high institutional collectivism, and high uncertainty avoidance, which show its social egalitarianism model. Germanic Europe has low humane orientation, low institutional collectivism, low in-group collectivism, low gender egalitarianism, but high performance orientation, high assertiveness, high future orientation, and high uncertainty avoidance, which typify its technical model. Further, Eastern Europe has low performance orientation, low future orientation, low humane orientation, low institutional collectivism, and low uncertainty avoidance, but high assertiveness orientation, high in-group orientation, and high gender egalitarianism, which typify its transitional communist model. Confucian Asia has high performance orientation, high future orientation, high institutional collectivism, and high in-group collectivism, which typify its Confucian ethic model. Southern Asia has high performance orientation, high humane orientation, high in-group collectivism, and high power distance, but low assertiveness, which typify its paternalistic model. The Middle Eastern cluster has low future orientation, low gender egalitarianism, and low uncertainty avoidance, but high in-group collectivism, which typify its desert life model. Finally, Sub-Saharan Africa has high humane orientation, which typifies its tribal model.

Next, we report the strategic significance of each of the nine cultural dimensions.

## Strategic Significance of Cultural Dimensions

*Performance Orientation*

The performance orientation dimension reflects the extent to which a society encourages and rewards improved performance, goal-oriented behavior, and innovation. Performance oriented societies put a thrust on achievement motivation, or need for achievement (McClelland, Atkinson, Clark, & Lowell, 1953). The achievement motive reflects a desire to perform in terms of standards of excellence or to be successful in competitive situations. The achievement motive translates into behavior through two major components: the hope for success (approach) and the fear of failure (avoidance). People with high achievement motive tend to approach rather than avoid tasks related to success, because for them success is a culmination of ability and hardwork about which they are confident of (Weiner, 1980). Once they select a performance goal, they are willing to put forth their best efforts (Atkinson, 1957; 1981). But in the face of continuing obstacles, they respond with a 'helplessness' response, involving avoidance of challenge and a deterioration of performance (Diener & Dweck, 1980). They seek positive feedback and focus their efforts in areas in which they have already been successful (Dweck, 1986; Dweck & Leggett, 1988). Their feedback-seeking is aimed at satisfaction of achievement and social endorsement of this achievement. It is less oriented towards formative information for reflection and learning from prior experiences (Dweck, 1986).

Consequently, in performance oriented societies, workforce, partners, and competitors would be intrinsically motivated by the need to perform tasks better and more innovatively, desire for progressive improvement, and the preference to work on tasks with moderate probabilities of success (McClelland, 1961). They also focus on knowledge accumulation, drive for challenge and exhibiting initiative (Fyans Jr., Salili, Maehr & Desai, 1983). They would value accomplishments and the feedback that allows assessment of the results, instead of emphasizing ascribed value characteristics such as age, education, family, and profession (Parsons & Shils, 1951). Further, the government in such societies may have only limited involvement in new product and technology development, measured in terms of its share in national R&D expenditures (Gupta, Sully & House, 2004). Thus, the market itself tends to be sufficiently open and efficient to allow the firms, local or foreign, to undertake innovative activities.

## *Assertiveness Orientation*

The dimension of assertiveness orientation is associated with a strong consciousness, expression, articulation, and communication of one's thoughts, feelings, beliefs, and rights; in public, political and social forums, and is related to physical and psychological aggressiveness and confrontation. People in assertive societies stand up for their individual or collective rights, and demonstrate strong interpersonal competence (Lange & Jakubowski, 1976). They tend to be adventurous, confident, and willing or eager to accept change in their environment. Assertiveness implies an action-oriented focus, founded on confident decision-making behavior, and characterized by strength, forcefulness, courage, initiative, conviction, and determination (Sarros & Woodman, 1993).

Assertive societies emphasize social skills and communication, direct personal influence and expression, and overall inter-personal effectiveness (Crawford, 1995). Here, people are willing to ask for what they want, deny what is not in their interest, and articulate positive and negative messages to others in an open and non-passive manner (Booream & Flowers, 1978). There is a focus on encouraging personal standards and the judgment of morality or ethics - people constantly question the establishment and its traditional wisdom, as well as universal value absolutes (Rakos, 1991). For instance, individuals and governments in assertive societies tend to take actions to stop the exports of natural resources, and focus instead on value-added manufactured and service product exports (Gupta, Sully & House, 2004).

*Future Orientation*

The dimension of future Ooientation is reflected in behaviors such as planning, preparing and investing for the future. It is related to the concept of short-term vs. long-term orientation (Hofstede, 2001). At a much deeper level, it is also associated with the distinction between materialistic vs. spiritual orientation (Cervantes & Ramirez, 1992). Less future oriented cultures focus on the short-term materialistic considerations of respecting traditions to avoid isolation from the society, and maintaining face to protect one's reputation and creditworthiness in the society (Hofstede, 2001). In contrast, more future oriented cultures emphasize long-term considerations of education for self-development, and the inner ability to persist in the face of obstacles for self-actualization. These cultures encourage planning, sacrifice and frugality, while lack of future orientation encourages consumption, spending, and materialistic display of income and wealth (Hofstede, 2001). Future oriented societies foster search for the opportunities consistent with the desired future states (Seginer & Schlesinger, 1998). Towards this end, they are inclined to support investments in intellectual property rights, such as trademarks and patents (Gupta, Sully & House, 2004). Spiritual orientation intensifies the sense of mission, purpose, vision and direction, which in turn supports the values of future orientation.

Future orientation tends to be associated with a higher rate of saving, a lower rate of consumption, and thus a lower level of life satisfaction. This is because consumption oriented material possessions are central to the life satisfaction measures (Leelakulthanit, Day, & Walters, 1991). In the less future oriented cultures, people seek material acquisitions to make their life more meaningful. While in the short-term cultures, matter is disassociated from the spirit, which contributes to the counter-opposing of need gratification and respecting musts; in future oriented cultures a strong concern for virtue allows a pragmatic integration of morals and practice (Hofstede, 2001: 363).

## Humane Orientation

The dimension of humane orientation is concerned with generosity, compassion, and empathy for others. The concept of humane orientation is quite old, and can be traced to the ancient works of Aristotle and Confucius, and the more recent writings of Mill (1863) and Dewey (1886). The concept of humane orientation has evolved partly as a critique of the doctrine of theology (Huxley, 1961; Solzhenitsyn, 1976). In contrast to the theological concerns of absolutes and transcendentalism, the value of humane orientation is deeply rooted in the human experience, and in the moral values arising from the situational and spontaneous demands of this human experience. In theological societies, "Belief in a supernatural after life leads to concentration on salvation in the other world and to a lack of concern for life in this world and its possible improvements" (Huxley, 1961: 39). But in humane oriented societies, the thrust is on striving for a good life in this world, not on a good life in the other world (Solzhenitsyn, 1976).

To this end, such humane oriented societies seek to control human dispositions of greed, envy, hatred, and cheating, and define behaviors based on the needs of the situation. They show constant striving for the betterment of the human experience, and rely upon the application of reason, the lessons of history, and personal experience to form an ethical/moral foundation and to create meaning in life (Kurtz, 2001). Also, in humane oriented societies there is a tendency to seek paternalistic or political interventions to temper the market forces for guaranteeing welfare and security for all people irrespective of their private property holdings or social power (Briggs, 1961). In societies that are concerned with the welfare of others, there is a limited emphasis on hedonic pleasure, personal comfort, and material success (Schwartz & Bilsky, 1987).

Five distinct characteristics of humane oriented societies can be identified (Kurtz, 2001). (1) Concern with Happiness: Humane oriented societies emphasize individual and social pursuit of happiness. The pursuit of happiness

– a key element of the Renaissance – implies striving for a full life in which the fruits of one's efforts contribute to a meaningful existence in this world. (2) Human Equality: Humane societies recognize equality and dignity of each person, and identify people as ends, not merely as means. This principle of human equality has been integral to democratic revolutions, and has inspired the overturning of authoritarian regimes and slavery, and the introduction of equal opportunity efforts. (3) Moral Freedom: Humane societies focus on the development of modern values of high intelligence, morality and aesthetics, and help individuals freely express their own needs and diverse views on life. (4) Respect for Diversity: Humane societies instill tolerance for diversity of values and norms in individuals and groups, and facilitate co-existence of diversity without forcing dogmatic similarity. They respect an unrepressed freedom of individuals to pursue their own interests, and thus encourage responsibility and consideration for others. Thus, these societies are founded on moral and civil virtues, such as honesty, uprightness, truth, sincerity, integrity, fairness and empathy. (5) Experiential Reason: Humane societies reject the absolute referential approach of the dogmatic theologians and religionists. They instead recognize the need for evolving and discovering new moral principles as societal situations change. The thrust is on using situational analysis to work out comprises and negotiate differences, and on pragmatically using technology for improving the common welfare of individuals and groups.

## Institutional Collectivism

The dimension of institutional collectivism is concerned with the inducements and rewards for collective behavior and norms, in contrast to incentives and rewards for individual freedom and contributions. Such collectivism is reflected in preferences for closer work relations and higher involvement with one's social unit. Environmental mastery, which refers to the ability to "choose or create environments suitable to his or her psychic conditions" (Ryff, 1989: 1071) gets a low priority in the institutionally collective cultures. Also, "the concept of an autonomous, bounded, abstract individual existing free of society yet living in society" is not typical in such cultures (Shweder & Bourne, 1984: 190). In the collectivistic Japanese society, for instance, social connections are an essential part of the culture (Nakamura, 1964). According to Rosenberger (1992: 4), "The very word for self in Japanese, jibun, implies that self is not an essentiality apart from the social realm." Read's (1955: 257) fieldwork in New Guinea showed that the institutionally collective societies refuse to "separate the individual from the social context" or grant a person "intrinsic moral value apart from that which attaches to him as the occupant of a particular social status." While the institutionally collective societies reject autonomy, they put priority on self-development for a place in the society. There "individuality supports a tribal purpose, a tribal identity" because "individuals are like the poles of a tipi - each has his own attitude and appearance but all look to the same center [heart] and support the same cover" (Strauss, 1982: 125).

In institutionally collectivist cultures, the people act with modesty, and demonstrate self-effacing and self-abnegating tendencies (Bond, 1986). The guiding principle tends to be, "the nail that sticks out gets pounded down." Self is largely construed interdependently, whereby worth and acceptability are diffused throughout the institutional fabric of the society and are not focused on the individual alone (Johnson, 1985). People are encouraged to seek self-critical and self-improving orientations as means to pursue the cultural goals associated with interdependence (Doi, 1973). In this manner, institutional collectivism emphasizes shared objectives, interchangeable interests, and common social behaviors of the people based on association with others in groups (Chatman, Polzer, Barsade & Neale, 1998). In contrast, a lack of institutional collectivism tends to be associated with a preoccupation with self-esteem (Bellah, Madsen, Sullivan, Swindler & Tipton, 1985). In less institutionally collective societies, people remember their past performance as much better than it actually was (Crary, 1966), claim more responsibility than their spouses give them credit for in household tasks (Ross & Sicoly, 1979), judge positive personality attributes to be more appropriate in describing themselves than in describing others (Alicke, 1985), and take credit for success, yet attribute failure to the situational variables (Zuckerman, 1979). Institutional collectivism tends to be greater in the Eastern parts of the world, which typically rely on stable informal institutions for social stability and economic activity, as compared to most societies in the West, which rely on more formalized institutions (Gupta, Sully & House, 2004).

## In-group Collectivism

The dimension of in-group collectivism relates to how the individuals relate to their family, as an autonomous identity or alternatively as consciousness of responsibilities towards their family. It is associated with 'pride in affiliation' and a general affective identification with, and a general affective commitment towards, family, group, community, and nation (Triandis, Bontempto, Villareal, Asai, & Lucca, 1988). In strong in-group collective cultures, "people from birth onwards are integrated into strong, cohesive in-groups, which throughout people's lifetime continue to protect them in exchange for unquestioning loyalty." (Hofstede, 1980: 51) In such cultures, there is an emphasis on collaboration, cohesiveness and harmony, as well as an effort by people to apply skills for the benefit of their family or in-group. The role of rationality is often abated, and enacting divisive goals and behaviors is discouraged, since they may destabilize harmony within the group (Schwartz, 1994: 101). Put differently, in-group collectivism represents a strong sense of 'family integrity' (Triandis et al., 1988). The moral suasion and discipline in group collectivism often results in less emphasis on due process because this function is internalized within the in-group norms (Gupta, Sully & House, 2004). Regard for the general association with the broader entity often carries moral imperatives in group collective cultures, but the thrust tends to be on the immediate ties and memberships. The responsibility and identity of the people begins with their immediate group, and then gradually extends outside.

   In-group collectivism emphasizes the innate and learned 'need to affiliate '. The in-group serves three basic needs: the need for affiliation, involvement, inclusion and belongingness; the need for intimacy, affection, and a sense of identity; and the need for social security, support, control, and power (Schutz, 1958; Festinger, 1954). In such societies, need for affiliation reflects the desire to be part of a group and to be accepted by a group (McClelland, 1985). Need for intimacy reflects a desire to experience warm, positive, and communicative relationships with others (Schutz, 1958). Need for social security, support, control and power is enacted by organizing and maintaining the group's processes (Schutz, 1958). Taken together, the three needs generate 'affective commitment' and a general identification, defined as 'pride in affiliation' by O'Reilly and Chatman (1986), with the family and group. Affective commitment, also referred to as an attitudinal commitment, indicates an "affective attachment to the goals and values of an organization, to one's role in relation to goals and values, and to the organization for its own sake, apart from its purely instrumental worth" (Buchanan, 1974: 533). It represents a high degree of emotional attachment and personal involvement of people in the larger group, and thus fosters an interest of the people in the overall best interests of the group (Allen & Meyer, 1990). In-group collectivism fosters connectivity to a group primarily because people want to be a member of the group and only secondarily because they ought to or need to.

## Gender Egalitarianism

The dimension of gender egalitarianism is concerned with the absence of a gender-dependent division of roles, expectations, evaluations, and power. In such societies, there are fewer gender stereotypes that characterize women as passive, weak, deferential and primarily domestically oriented. Gender egalitarianism influences role differences between men and women, as well as the common values of men and women. Low gender egalitarianism is associated with a more orthodox role for women, as well as an orthodox worldview of both men and women. In gender egalitarian societies, gender discrimination is mitigated, allowing both men and women to effectively participate in the labor force and contribute to their families on an equal basis. Men actively participate in child rearing and family maintenance activities. This enables women to engage fully in both the public and the community domains (Coltrane, 1988).

In contrast, in most societies of the world where men traditionally are engaged in jobs that do not sufficiently reward women for their labor, women often work part-time in 'feminine' jobs for the purposes of supplementing the incomes of men. Feminine jobs largely involve family maintenance activities, nurturance, and relationships with others in a service capacity. In low gender egalitarian societies, economic development only increases returns to both men and women within their traditional gender domains, while keeping the roles of men and women separate. Gender egalitarianism, on the other hand, is related to the male-female societal equality and a higher share of women engaged in earned income, rather than domestic, activities. More than economic modernization, gender egalitarianism reflects an inherent understanding between men and women, which enhances their ability to work together in social and economic spheres (Gupta, Sully & House, 2004).

Further, gender egalitarian societies encourage people to relate better to the concept of unity in diversity as an expression of unity, without uniformity and without fragmentation. They are less likely to encourage cultural hegemony, and thus are more encouraging of ethnic diversity. To them, a diverse community represents a rich source of ideas and techniques. Gender egalitarianism connotes a 'gendered' social construction of both men and women. It influences the very epistemological roots of people's worldview: how they see the world, how they know what they see, and what they regard as truth. Thus, gender egalitarianism constitutes a lens that enables people to see an otherwise hidden dimension of social relationships, namely connection with others. Gender egalitarian societies not only tolerate diversity, but also emphasize understanding, respect, and the nurturing of diversity in their communities, through sustained committed efforts (Martin, 1993).

*Power Distance*

The dimension of power distance reflects the extent to which members of a cultural group expect and agree that power should be shared unequally. In high power distance societies, there are considerable inequalities among people with respect to factors such as power, authority, prestige, status, wealth, and material possessions (Hofstede, 1980). In these societies, there is often strong endorsement of leaders and their power. Such endorsement may degenerate in practice, into an obligated and blind acceptance of the legitimacy, position, or authority of the leaders. Leaders in high power distance societies tend to practice paternalistic benevolence with those who support them, but levy autocratic suppression to those who try to revolt. The society and economy is vertically differentiated into classes, and there is limited upward mobility socially as well as occupationally. There are constant attempts by more powerful people both to distance themselves from the less powerful people, and to endear themselves to the higher-ranking elites (Mulder, 1977). Further, power distance is related to an unequal distribution of income in the society, and the control of wealth and productive resources by the privileged classes (Gupta, Sully & House, 2004).

Societies with high power distance make the need for power, as well as the manifest tendencies associated with need for power, highly salient. Individuals with a high need for power seek to have an impact on the lives of other people – by convincing them of their perspective or empowering others around them, by finding ways to be involved, or associated with, powerful people and to be highly competitive (McClelland, 1965). Since high need for power is associated with social influence behaviors, it is an important element of leadership effectiveness, when coupled with a strong concern for the moral use of power (McClelland & Burnham, 1976). Individuals with a high need for power and concern for the moral use of power organize the efforts of others to further the goals of their organization or the society (McClelland & Burnham, 1976).

However, unless constrained by a strong concern for the moral use of power, the need for power also motivates the exercise of power in an aggressive manner for self-aggrandizing purposes, to the detriment of the society (McCelland, 1965).

House, Spangler and Woycke (1991: 367) in their study of US Presidents reported that activity inhibition defined as "the extent to which an individual uses available power to achieve institutional or social goals rather than purely personal goals" was positively related to presidential performance.

Situations that demand considerable leadership resources often generate a positive endorsement of power. Such situations call upon the leaders to practice empowerment, and to delegate their power onto followers on a consistent basis (Morand, 1996). However, the use of power as a mechanism for creating social distance would degenerate into a culture of dependency and stagnation.

## Uncertainty Avoidance

The dimension of uncertainty avoidance is concerned with the extent to which people seek orderliness, consistency, structure, formalized procedures, and laws to deal with naturally occurring uncertain and important events in their daily lives. It is related with the use of procedures, such as standardized decision rules, which can minimize the need to predict uncertain events in the future (Cyert & March, 1963). It is also associated with social reliance on experts, technology, money and material possessions, need for security, and social organization, legislation, and governance. The concept of uncertainty avoidance is rooted in the emotional and psychological 'need for security', oriented towards pacification and control of anxiety about the unknown (Hofstede, 2001).

People socialized to have a high need for security are likely to resist change because it threatens their feelings of safety. The need for security is related to the need for knowledge - the more people know about their environment, the more secure they are likely to feel about their ability to navigate their way through it. Further, the need for security is related more to the social forms of knowledge, as opposed to the personal forms of knowledge. Each person's knowledge acquisition capability is limited. Reliance on social knowledge helps to pool the effort and competence of different people, and thus grants greater confidence and security to each person. By the same token, uncertainty avoidance is also related to a preference for social action and social democracy. In higher uncertainty avoidance societies, more priority is given to the training of experts rather than lay people for particular tasks (Hofstede, 2001). Here, "Citizens are not only more dependent on government, but they want it that way." (Hofstede, 2001: 172) Uncertainty avoidance is also associated with 'tight' societies, where social solidarity and stability is emphasized (Hofstede, 2001). Thus, uncertainty avoidance is related to the values of personal conformity, resistance to social change, interest in national rather than international affairs, and a call for national leadership (Eckhardt, 1971). On the other hand, the 'loose' societies tend to be less uncertainty avoiding. Here the values of group organization, formality, permanence, durability and solidarity are undeveloped, and deviant behavior is easily tolerated (Pelto, 1968).

Societies characterized by greater uncertainty avoidance tend to seek continuous feedback for adaptation and perfecting behavior. While decisions for making exploratory investments in new product and technology development are related to low uncertainty avoidance, the implementation of such decisions is associated with the use of controls related to uncertainty avoidance (Nakata & Sivakumar, 1996). Uncertainty avoidance practices foster mass availability of information technologies, as measured by information processing technologies such as fax machines, internet connections, computers, telephones, and televisions, for reducing uncertainty from the lack of knowledge (Gupta, Sully & House, 2004). People in high uncertainty avoidance cultures have a heightened sense of concern with the need for effective communication and coordination. Therefore, they are more willing to invest in reliable technological support systems, to help them effectively access social information and support. Technological support systems reflect an institutionalized form of knowledge diffusion, because they incorporate the collective social knowledge about the solutions to their societal problems. In uncertainty avoiding societies, the positive outcomes tend to be less attributed to people's abilities, and more to technology and investments into security and social organization (Chandler, Sharma & Wolf, 1983; Yan & Gaier, 1994). Put differently, there is greater thrust on systemic and social competence, and less emphasis on citizen and human competence (Hofstede, 2001).

Having identified the significance of the nine GLOBE cultural dimensions, we next highlight how these can be used for cross-cultural leadership.

## Leveraging Cultural Dimensions for Effective Cross-cultural Leadership

What is expected of leaders, what leaders may or may not do, and the status and influence bestowed on leaders vary considerably in accordance with the cultural forces in the countries or regions in which the leaders function (House, Hanges, Ruiz-Quintanilla, Dorfman, Javidan, Dickson, Gupta, and GLOBE associates, 1999). For instance, the Dutch, and other Nordic societies, place emphasis on egalitarianism and are skeptical about the value of leadership. Terms like leader and manager carry a stigma. If a father is employed as a manager, Dutch children will not admit it to their schoolmates. In contrast, Americans, and other Anglo societies, respect entrepreneurial leaders, characterized by two sets of behaviors: scenario enactment and cast enactment (Gupta, Macmillan, & Surie, 2002). Effective scenario enactors are bold, forceful, and confident, as personified by John Wayne. Effective cast enactors empower their subordinates. Malaysians, and other Southern Asian societies, expect their leaders to behave in a manner that is humble, modest, and dignified. Further, the French, and other Latin European societies, expect leaders to be "cultivated" - highly educated in the liberal arts.

Given the increased globalization of industrial organizations and increased interdependency among nations, the need for better understanding of cultural influences on leadership has never been greater. From scientific and theoretical perspectives, compelling reasons exist for considering the role of the societal culture in influencing leadership processes. In addition, because the goal of science is to develop universally valid theories and principles, there is a need for leadership theories that apply across cultures (House et al.. 1999). There are inherent limitations in transferring theories across cultures. What works in one culture (i.e. a culturally endorsed implicit theory of leadership) may not work in another culture. As Triandis (1993) suggests, leadership researchers will be able to 'fine tune' theories by investigating cultural variations as parameters of those theories. In addition, a focus on cross-cultural issues can help researchers uncover new relationships by forcing investigators to include a much broader range of variables, often not considered in contemporary theories, such as the importance of religion, language, history, and political systems (Dorfman, 1996).

The GLOBE project has classified cross-cultural leadership into six broad types of culturally endorsed implicit leadership theories: (1) Value-based/Charismatic leadership, (2) Team oriented Leadership, (3) Participative Leadership, (4) Humane Leadership, (5) Self-protective Leadership, and (6) Autonomous Leadership (House et. al., 1999). Hartog, House, Hanges, Ruiz-Quintanilla and GLOBE associates (1999) report that value-based/charismatic and team-oriented leadership are universally deemed as effective. On the other hand, participative, humane, self-protective, and autonomous are culturally contingent - in some societies they are deemed as effective, and in others they are perceived to be counter-productive. House et. al. (1999) reported that cultural dimensions significantly influence universal as well as culturally contingent leadership theories. For instance, the cultures that value performance orientation tend to endorse value-based/charismatic leadership more strongly, and the cultures that value institutional and family collectivism tend to endorse team-oriented leadership more strongly. Similarly, the cultures that value power distance and uncertainty avoidance tend not to endorse participative leadership, and the cultures that value human orientation more strongly endorse humane leadership. Based on these, we speculate that leader behavior, which is congruent with a culturally endorsed implicit theory of leadership, will lead to greater organizational effectiveness.

However, there may be times when leaders need to violate the culturally implicit theory of leadership to help their organizations to be effective. For example, in low performance oriented regions such as Middle East and Eastern Europe, it may be necessary for the leader to enforce high-performance standards. This can be accomplished by careful selection and development of organizational members, and/or by the use of expatriates from countries with high-performance standards. Similarly, in high-power distance cultures, or cultures that are low on the participative leader dimension, there may be some tasks - such as the employee being in direct contact with the customer and needing to make on the spot decisions -- that require a high degree of empowerment and delegation to organizational members.

In addition to leveraging the knowledge of cultural dimensions for managing within cultures, the leaders can also use knowledge of differences in societal cultures to help improve the quality of global strategic decision-making. Next, we develop a set of implications of cross-cultural differentials for the management of multinational firms, and for further research on cross-cultural management.

## Leveraging Cultural Differentials for Global Strategic Advantage

Knowledge about cultural dimensions can be used by organizations as an aid to their global decision-making, and for gaining a strategic advantage in the global marketplace. Here, we show how cultural knowledge and cultural differentials can guide decisions related to the sequence of global investments, mode of international entry, design of value chain organization, multi-constituency leadership, and human resource diversity.

## Sequence of Global Investments

When establishing international operations, firms suffer a cost of foreignness since they lack insider market knowledge (Hymer, 1976). They also find it difficult to interpret the available market information in terms that are meaningful and relevant for the local culture ((Johanson & Vahlne, 1977; Andersen, 1993), since the meaning from the insider's perspective tends to differ substantially from the meaning from the outsider's perspective. The gap between insiders' and outsiders' interpretations of meanings is a function of psychic distance, which reflects "factors preventing or disturbing firms learning about and understanding a foreign environment" (Nordstrom & Vahlne, 1994: 42). Psychic distance includes cultural differences such as values and practices, institutional differences such as legal and administrative systems, and structural differences such as competitive market structures among nations. Psychic factors, derived from the similarities or differences in cultural dimensions, are a critical guiding factor in the development of multinational enterprises.

The sustainable growth of large, surviving multinationals is frequently distinguished by a series of small, cumulative steps over a period of time (Johanson & Wiedersheim-Paul, 1975), first "moving into those markets that they can most easily understand, entering more distant markets only at a later stage" (Benito & Gripsrud, 1992: 464). To illustrate, many successful American firms began their internationalization first in Canada (both in the Anglo cluster), Austrian firms first began their internationalization in Germany (both in the Germanic cluster), Japanese firms first began their internationalization in Taiwan (both in the Confucian Asia cluster),and Indian firms began their internationalization in Malaysia (both in the Southern Asia cluster). By focusing initially on the nations that share similar cultures, the firms can rapidly build economies of scale and develop regional value chains, without being burdened by unusual costs of foreignness and psychic distance. With a strong foundation in societies with similar cultures, it becomes easier for firms to expand into other cultures.

Precise knowledge about specific dimensions of cultures on which the societies differ can help organizations to develop a sequential strategy for globalization. Two dimensions are particularly relevant in organizational design: power distance and uncertainty avoidance.

A high degree of power distance as a societal attribute cultivates hierarchical structures, while a low degree of power distance nurtures horizontal structures. A high degree of uncertainty avoidance cultivates formal mechanistic structures, while a low degree of uncertainty avoidance supports organic structures. More hierarchical and mechanistic structures tend to be effective for products in mature life cycles, with cost-sensitive demand, and standardized technologies. Hierarchical firms can establish and enforce standards quickly, and maintain tight control of operations by giving incentives for following the mechanistic norms (Saloner, Shepard, & Podolny, 2001). Therefore we speculate that

Proposition 1.1: Firms whose competitive advantage depends on rapidly standardizing the established product lines and aggressive price cuts should seek to establish factories and sourcing networks in societies that are high in power distance and uncertainty avoidance.

On the other hand, horizontal and organic structures tend to be more effective for products that require substantial experience, tacit knowledge, customization, and service content. They also tend to be more effective, in an emerging and developmental life cycle (Saloner, Shepard, and Podolny, 2001). Horizontal firms can flexibly respond to the changing customer and market needs, and creatively sample and select emerging technologies and knowledge opportunities. Therefore, we speculate that

Proposition 1.2: Firms whose competitive advantage relies on fast-paced 'time to market' strategies and personalization should seek to establish core operations in societies that are low in power distance and uncertainty avoidance.

Finally, cultural dimensions can also help firms systematically plan and implement organizational learning projects.

Proposition 1.3: To turn around the markets that are becoming increasingly commodity-like and price sensitive, firms should expand into and grant special mandates to low power distance and low uncertainty avoidance societies for developing higher value-adding service modules.

Proposition 1.4: Similarly, to expand the markets for costly services, firms should leverage operations in high power distance and high uncertainty avoidance societies to standardize the systems and to reach out to a larger mass market.

## Mode of International Entry

Psychic distance and cultural difference makes international entry prone to high levels of uncertainty, and forces many firms to use a large risk adjustment factor in assessing the effects of cultural and market differences. Better cultural knowledge and a systematic process of learning about different cultures can help make the risks of international entry more manageable (Kogut & Singh, 1998), and yield the advantages of globalization to the firms. To make the risks of cultural differences predictable and quantifiable, a common approach of successful firms is to rely on joint ventures and acquisitions for their first entry into other societies, especially when those societies differ substantially in terms of culture. The joint ventures and acquisitions give access to cultural skills and learning that can prove very costly and time consuming for a firm that tries to enter the market using its own resources (Barkema, Bell, & Pennings, 1996). However when the opportunities exist, the multinational enterprises prefer full acquisitions, as opposed to partial acquisitions and joint ventures, for entering the societies that have a different culture. Partial acquisitions and joint ventures add an intricate layer of complexity, because the firms must typically negotiate, coordinate, communicate, and share control with a local partner. For effective partner relationships, a high level of local cultural competence is generally needed - else the venture becomes unduly vulnerable to transactional difficulties, performance failure, and early dissolution (Lane & Beamish, 1990). To illustrate, in a recent joint venture among Asahi Glass of Japan, Samsung Group of South Korea, and Corning of the United States, the first two teamed together because of their shared priority on group collectivism and non-assertiveness in their communications, while Corning was isolated because of its focus on uncertainty avoidance and assertive performance orientation. This caused the failure of the venture (Griffith & Harvey, 2001). However, a full acquisition strategy is also not free from risks. In fact, when an overseas unit is fully acquired, success depends on the ability of firms to integrate their new overseas unit with its other international operations. Since the overseas units may have a distinct organizational culture, such integration is often quite difficult (Barkema, Bell, & Pennings, 1996).

Cultural dimensions can help design a more robust framework for selecting the mode of international entry. Cross-cultural integration and communication competence is particularly sensitive to the dimensions of group collectivism and assertiveness. A high degree of in-group collectivism inculcates a sense of belongingness to a group, resulting in a feeling of demarcation of in-group vs. out-group, while a low degree of group collectivism nurtures a contractual view of relationships. A high degree of assertiveness generates a sense of confidence carrying conviction and acceptance of one's worldview by others, while a low degree of assertiveness supports a sense of assimilation and adaptation. Therefore we speculate that

Proposition 2.1: Full acquisitions are likely to be more effective than the partial acquisitions as a mode of entry when the society of the acquired organization has a high degree of in-group collectivism and q high degree of assertiveness.

In-group oriented and assertive employees would be more committed to the corporate group if they saw themselves as part of it, and would be more willing to be its brand ambassadors in the host society. On the other hand, we speculate that

Proposition 2.2: Joint ventures and partial acquisitions should be preferred when the host society has a low degree group collectivism and assertiveness.

Less group-oriented overseas partners and employees would rise above their own group interests and seek to identify areas of mutual interests. Also, less assertive overseas partners and employees would not single-mindedly pursue their own point of view, rather they could be engaged in a fruitful two-way dialogue for exchange of knowledge, collaborative problem-solving, and joint learning. Finally, contractual, non-assertive problem solving in joint ventures and partial acquisitions can be a platform for handling the tasks that are outside the core competence and knowledge base of the acquiring firm. On the other hand, relational, assertive initiatives in fully integrated acquisitions would be best suited for the areas within the primary capability set of the firm. Also, as the firm develops cultural competence, it can launch independent investments to exploit derivative project opportunities, and forge strategic alliances with a broader network of partners in the host cultures.

## Design of Value Chain Organization

There is much interest in an effective international organization of the value chain – the sequence of activities through which a firm adds value for the customers (Krugman, 1995). The differences in cultures and associated competencies can form a solid basis for a distributed organization of value chain at a global level. For instance, Nordic societies tend to be adept at gender management, and Germanic societies are adept in enforcing autonomous discipline and control through the use of information and communications technology. Therefore, Nordic operations may be given an international mandate for implementing processes for gender empowerment, while the Germanic operations may act as facilitators in applying information technology for reducing the costs of centralized control. In this way, organizations from both societies contribute to each other additional knowledge and competencies.

There is a growing imperative for time-based competition, including managing new product development projects in a time-bound fashion.

However, not all learning can be planned in advance because a large component of knowledge may be tacit. Further, exchange of knowledge evolves in a chaotic fashion through spontaneous experiments and unanticipated discoveries. The firms can introduce a degree of structure to these varied kinds of learning, and also mandate strategic responsibilities to operations in different societies by using cultural dimensions as an organizing principle. The cultural dimensions of future orientation and performance orientation are particularly important in this regard.

In more future oriented societies, the thrust is on long-term planning horizons, and predictable behaviors, while in less future oriented societies, spontaneous behaviors and experimental actions are typical. In more performance-oriented societies, the behaviors and rewards are oriented towards specific, measurable goals; but in less performance-oriented societies, the behaviors and rewards are guided by a diverse set of fluid forces including social desirability issues. The firms can organize their value chain vertically along the future orientation dimension. Upstream activities, such as new product development and other research projects, typically require long-term planning to contain costs and maximize value. We speculate that

Proposition 3.1: Upstream activities are best assigned to more future oriented societies.

Downstream activities, such as customization and customer relationship management, on the other hand depend on spontaneous encounters in the market place. We speculate that

Proposition 3.2: Less future oriented societies are likely to handle downstream activities more effectively.

Similarly, the performance orientation dimension can guide the horizontal organization of the value chain. Within each segment of the value chain, measurable goals are less meaningful for more mature activities, where reliance on established standards is less valuable for competitive advantage. On the other hand, for innovative and emerging activities, it is critical to anchor compensation on clear standards for codification of the knowledge-base and best practices relevant to the activities, abstraction of the links with organizational capabilities, and diffusion of the knowledge throughout the organization.   Thus, a strong performance orientation is essential.   Thus, we speculate that:

> Proposition 3.3: For greater effectiveness, mature activities should be assigned to societies that have a   low degree of   performance orientation, and emerging, innovative activities to those that have a   high degree of   performance orientation.

Thereafter, different process elements of the project may be allocated to different firms in individual societies, depending on the level of their organizational resources and technical skill sets, to allow accomplishment of the desired time, cost and quality goals.

## Multi-Constituency Leadership

Increasingly, organizational effectiveness is contingent on the leadership skills that balance diverse goals of multiple constituencies, and on a leadership perspective that focuses on building sustainable relationships with ecology, community, customers, suppliers, workers, and competing and collaborating organizations. Competitive advantage is less and less dependent on a view of strategic decision making that sees leaders as agents of the stockholders, wherein leader interest is fundamentally at variance with that of the stockholder as both seek to promote their own self-interest. Instead, with globalization, outstanding leaders are taking a 'stewardship' role, seeking to generate and enhance value for the relationship between both organizations. To build and sustain relational networks, an effective communication framework is imperative (Palmer, 1997; Koza & Lewin, 2000). Specifically, sufficient commonality and consistency in cultural frameworks is necessary to enable correct 'translation' of the messages by recipients to maintain the true meaning by the sender (Kim, 1992). While a common cultural framework facilitates relation building, it also acts as a conduit for a faster diffusion of tacit knowledge of the competing firms from societies with similar cultures.

Consider the case of the Confucian Asia cluster, which includes societies such as Japan, Korea and Taiwan. The growth of Japanese firms after World War II precipitated the rise of Korean and Taiwanese competition in similar and related industry areas within decades, and led to a loss of the Japanese share in multiple global markets. With effective leadership, the firms can benefit from the propensity of knowledge to diffuse more efficiently across societies with similar cultures. Thus, more recently, Japanese firms have taken to designing innovative products within Japan, and then moving the production to their factories and affiliates in China to secure cost efficiencies. The similarity in cultural norms within the Confucian Asia cluster has facilitated effective transfer of production methods, organizing principles, and learning from one nation to the other (Abo, 1996), and thereby helped Japanese firms limit the losses in their global market positions.

The societal culture also plays an important role in shaping the form of a competitive advantage model. Thus, Anglo societies tend to rely on a market-contract model, Confucian societies on a relational-contract model, and Germanic societies on a professional bureaucracy model (Dore, 1973; Hofstede, 2001). Increasingly, the competitive advantage of the firms is being subject to issues related to social capital, ethics, and human rights. Cultural dimensions such as institutional collectivism and humane orientation are likely to be especially relevant for meeting these new competitive and legitimacy challenges. High institutional collectivism relates to a thrust on holistic and integrated behavior where one's self identity is substantially based on the collectivity of which they are members, while low institutional collectivism is associated with autonomous self-perceptions. High humane orientation emphasizes a secular concept of public morality and ethics, something that is of limited concern under low humane orientation. Increasingly, international firms are also being challenged to be responsive to the values of host societies that have varying degrees of institutional collectivism and humane orientation. For instance, managers must recognize that in some societies it is legitimate for businesses to be managed primarily for profit, while in other societies the issues related to sustainable ecology, employee welfare, and corporate citizenship are pertinent. Therefore we suggest that:

Proposition 4: To develop a secular policy that is responsive to both profit-making as well as corporate citizenship goals, firms would need to identify and adopt the best practices from different cultures.

The recent trends do suggest that the firms are organizing practice development initiatives in coordinated international networks, rather than accepting separate practices in each society or enforcing dominant practices of one society on the rest of their operations (Bartlett & Ghoshal, 1994).

## Human Resource Diversity

Culture plays an important role in the design of human resource management systems that are responsive to the diverse needs and preferences of people. Culturally responsive human resource management systems can facilitate cross-cultural teamwork, offer fair compensation and rewards, and support constructive careers and training in the organization. To illustrate, there exist substantial cross-cultural differences among people in their attitudes towards relationships with the group (Triandis et. al, 1988). The Anglo societies, for instance, tend to favor individualistic, impersonal, and rational decision-making, while the Confucian Asian societies pay regard to interpersonal feelings, relationships, and group orientation (England, 1983; Hofstede, 1980). Recognition of this factor has led many firms in the Anglo cultures to encourage their employees to exchange information with their team members, address the points of disagreement, and strive to clarify issues to expeditiously reach a closure (Moran, 1987). Such an approach inculcates a sense of pride in the ability of the team to expeditiously accomplish outstanding results, and in the quality of team members that allows employees to also perform effectively.

Similarly, the factors influencing motivation of people vary significantly across cultures. Vroom (1964) suggested valence (importance of an award), expectancy (effort-performance relationship), and instrumentality (performance-award relationship) as the core determinants of motivation. Though there has been only partial empirical support for Vroom's theory in the American context, it provides a nice framework for examining cross-cultural motivation.

Intrinsic vs. extrinsic motivational orientation is a key factor influencing the valence. Intrinsic motivation, in particular, contributes positively to overall performance, as well as, to the specific dimensions of technical knowledge, providing information, and controlling expense (Goolsby, Lagace & Boorom 1992). The intrinsic vs. extrinsic motivation orientation differs across cultures: Southern Asian clusters, for instance, tend to be highly motivated by intrinsic goals, because of their concern with humane, group oriented, and performance oriented dimensions (See Table 2). Valence is also influenced by need satisfaction, which also varies across cultures. Similarly, the expectancy of effort-performance linkage differs across cultures. In Confucian Asian cultures, people tend to discount their efforts, and tend to attribute performance more to group maintenance and harmony of factors because of a high degree of institutional collectivism (see Table 2). As a result, one's effort is not expected to lead to very high levels of performance. Also, if the performance is indeed high, then the firm is expected to share the rewards with the whole group, and not with one individual. Finally, the instrumental relationship between performance and award also varies by cultures. In Anglo cultures (with high performance orientation), performance-based pay systems, founded on measurable and verifiable performance measures, may be sufficient to establish this instrumentality (see Table 2).

Clearly, firms need to introduce careful selection of employees, orientation/training programs or incentive system adaptations to be congruent with cross-cultural variations. In addition, careers and training systems should also be sensitive to more subtle, emic aspects of cultures.

While discussing the issue of effective learning of languages, Brooks (1964) distinguished between Culture with a capital C, which referred to formal culture and culture with a small c, or deep culture, which referred to 'way-of-life' culture. In practice, training of culture as 'way of life' tends to be difficult and costly to implement. Since cultural dimensions tend to be holistically inter-related, it may be useful to organize societies into clusters that share similar patterns of different cultural dimensions. A cultural cluster-based career and training system can allow the firms to develop a critical knowledge pool about a broad group of societies, which can then be used as a platform for further cross-cultural learning about the particular country to which one is being assigned. Therefore, we propose that:

> Proposition 5: By giving their key executives exposure to the major cultural clusters, and some important markets within each cluster, the firms can ensure stronger retention and exploitation of cultural knowledge and expertise.

## Conclusions

Project GLOBE provides managers with an interesting starting point for gaining a deeper understanding about cultures, and ways to begin leveraging cultural differentials for strategic advantages in the global marketplace. Strategic knowledge about cultural dimensions is, however, just the first step in a systematic organization of cultural resources, capabilities, and learning. It is important to recognize that the societies that appear quite similar in terms of several cultural dimensions may still be substantially different in other aspects. In the Anglo cluster, for instance, the United States is renowned for its technological leadership. Canada, Australia, New Zealand, and South Africa remain technological followers. These differences are partly a reflection of the varying work-culture and work-climate of different societies, associated with the structural differences in economic, political, civic, and social institutions (Dunphy & Herbig, 1994). The nations differ in their priority on the protection of property rights, government funding of research and university education, venture capital, anti-trust, and labor and environment protection laws. For instance, Canada, Australia, New Zealand and South Africa have a market size even smaller than that of the UK, their military budgets are very low, and their economy is based pre-dominantly on natural resources, which crowd out innovations in the other sectors by bidding up the cost of human resources.

The manifestation of each cultural dimension within any given society also tends to be pluralistic in nature. Societal culture analysis should be used for the purposes of inclusion, involvement, and equal representation to members of all societies, rather than for the purposes of differentiating them for preferential treatment. Each ethnological group has its distinctive values and norms, which shape the behavior of the members identifying with, or influenced by, them (Howard & Scott, 1981). While factors such as forced assimilation by the dominant group, government policy, education, technology and media exposure could result in partial convergence during some periods and in some elements, other countervailing forces like renewed interest in traditions and identity as a result of post-modernism may make segregation more salient (Berry, Poortinga, Segall, & Dasen, 1992). Pineda & Whitehead's (1997) study on subcultures in the Philippines, noted that despite differences in language, northern and southern regions share a strong bond based on shared history, religion and ethnicity. On the other hand, ethnic Chinese differ in their language, religion (Buddhism), and history, from the ethnic Malays/Filipinos. A majority of ethnic Chinese live in urban cities in self-contained communities, and control 70% of the economy, though they constitute only 3% of the population (Naisbitt, 1996). Most of the ethnic Filipino workforce has received US-style education, and their culture was subject to more than 300 years of Spanish/Mexican influence. They put higher value on self-esteem and personal judgment, partly because they have more experience with the local institutions (Pineda & Whitehead, 1997). Subculture differentiation may also arise due to generation, gender, education, occupation, and income differences. The implications of these differentiating factors should be duly recognized while implementing a cultural strategy.

Finally, globalization of information, research, education, media, trade, investments, organizations, language, and technology has contributed to significant convergence in some cultural practices and norms across many societies. Discounting these universal, common, and shared cultural elements could prevent managers from exploiting the benefits of economies of scale, agglomeration, and mass customization. Under appropriate and supportive conditions, these universal norms can be the basis for self-organizing interaction, communication, and learning among people and organizational units from different societies. Therefore, it is essential to not take a mechanistic view of societal cultures, but instead to allow an organic interaction between members of different societies. When the firms use cultural data as the basis for designing their organizational structures and strategies, they should also encourage the use of task forces, web, and other vehicles for organic cross-cultural exchange and linkages.

In summary, cross-cluster cultural competence, learning, knowledge, and perspectives built on the basis of the GLOBE study can help firms develop robust models for organizational transformation across cultures. Those interested in knowing more about the project and its findings are referred to the GLOBE website at mgmt3.ucalgary.ca/web/globe.nsf/index.

# References

Abo, T. (1996). "The Japanese production system: the process of adaptation to national settings." In R. Boyer & D. Drache (eds.) *States Against Markets: The Limits of Globalization.*( pp 136-154) London: Routledge.

Alicke, M. D. (1985). "Global self-evaluation as determined by the desirability and controllability of trait adjectives". *Journal of Personality and Social Psychology*, **49**, 1621-1630.

Allen, N.J., and Meyer, J.P. (1990). "The measurement and antecedents of affective, continuance, and normative commitment". *Journal of Occupational Psychology*, **63**, 1-18.

Andersen, O. (1993). "On the internationalization process of firms: A critical analysis". *Journal of International Business Studies*, **24** (2), 209-232.

Atkinson, J. W. (1957). "Motivational determinants of risk-taking behavior." *Psychological Review*, **64**, 359-372.

Atkinson, J. W. (1981). "Thematic apperceptive measurement of motivation in 1950 and 1980." In G. d'Ydewalle & W. Lens (Eds.), *Cognition in Human Motivation and Learning* (pp.159-198). Hillsdale, NJ: Lawrence Erlbaum Associates.

Barkema, H. G., Bell, J. & Pennings, J.M. (1996). "Foreign entry, cultural barriers, and learning." *Strategic Management Journal,* **17**, 151-166.

Bartlett, C.A. & Ghoshal, S. (1991). *Managing Across Borders: The Transnational Solution.* MA: Harvard Business School Press.

Bellah, R. N., Madsen, R., Sullivan, W. M., Swindler, A., & Tipton, S. M. (1985). *Habits of the Heart: Individualism and Commitment in American Life*. Berkeley: University of California Press.

Benito, G. & Gripsrud, G. (1992). "The expansion of foreign direct investment: discrete rational location choices or a cultural learning process?" *Journal of International Business Studies*, **23**(3), 461-476.

Berry, J.W, Poortinga, YH, Segall, MH, & Dasen, PR (1992). *Cross-cultural Psychology: Research and Applications*. Cambridge: Cambridge University Press.

Bond, M. H. (Ed.). (1986). *The Psychology of the Chinese People*. New York: Oxford.

Booream, C.D. & Flowers, J.V. (1978). "A procedural model for training of assertive behavior." In J.M. Whitely and J.V. Flowers (eds.) *Approaches to Assertion Training*, (pp. 15-46), CA: Brooks/Cole.

Briggs, A. (1961). "The Welfare State in Historical Perspective." *Archives Europeennes de Sociologie*, **2**, 221-258.

Brooks, N.H. (1964). *Language and language learning: Theory and practice*. New York: Harcourt, Brace & World.

Buchanan, B. (1974). "Building organizational commitment: The socialization of managers in work organizations." *Administrative Science Quarterly*, **19**, 533-546.

Cervantes, J.M., & Ramirez, O. (1992). "Spirituality and family dynamics in psychotherapy with Latino children." In L.A. Vargas & J.D. Koss-Chioino (Eds.). *Working with Culture* (pp. 103-128). San Francisco: Jossey Bass.

Chandler, T. A., Sharma, D. D., and Wolf, F. M. (1983). "Gender differences in achievement and affiliation attributions: A five nation study." *Journal of Cross-cultural Psychology*, **14**, 241-256.

Chatman, T. A., Polzer, J.T., Barsade, S.G., and Neale, M.A. (1998). "Being different yet feeling similar: The influence of demographic composition and organizational culture on work processes and outcomes." *Administrative Science Quarterly*. **43**, 749-780.

Coltrane, S. (1988). "Father-child relationships and the status of women: A cross-cultural study." *American Journal of Sociology*, **93**, 1060-1095

Crary, W. G. (1966). "Reactions to incongruent self-experiences." *Journal of Consulting Psychology*, **30**, 246-252.

Crawford, M. (1995). *Talking Difference: On Gender and Language*. London: Sage.

Cyert, R.M., and March, J.G. (1963). *A Behavioral Theory of the Firm*. NJ: Prentice Hall.

Dewey, J. (1886); "The psychological standpoint". *Mind*. **11**, 1-19.

Diener, C.I. and Dweck, C.S. (1980). "An analysis of learned helplessness II. The processing of success." *Journal of Personality and Social Psychology*, **39**, 940-952.

Doi, T. (1973). *The Anatomy of Dependence*. Tokyo: Kodansha.

Dore, R. (1973). *British Factory-Japanese Factory*. Berkeley: University of California Press.

Dorfman, P. W. (1996). "International and Cross-cultural Leadership Research." In B J Punnett & O Shenkar (Eds.) *Handbook for International Management Research*, (pp267-349), UK: Blackwell.

Dunphy, S. & Herbig, P. (1994). "A Comparison of Innovative Capabilities among the Anglo-American Countries: The Case for Structural Influences on Innovation." *Management Decisions*, **32**(8), 50-58.

Dweck, C.S. (1986). "Motivational processes affecting learning." *American Psychologist*, **41**, 1040-1048.

Dweck, C.S. & Leggett, EL. (1988). "A social-cognitive approach to motivation and personality." *Psychological Review,* **95**, 256-273.

Eckhardt, W. (1971). "Conservatism, East and West." *Journal of Cross-cultural Psychology*. **2**, 109-128.

England, G.W. (1983). "Japanese and American Management: Theory Z and Beyond." *Journal of International Business Studies*. **14**, 131-142.

Festinger, L. (1954). "A theory of social comparison processes." *Human Relations*, **7**, 117-140.

Fyans, Jr., L.J.; Salili F.; Maehr M.L., and Desai K.A. (1983). "A cross-cultural exploration into the meaning of achievement." *Journal of Personality and Social Psychology*, **44**(5), 1000-1013.

Goolsby, J. R., Lagace, R. R, & Boorom, M. L. (1992). "Psychological Adaptiveness and Sales Performance." *Journal of Personal Selling and Sales Management,* **12**(2), 51-55.

Griffith, D.A. & Harvey, M.G. (2001). "Executive insights: An intercultural communication model for use in global interorganizational networks." *Journal of International Marketing,* **9** (3), 87-102.

Gupta, V., & Hanges P. J. (2004). "A Taxonomy of GLOBE Cultural Clusters." In House R J, Hanges P J, Javidan M, Dorfman P, Gupta V. (Eds.) *Leadership, Cultures, and Organizations: The GLOBE Study of 62 Societies,* CA: Sage Publications.

Gupta, V., Macmillan I. C., & Surie G. (2002). "Entrepreneurial Leadership: Developing and Measuring a Cross-cultural Construct." *Academy of Management,* Denver, CO.

Gupta, V., Sully, M., & House, R. J. (2004). "Developing Validation Measures of GLOBE's Societal Culture Scales." In House R J, Hanges P J, Javidan M, Dorfman P, Gupta V. (Eds.) *Leadership, Cultures, and Organizations: The GLOBE Study of 62 Societies,* CA: Sage Publications.

Hanges P. J & Dickson M. (2004). "Statistical Validation of GLOBE Scales." In House R J, Hanges P J, Javidan M, Dorfman P, Gupta V. (Eds.) *Leadership, Cultures, and Organizations: The GLOBE Study of 62 Societies,* CA: Sage Publications.

Hartog D., House R.J, Hanges P.J, Ruiz-Quintanilla S.A., & GLOBE associates (1999). "Emics and Etics of Culturally-Endorsed Implicit Leadership Theories: Are Attributes of Charismatic/Transformational Leadership Universally Endorsed?" *Leadership Quarterly,* **10**(2), 219-256.

Hofstede, G.; (1980). *Culture's Consequences.* Beverly Hills: Sage.

Hofstede, G. (2001). *Culture's Consequences: Comparing Values, Behaviors, Institutions, and Organizations Across Nations.* Second Edition. CA: Sage Publications.

House, R.J. (1977). "A 1976 Theory of Charismatic Leadership." in Hunt, J.G. and Larsons, L.L. (Eds), *Leadership: The Cutting Edge,* Southern Illinois University Press, IL.

House, R.J., Hanges P.J, Ruiz-Quintanilla S.A., Dorfman PW, Javidan M, Dickson M, Gupta V., & GLOBE associates (1999). "Cultural influences on leadership and organizations: Project GLOBE." *Advances in Global Leadership*, **1**, 171-233.

House, R. J., Spangler W. D., & Woycke J. (1991). "Personality and Charisma in the U.S. Presidency: A psychological theory of leader effectiveness." *Administrative Science Quarterly*, **36**, 364-396.

Howard, A. and Scott, R.A. (1981). *The minority groups in complex societies.* In: R.H.

Huxley, J.S. *The Humanist Frame.* Harper & Bros., New York, 1961.

Hymer, S. (1976). *The International Operations of National Firms: Study of Direct Foreign Investment.* Cambridge, Mass.: MIT Press. (Ph.D. Dissertation).

Inglehart, R. (1997). *Modernization and Postmodernization: Cultural, Economic and Political Change in 43 Societies.* NJ: Princeton University Press.

Jackson, D. N., Ahmed, S. A. & Heapy, N. A. (1973). "Is achievement a unitary construct?" University of Western Ontario, *Research Bulletin,* 273.

Javidan, M. & House, R J. (2001). "Cultural Acumen for the Global Manager: Lessons from Project GLOBE." *Organizational Dynamics*, **29**(4), 289-305.

Johanson, J. & Vahlne, J-E (1977). "The internationalization process of the firm - a model of knowledge development and increasing foreign market commitments." *Journal of International Business Studies*, **8** (1), 23-32.

Johanson, J. & Wiedersheim-Paul, F. (1975), "The internationalization of the firm - Four Swedish cases." *Journal of Management Studies*, **12** (3), 305-322.

Johnson, F. (1985). "The Western concept of the self." In A. J. Marsella, G. DeVos, & F. L. K. Hsu (Eds.), *Culture and Self: Asian and Western Perspectives* (pp. 91-138). Honolulu: University of Hawaii Press.

Kim, Y.Y. (1992). "Intercultural Communication Competence. A Systems Theoretic View." In S. Ting-Toomey & F. Korzenny (Eds.). *Cross-cultural Interpersonal Communication* (pp. 259-275). Newbury Park, CA: Sage Publications.

Kluckhohn, F. R.. & Strodtbeck, F. L. (1961). *Variations in Value Orientations.* NY: HarperCollins.

Kogut B., & Singh H. (1998). "The effect of national culture on the choice of entry mode." *Journal of International Business Studies*, **29**, 411-432.

Koza, M. P. & Lewin, A. Y. (2000). "Managing Partnerships and Strategic Alliances: Raising the Odds of Success." *European Management Journal*, **18**(2): 146-151.

Krugman, P. (1995). *Development, Geography and Economic Theory*. MA: MIT Press.

Kurtz, P. (2001); "Two Competing Moralities." **21**(3), Free Inquiry Magazine.

Lane, H. W., & Beamish, P. W. (1990). "Cross-cultural cooperative behavior in joint ventures in LDCs." *Management International Review*, 30 (special issue): 87-102.

Lange, A., & Jakubowski, P. (1976). *Responsible Assertive Behavior.* Champaign, IL: Research Press.

Leelakulthanit O., Day R., and Walters R. (1991). "Investigating the relationship between Marketing and Overall Satisfaction with Life in a Developing Country." *Journal of Macromarketing*, **11**: 3-23.

Martin, P. Y. (1993). "Feminist Practice in Organizations: Implications for Management." In Fagenson S. (Ed) *Women in Management: Trends, Perspectives and Challenges*, CA: Sage.

Maslow, A.H. (1970). *Motivation and Personality*. New York: Harper & Row.

McClelland, D.C. (1961). *The Achieving Society*. NJ: D.Van Nostrand Co.

McClelland, D.C. (1965). "Wanted: A new self-image for women." In R.J. Lifton (Ed.). *The Woman in America.* 173-192. Boston: Houghton Mifflin.

McClelland, D. C. (1985). *Human Motivation* IL: Scott, Foresman, & CO.

McClelland, D. C., Atkinson, J. W., Clark, R. A., & Lowell, E. L. (1953). *The Achievement Motive*. Englewood Cliffs: NJ: Prentice-Hall.

McClelland, D. C. & Burnham, D H (1976). "Power is the great motivator." *Harvard Business Review*. **54**(4), 100-110.

Mill, J. S. (1863). *Utilitarianism*. London: Parker, Son and Bourn.

Moran, R.T. (1987). *Getting Your Yen's Worth: How to Negotiate with Japan, Inc.* TX: Gulf.

Morand, D.A.; (1996). "What's in a name?" *Management Communication Quarterly*, **9**(4), 4-22.

Mulder, M. (1977). "Power equalization through participation." *Administrative Science Quarterly*, **16**, 31-38.

Munroe, R.L. Munroe and B. Whiting (eds), *Handbook of Cross-Cultural Human Development*, New York: Garland STPM Press.

Murdock, G. (1972). *The Outline of World Cultures*. 4th ed. New Haven, CT: Human Relations Area Files.

Naisbitt, J. (1996). *Mega trends Asia*. New York: Simon & Schuster.

Nakamura, H. (1964). *Ways of Thinking of Eastern Peoples*. Honolulu: University of Hawaii Press.

Nakata, C., and Sivakumar, K., (1996). "National Culture and new product development: An integrative review." *Journal of Marketing*. **60**, 61-72.

Nordstrom, K. & Vahlne J-E (1994). "Is the globe shrinking? Psychic distance and the establishment of Swedish sales subsidiaries during the last 100 years." In M. Landeck, editor, *International Trade: Regional and Global Issues*. United Sates: St. Martin's Press.

O'Reilly III, and Chatman J. (1986). "Organizational commitment and psychological adjustment: the effects of compliance, identification, and internalization on presocial behavior." *Journal of Applied Psychology*, **71**, 492-499.

Palmer, A. (1997). "Defining relationship marketing: an international perspective." *Management Decision*, **35**(4), 319-329.

Parsons, T., and Shils, E.A. (1951). *Towards a General Theory of Action*. MA: Harvard University Press.

Pelto, P. J. (1968). "The differences between "tight" and "loose" societies." *Transaction*. **5**, 37-40.

Perlmutter, H.V. (1969). "The tortuous evolution of the multinational corporation." *Columbia Journal of World Business*, **4**, 24-31.

Pineda, R.C. & Whitehead C. J. (1997). "The effects of ethnic group culture on managerial task activities." *Group & Organization Management*, **22**(1), 31-52.

Rakos, R.F. (1991). *Assertive Behavior: Theory, Research and Training*. London: Routledge.

Read, K. E. (1955). "Morality and the concept of the person among the Gahuku-Gama." *Oceania*, **25**, 233-282

Rosenberger, N. R. (1992). *Japanese Sense of Self.* Cambridge: Cambridge University Press.

Ross, M., & Sicoly, F. (1979). "Egocentric biases in availability and attribution." *Journal of Personality and Social Psychology*, **37**, 322-336.

Ryff, C. D. (1989). "Happiness is everything or is it? Explorations on the meaning of psychological well-being." *Journal of Personality and Social Psychology*, **57**, 1069-1081.

Saloner, G., Shepard, A, & Podolny, J. (2001). *Strategic Management.* NY: John Wiley.

Sarros, J C & Woodman, D S (1993). "Leadership in Australia and its organizational outcomes." *Leadership & Organization Development Journal.* **14**(4), 3-9.

Schutz, W. C. (1958). *FIRO: A Three-dimensional Theory of Interpersonal Behavior.* NY: Holt, Rinehart & Winston.

Schwartz, S.H. (1994). "Beyond individualism and collectivism: New cultural dimensions of values.' In U. Kim, H.C. Triandis, C. Kagitcibasi, S-C Choi, and G. Yoon (eds.) *Individualism and Collectivism: Theory, Method, and Applications*, (pp. 85-122), CA: Sage.

Schwartz, S.H. & Bilsky, W. (1987). "Towards a Universal Psychological Structure of Human Values." *Journal of Personality and Social Psychology*, **53**(3): 550-562.

Seginer, R., and Schlesinger, R. (1998). "Adolescent's future orientation in time and place: The Case of the Israeli Kibbutz", *International Journal of Behavioral Development*, **22**, 151-167.

Shweder, R. A., & Bourne, E. J. (1984). "Does the concept of the person vary cross-culturally?" In R. A. Shweder & R. A. LeVine (Eds.), *Culture Theory: Essays on Mind, Self, and Emotion* (pp. 158-199). New York: Cambridge University Press.

Solzhenitsyn, A., (1976). *Warning to the West.* NY: Farrar, Strauss and Giroux.

Strauss, A. S. (1982). "The structure of the self in Northern Cheyenne culture." In B. Lee (Ed.), *Psychosocial Theories of the Self* (pp. 111-128). New York: Plenum.

Triandis, H. C. (1993). "The contingency model in cross-cultural perspective."
    In M M Chemers & R Ayman (Eds.) *Leadership Theory and Research:
    Perspectives and Directions*, ( pp.167-188), San Diego: Academic Press.

Triandis, H.C., Bontempto, R., Villareal, M.J., Asai, M., and Lucca, N. (1988).
    "Individualism and Collectivism: Cross cultural perspectives on self-in-
    group relationships." *Journal of Personality and Social Psychology*, **54**,
    323-338.

Trompenaars, F. (1993). *Riding the Waves of Culture: Understanding
    CulturalDiversity in Business*. London: Economist Books.

Vroom, V.H. (1964). *Work and Motivation*. New York: Wiley.

Weiner, B. (1980). *Human Motivation*. New York: Holt, Rinehart, and
    Winston.

Yan, W. F. and Gaier, E L (1994). "Causal attributions for college success and
    failure: An Asia-American Comparison." *Journal of Cross-cultural
    Psychology*, **25**, 146-158.

Zuckerman, M. (1979). "Attribution of success and failure revisited, or: The
    motivational bias is alive and well in attribution theory." *Journal of
    Personality*, **47**, 245-287.

## Chapter 3

# Leadership Strategies and Relationship Competence Development[1]

Zhong-Ming Wang
School of Management, Zhejiang University, CHINA

## Introduction

With the rapid development of the Chinese economy and organizational reform, leadership, entrepreneurship and teamwork have become active areas of research and applications in China. In the recent years, the focus of research has shifted from leadership patterns and general selection to leadership and entrepreneurship competence, and leadership team development in relation to the areas of strategic human resource management (Wang, 1989a; Wang, 1990; Li, Tsui, Xin & Hambrick, 1999; Wang, 1999b; Wang 2000). As China enters into WTO, leadership in the international business setting is becoming a new focus. Cross-regional joint ventures and wholly-owned ventures have been the most frequent entry mode for overseas Chinese entrepreneurs, small and medium-sized international firms, and leading multinational companies. As a result,

[1] This chapter is supported by the Chinese National Science Foundation Grants (Project No. 70071050 and Project No. 70232010) to the author.

cross-regional mergers and acquisitions are becoming more and more popular forms of new business ventures in China (Wang, 1992; Leung, Smith, Wang & Sun, 1996; Wang, 1999a; Chen, et al 2002; Tsui & Lau, 2002). Many local Chinese companies are facing the challenge of developing effective strategies for cross-cultural leadership and cross-regional entrepreneurship and business management. Specifically, leadership studies are carried out in such areas as leadership competence structure and its assessment, relationship management, teamwork leadership, conflict resolution, entrepreneurship and organizational change. In this chapter, we shall first present some recent research findings on relationship structure and leadership competence, and then discuss the progresses in studies on leadership strategies and teamwork in China.

## Relationship Management and Implicit Leadership

Although the importance of *Guanxi* and relationship-building in business and in other types of negotiations in Asia and in other high-context societies has been stressed by a number of authors, we still need more empirical evidence to describe the concept of relationships and relationship-building in leadership and business. Though it has been suggested that *Guanxi* and relationship-building is central to successful business and management in Asia, many questions remain unanswered before we can understand the role and process of relationship strategy. Relationship competence seems to be among the central components of implicit leadership in China (Guzzo & Shea, 1992; Wang, 1995; Lou, 1997; Dyer & Singh, 1998; Tjosvold, Hui, and Law, 1998; Miles, 2000; Wang, 2000; Li & Labig, 2001).

*The Relationship Concept* What are the features of relationship concept in China? In order to understand this question, Yang (1995) suggested adopting the social-oriented approach to Chinese personality and behavior. In the studies on the relationship between personality and performance, Wang (2000) found that interpersonal relationship building proved to be an effective performance predictor for Chinese employees and managers. Also, Wang and Liang (2003) reviewed recent literature and conducted a series of field interviews on relationship and its key elements under the Chinese work setting. They concluded that in general, the Chinese relationship orientation included at least three components: Harmony seeking, *Renqing-Face* concern, and group-others consideration. Here are the implications of these components.

1. Harmony seeking. The first element of the Chinese relationship orientation is "harmony seeking". The Chinese society has, for a long time, emphasized interpersonal harmony and valued harmonic relationships. The rule of royalty and benevolence was seen as the fundamental principle of dealing with interpersonal relationships under the tradition of Confucian culture (Pang, 1997). Therefore, both compromising strategies and accommodation strategies were mostly adopted in coping with relationship problems in China. For example, It was found that in a collectivist society, people tended to choose both compromising and accommodation strategies to solve conflicts in organizations. Ho and Chiu (1996) analyzed 2,056 proverbs and demonstrated two main cultural characteristics: altruism, and harmony maintenance. The study on relationship leadership found that social morality was the highest loading factor of scarifying individual interests and maintaining group harmony among Chinese employees.

2. *Renqing* (interpersonal affection) and *Face* concern. The second element of the Chinese Relationship orientation is the "*Renqing* and *Face* concern". The Chinese approach to relationship is affected by the Chinese traditions of *Renqing* and *Face*. A number of studies noticed that *Guanxi* networking and social exchange behavior were popular and dominating under the Chinese social and business practice (e.g., Luo, 1997). Huang (1988) also demonstrated that *Renqing* had been used as a social resource while *Face* was a function of the person's social status and reputation. *Renqing* was usually reciprocative involving judgment from both sides, which mediated the business connections and subordinate-supervisor relationship.

3. Group-others consideration. The third element of the Chinese relationship orientation is "group and others consideration". Studies showed that the Chinese interpersonal interaction was more to give an impression of participation and that under the group-oriented culture,

individuals expressed an interdependent self-concept and paid more attention to others' needs, expectations and goals (Markus, & Kitayama, 1991). Even achievement motivation has a social and group element. As Zhu (1989) pointed out, the Chinese achievement motivation involved a key element of personal image in front of the social public. Therefore behaviors such as social comparison, seeking satisfaction from others, avoiding responsibilities, and making judgment by others' feedback were often emphasized.

In a recent empirical study, we used a relationship scale and discovered four key factors: Harmony seeking, social support, information channel and task accomplishment. Inter-correlations among those factors indicated two more general factors: social harmony (harmony seeking and social support) and task channel (information channel and task accomplishment). Among others, harmony seeking was positively correlated with both information channel and task accomplishment, whereas information channel was positively correlated with task accomplishment. However, harmony seeking was negatively correlated with social support, indicating a *Renqing* dilemma.

*Implicit Leadership Theory* Relationship management is largely implicit. Implicit leadership theories became popular in the 1990s (e.g., Kenney, Schwardta-Kenney & Blascorich 1996). In an early work on leadership assessment, the Chinese concept of leadership was studied in order to achieve two objectives of research:

1. To change the traditional way of evaluating enterprise leaders by personal impressions or only political affiliations, and
2. To build up a comprehensive and scientific assessment system for cadre selection and promotion.

To test the hypotheses, a large-scale assessment of leadership behavior was developed and conducted on the basis of a Japanese two–dimensional instrument for leadership assessment (Misumi 1985). This was done in order to measure task performance and relationship maintenance (so-called Performance–Maintenance Scale or PM Scale) among the Chinese managers from the middle and top management positions. Eight situational criteria were used in this PM study:

1. Work motivation,
2. Income satisfaction,
3. Work environment,
4. Mental hygiene,
5. Teamwork,
6. Efficiency of meetings,
7. Communications, and
8. Performance.

This leadership assessment involved 16,260 respondents from 53 factories in various industries in China (Xu, 1987; 1989). The results showed that despite some cultural similarities between China and Japan, moral character emerged as the third dimension of leadership assessment in addition to the original two dimensions of performance and maintenance (Lin, Chen & Wang, 1987; Lin, 1989). The moral character factor was apparently an important cultural characteristic of the leadership concept in Chinese society, generally including personal characteristics such as honesty, integrity, positive attitudes toward employees and party leadership, virtual team cooperation, and organizational commitment. It was believed that any leadership perspective that does not emphasize the moral character of leaders is incomplete (Peterson, Smith, Misumi & Bond, 1990). Therefore, the PM scale was modified into a three–dimensional scale including character, performance and maintenance (CPM) and implemented in a number of Chinese governmental organizations and industrial enterprises. It proved to be a reliable and valid assessment of leadership competence and management behavior. In an attempt to identify the implicit theory of leadership among Chinese people, Lin, Chia and Fang (2000) developed the Chinese Implicit Leadership Scale (CILS) and administered it to 622 Chinese employees from five occupational groups, to explore differences in their perception of leadership. Factor analysis yielded four factors of leadership: personal morality, goal efficiency, interpersonal competence, and versatility. Social groups differing in age, gender, education level, and occupation rated these factors. Results showed no significant gender differences, and the underlying cause for social group differences was education level. The highest ratings to "interpersonal competence" reflected its importance in leadership perception, which is consistent with Chinese collectivist values.

*Relationship as a Competence Structural Component for Leadership and Entrepreneurship* What characterizes the leadership and entrepreneurship competence in China? In a recent study on managerial competency modeling for assessment and selection, Wang and Chen (2002) and Wang (2002a) used a strategic and hierarchical job analysis technique and conducted a leadership critical incident analysis among 568 entrepreneurs and their deputy managers from different companies in China. The main purpose of research was to link work activity, competency elements, and work context with strategic objectives. The leadership competency structure was based on job requirements according to the strategic objectives in the organizations. A competence-performance model of leadership was used as a framework. Both criticality and frequency of leadership competencies for manager and deputy positions were analyzed. Based upon the results from the structured interview and managerial job analysis, a five-factor model was built up. The five factors of leadership competency modeling are:

1. *Moral quality:* including leadership integrity, work values, and job commitment.
2. *Personality:* consisting of conscientiousness, emotional stability, group compatibility, extraversion, and openness.
3. *Motivation:* referring to achievement motive, power motive, and relationship motive.
4. *Managerial skills:* including strategic decision-making skills, relationship coordination skills, empowerment and facilitation skills, business monitoring skills, and innovation skills.
5. *Managerial performance:* focusing on the performance process in terms of behavioral performance, functional performance and organizational performance.

The general results of structural equation modeling showed that there was an implicit managerial competency mental model (based upon higher-order factors) behind the leadership competency factors. The relationship-based constructs gathered around a second-order factor hierarchy. Figure 1 presents the structure of both first- and second-order competency factors. As shown in Figure 1, relationship-based competencies do not appear to be independent first-order factors but go behind and form a second-order factorial hierarchy of leadership competency, indicating that under the Chinese context, relationship-based constructs were dominating the competency modeling process and may affect the general mental model of assessment.

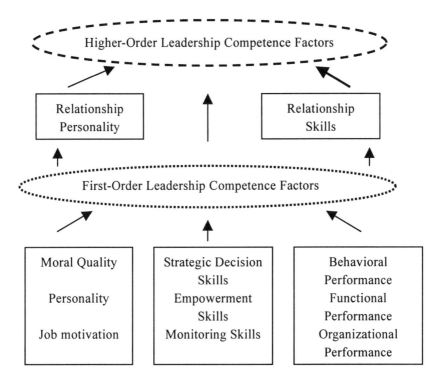

**Figure 1: Factorial structure of leadership competencies in China**

*Relationship Competence and Guanxi Orientation* A closely relevant concept is *Guanxi* (connection and relationship) (e.g., Luo, 1997), particularly leader-member exchange relationship (Graen & Schieman, 1978; Graen & Uhl-Bien, 1995). In a recent review of Chinese management studies, Tsui, Farth and Xin (2000) identified six *Guanxi* bases:

1. Being related to each other;
2. Belonging to the same political party;
3. Being former colleagues;
4. Being former classmates;
5. Being former neighbours; and
6. Being from the same place.

The research also suggested that *Guanxi* was more pervasive and important in lateral than in vertical dyads, indicating that relationship-based constructs are more closely connected with networks and across other aspects of work behaviour or competence. In another study involving more than 250 employees, Wang and Liang (2003) demonstrated a multidimensional structure of relationship (and/or *Guanxi*) orientation. The four dimensions of relationship orientation are:

- Task accomplishment,
- Harmony maintenance,
- Social support, and
- Information channel.

Among them, task accomplishment was shown to be a habitual tendency of solving problems through various kinds of relationship and social networks; harmony maintenance shows the conflict avoidance in interpersonal interactions; social support represents a relationship behavior in obtaining sentimental or task support from other people, whereas information channel means impression management behavior through various types of information channels.

## Leadership Strategy and Organizational Change

One of the significant developments in recent Chinese leadership studies has been its emphasis on leadership strategy in business development and organizational change (Xu, 1986; Warner, 1987; Wang, 1988; Laaksonen, 1988; Chen, 1989; Wang, 1989b; Wang & He, 1991; Redding & Wong, 1996; Tsui & Lau, 2002). There has been a clear shift of international business investment from joint ventures to the wholly-owned ventures and a rapid development of cross-regional business and international ventures.

*Leadership Strategies and Organizational Change* While more and more Chinese companies have adopted a cross-regional business development strategy and been actively involved in joint ventures, mergers and acquisitions, leadership strategies under cross-regional organizational changes is becoming an important topic for research and applications (Wang, 1999b, 1999c). These changes are closely related to the Chinese cultural values (Bond, 1996; Pervaiz & Li, 1996; Leung, 1997).

What are the effective leadership strategies for the mergers and acquisitions in China? Wang and Feng (2003) studied leadership strategies in joint ventures, mergers and acquisitions among 180 managers from 36 Chinese local companies who were involved in organizational re-structuring and changes. The research showed that the key was to effectively integrate the resources and businesses from different parties in the process of organizational change. There were two categories of leadership integration strategies more frequently used in recent practice: *task integration strategy*, and *behavioral integration strategy*.

Under the task integration leadership strategy, there are two key elements:

1. Strategic task leadership, focusing on long-term structural and business changes, and
2. Operational task leadership, emphasizing short-term role allocation and task re-design.

However, under the behavioral integration leadership strategy, there are two other key elements:

1.  Change process behavior, facilitating proactive actions in the organizational change process, and
2.  Cross-functional interactive behavior, encouraging teamwork and multi-level communication.

Among those 36 Chinese companies in the study, collectivistic behavioral integration leadership had a significantly positive impact on contextual performance under changes, whereas career objective and change process (e.g., speed of change) leadership had negative effects on contextual performance. In the meantime, factors such as team loyalty, organizational innovation and cross-functional interactive leadership behavior showed significantly positive effects on organizational performance among those companies.

*Transformational and transactional leadership* Under the cross-regional or cross-cultural business setting, a transformational leadership approach may be more widely adopted. In a recent study, Wang (2003) tested the model of transformational leadership vs transactional leadership under cross-regional entrepreneurial strategies in comparison with local entrepreneurial strategies. A series of interviews demonstrated three key leadership competencies for managers working under a cross-regional business and entrepreneurship setting:

1.  Cross-functional management competency: Managers need to share knowledge of business, administration, technology as well as marketing in order to implement policies and assignments from the headquarters.
2.  Local resources integration competency: Managers need to be able to rapidly integrate local resources and establish a good relationship with local governments, suppliers and customers. This is particularly true at the start-up stage of the new ventures.
3.  Multi-level communication competency: Managers need to develop channels of effective communication with subsidiaries, headquarters, subordinates and external parties.

Research suggested that the transformational leadership approach was more dominating at the start-up phase of an entrepreneurial company while the transactional leadership approach was more significant at the developing phase (second phase) of entrepreneurship development. Also, among companies under different ownerships (state-owned, privately-owned, and international joint ventures), there were significant differences in using the transformational leadership approach, but no difference in transactional leadership approach. Managers in joint ventures showed higher levels of transformational leadership behavior than that of state- and privately-owned companies. Besides, the transformational leadership approach was rated higher in smaller companies than that of medium- and large-sized companies. Interestingly, the transformation leadership approach had a higher predicting power to individual performance and satisfaction and led to stronger affective commitment than that of the transactional leadership.

Recent empirical studies in China demonstrated that transformational leadership was more effective under a cross-regional entrepreneurship setting, and transactional leadership was more popular under non-regional business situations. Specifically, under a cross-regional entrepreneurship strategy, transformational leadership (emphasizing charismatic motivational strategy, contingency rewards, and intellectual incentive) could lead to a high level of organizational commitment, job satisfaction and individual performance. However, under local business strategy, leaders showed a more transactional leadership approach. The effects of transformational leadership were mediated by organizational support culture (Wang, 2003). As Zhang's (2003) study on the transformational leadership and its effects on organizational change in the Chinese local entrepreneurial companies showed, organizational climate was an important mediating factor in explaining the positive relationship between transformational leadership and change strategies.

A crucial aspect of leadership strategies under business and organizational change is to develop effective leadership teams. In a three-year longitudinal study on cross-cultural leadership teams, Wang and Schneider (2003) demonstrated the framework of Third Culture principles for leadership strategies and development in joint-ventures in China. The

Third Culture is defined as an approach to leadership partnership and interactive teamwork climate. It emphasizes an alternative, innovative, joint and trustful culture rather than focusing on a one-partner culture, such as the traditional culture or the overseas culture or the Chinese culture. The Third Culture includes four key components: cross-cultural awareness, team member compatibility, competency-based learning, and performance accountability (Wang 2003). The longitudinal research showed that the Third Culture could be effectively achieved through two approaches:

1. Tailor-made leadership development programs, focusing on HR skills and team learning, and
2. Joint business-strategy-redesign programs, focusing on strategic business planning and collaborative redesigning team meetings.

## Leadership Team and Event Management

China has a tradition of promoting groups and team development at work. Since the early 1950s, titles such as excellent team and excellent enterprise have been used as a social reward for high morale and performance work groups or organizations (Wang 1993). During the 1950s and early 1960s, the excellent team movement focused mostly upon team technical innovations and cooperation. More recently, the emphasis has been shifted towards high performance teams, management leadership teams, cross-cultural work teams and virtual teams. Wang Z. M. (1989b) proposed a process model to define the effects of influence and power-sharing on both competence utilization and managerial transparency (two-way communication and sound psychological climate for goal-pursuing), which in turn lead to changes under organizational uncertainty, performance, satisfaction, and managerial success.

*Leadership Strategies in Team Conflict Management* The concept of conflict has cross-cultural differences. In the Chinese language, the term "conflict" has a strong negative implication so we would rather use "contradiction" instead. Studies were carried out to examine the effective, empowering, managerial leadership in the Chinese organizational setting. Field interviews of Chinese managers and employees in Hong Kong indicated that cooperative goals contributed to constructive discussions between managers and employees and such discussions, in turn, resulted in productive work and stronger work relationships (Wang, 1995; Wang, 1998; Tjosvold, Hui & Law, 2001). The results suggested that Chinese and North American managers operationalized goals and controversy differently.

In fact, even the concepts such as conflict and conflict management may have different meanings in different cultures. As one of the first empirical research attempts to find out the difference, Chen (1998) conducted a survey to find out the conceptual difference between conflict and conflict management among Chinese employees and western students studying in China. The results showed that the concept of conflict among western students was more explicitly related to two-sided contradictions in opinions or interests and more result-oriented, whereas the concept among Chinese employees was more implicit and process-oriented. When testing the usage of different conflict resolution strategies among managers from state-owned, privately-owned, and joint ventures in dealing with either intra-cultural conflict situations or inter-cultural conflict situations, six strategies were revealed: integration, control, compromising, avoidance, conforming, and flexibility strategies. The results showed that in general, managers from joint ventures adopted significantly different strategies than that of state-owned and privately-owned companies. Specifically, for intra-cultural conflict resolutions, Chinese SOEs' managers mainly used conforming strategies and then integration strategies, joint-venture managers mainly adopted flexibility strategies and then integration strategies while managers from the privately-owned firms more integration strategy and then conforming strategy. However, for inter-cultural conflict resolutions, both Chinese SOEs' and joint venture managers more adopted control and conforming strategies while privately-owned managers used integration and control more dominantly and then compromising strategies. Therefore, in general the most common conflict resolution strategy among the Chinese managers is the conforming strategy given the cultural tradition. They adopted very different strategies between intra- and inter-cultural conflict resolutions. In a comparison between top managers and middle managers in their dealing with conflicts, it was found that top managers more adopted integration strategies while middle managers more used compromising strategies. Compared with intra-cultural conflict resolution, the use of integration strategies decreased with the control strategy being enhanced and the difference between top managers and middle managers decreased under intercultural conflict management situations.

Conflict management is closely related with team development and team leadership. In a field study on team conflict management among 315 managers from 61 work teams in China investigated the conflict management characteristics and their relationships with team climate and performance under different ownership systems and sectors (Wang and Hu 2003). Three conflict management factors were revealed:  team sharing, conflict efficacy and team dependency, while three team climate factors included team innovation, goal commitment, and result-orientation. The two team management factors were: initiative and efficiency. Statistical analysis showed that there were significant differences among ownership and sectors. Teams in joint ventures had significantly higher levels of team dependency and conflict efficacy but lower team sharing than that of other ownerships and systems.   Teams in manufacturing sector, however, showed significantly higher level of conflict efficacy than that of service sector. Further analysis indicated that team sharing was positively correlated with both team work initiative and team performance while conflict efficacy closely correlated to work initiative. However, team sharing was negatively correlated with work initiative and performance in those 61 work teams when relationship orientation was still dominating the work teams. Specifically, under the state- and privately-owned organizational settings, team-sharing had the most significant effects on team climate factor such as team innovation, goal commitment and result-orientation, whereas under the joint venture setting, conflict efficacy played a more important role in determining those team climate factors. These findings provide useful implications for improving team climate and conflict efficacy in the Chinese organizations.

*Roles of Cultural Values in Conflict Management* Cultural values may play an important role in Chinese management (e.g., Nevis, 1983; Leung & Bond, 1984; Wang, 2000). Tjosvold, Hui and Law's study (2001) suggested that the Chinese value of harmony was often considered as the need to avoid conflict. Recent experiments have shown that Chinese people can value and use conflict to explore issues, make effective decisions, and strengthen relationships when they communicate that they want to manage the conflict for mutual benefit rather than win at the other's expense. Field studies document that cooperative conflict dynamics contribute to effective teamwork, quality service, and leadership in China. Chinese managers and employees are able to use participation and other management innovations to become partners in discussing issues and solving problems. The Chinese and their international partners appear to be able to use cooperative conflict to discuss their differences open-mindedly and forge productive, market-oriented organizations. Another study among 800 employees in China by Xie and Johns (2000) demonstrated the interactive effects of group cohesiveness and absence culture salience on absence. Consistent support for the interactive effects of cohesiveness and salience was provided by group, individual, and cross-level analyses. Group absence norms mediated the effects of cohesiveness, cultural salience, and their interaction on self-reported absenteeism.

Leadership strategies in conflict management may differ in dealing with intra-cultural conflicts and intercultural conflicts (Wang 1998). Managers working in bicultural teams are expected to adopt different strategies to manage conflicts with employees from a different culture or the same culture. Wang (2002) conducted a research project among Chinese and American managers who were working at Sino-American joint ventures in China. The focuses of research were on (a) cross-cultural differences in intra-cultural conflict management, and (b) differences between intercultural and intra-cultural conflict. Those managers were asked to handle situational intra-cultural and intercultural conflicts in their bicultural teams. The results indicated that there was a three dimensional solution for American intercultural conflict. The results showed that the responses could be classified into three categories: Joint response (active versus passive), conciliatory attempt (teamwork versus individual work), and coordinative response (disruptive versus accommodating). For the Chinese intra-cultural conflict, a two dimensional solution was obtained: a response of direct versus indirect, and a response of maintaining or disrupting harmony in the workplace.

*Leadership Styles and Event Management* Leadership styles may differ from different management events and under different cultural systems.

Country differences were also obtained in how the way that events were handled was related to performance criteria (Smith, Peterson and Misumi, 1994). The sources used in a country will depend upon generalized societal preferences for particular sorts of social processes and to typical organization forms institutionalized within that country (e.g., different ownerships, management systems, SMEs, etc.), as is the case (Redding & Wong 1996). Smith, Peterson and Wang (1996) conducted a cross-cultural study on event management styles of managers in China, the USA and Britain. Those managers were asked to describe the extent to which they used different sources (reliance on rules and procedures; superiors; colleagues; subordinates; self; own experience and training;) for handling nine managerial events as follows:

1.  Choosing a new subordinate to work with you.
2.  Rewarding your subordinates when they do good work.
3.  Changing work procedures used by your subordinates.
4.  Dealing with your subordinates when their work is unsatisfactory.
5.  Improving the quality of work in your department.
6.  Deciding how to use raw materials more effectively.
7.  Improving coordination with other departments.
8.  Improving your department's communications with senior management.
9.  Improving teamwork within your department.

The results showed that Western managers relied more upon their own experience and training, while the Chinese managers relied more on rules and procedures.  For most events, Western managers who described themselves as relying on their own experience and training believed that the events had been well handled. They reported that events were less well handled to the extent that they referred to their superiors. Reliance on the superior was associated with role ambiguity among Western managers but not in China. Even though Chinese managers relied more upon rules and procedures they too evaluated events more positively when they had relied on their own experience and training. In a more recent study on event management approaches across joint ventures with different partnerships, Wang (2003) conducted follow-up interviews and made further analysis on leadership styles and event management in joint ventures. The results indicated that there were three types of leadership approaches in event management:

1. The Chinese approach: Event management by social norms, more relying upon widespread beliefs in dealing with key leadership events;
2. The Asian-pacific approach: Event management by line systems, more relying on sources from superiors and subordinates in dealing with key leadership events;
3. The European approach: Event management by task expertise, more relying on own experience and training in dealing with key leadership events (Smith, Wang, & Leung, 1997).

## Relationship Leadership in Virtual Teamwork

With the development of IT networking and multiple business modeling, leadership strategies and HR approaches for virtual teams and organizations are becoming new areas of research both in China and overseas (Townsend, DeMarie, & Hendrickson, 1998; Cascio 2000; Heneman & Greenberger 2002). From the recent empirical studies on virtual teams in the Chinese organizations, three successful contingencies were revealed (Wang, 2002b):

1. *The contingent factor of developing an adaptive knowledge sharing mechanism.* In developing E-commerce systems, it would be important to develop an adaptive leadership knowledge sharing mechanism in order to formulate communication systems and achieve better resource-sharing, reliable coordination and low-cost teamwork.
2. *The contingent factor of facilitating process control and result-orientation organizational climate.* Managers in cross-organization leadership should be prepared to work in parallel and communicate across organizational levels. This multi-level communication competence could be developed under the result-orientation organizational climate.
3. *The contingent factor of establishing teamwork competence-mentoring program.* As partners in the E-commerce projects would establish a

mentoring relationship with formal paths and project rules to ensure effective virtual teamwork. This could be done through a teamwork competence-mentoring program.

Based upon a distributed task analysis on virtual teams, Wang (2003) studied 38 virtual teams and 37 face-to-face teams. Altogether, 340 team members were asked to complete a teamwork questionnaire. The results demonstrated six characteristics of virtual team tasks and four key competencies for effective team leadership.

1.  Six virtual team task characteristics are:

   ● Multi-level structure,
   ● Distributive difficulty,
   ● Multi-goal orientation,
   ● Cross-hierarchy dependence,
   ● Cross-functional expertise,
   ● Internet communicative dependence.

2.  Four key competencies are:

   ● Learning and innovation skills,
   ● Communication and coordination skills,
   ● Technical knowledge and information skills.
   ● Self-management skills.

The competencies of team members are closely correlated with performance: the self-management skills, technical skills, communication skills, learning and innovation skills have significant impacts on task performance, while communication and coordination skills, and information skills are significantly related to contextual performance. Furthermore, team climate influences team performance. For example, team climate elements such as innovation orientation, goal commitment, communication, participation and trust all affected team task performance, while trust, communication and participation, and innovation orientation also influenced team contextual performance. In general, the virtual team is significantly different from the face-to-face team in task cross-functioning, internet task dependence and task goal orientation.

What are the implications of these studies for strategic HRM and leadership?

1. *Virtual organizations need strategic objectives driven for long-term benefits.* Under the E-commerce setting, virtual organizational goal-setting will be crucial at the early stage of project development. A typical E-commerce development model should include four incremental phases: phases of corporate network building, office automation, core business management systems, and value-added e-business.

2. *Virtual organizations need active task re-grouping to achieve high-levels of member-team fit and team compatibility.* A flexible leadership approach proved to be useful for ensuring on-site regrouping for member-team fit in virtual team HR development. Wang (1998) identified three components of team compatibility: active cooperation, communicative coordination and information sharing. Through active re-grouping, three levels of team compatibility will be ensured across virtual organizations: strategy compatibility (the managerial compatibility of the strategies adopted by various parties), group compatibility (the psychological compatibility among team members from different organizations), and performance compatibility (the operational compatibility among performance criteria and systems).

3. *Virtual organizations need more competence mentoring from the managers, particularly for skills of networking, goal-setting and result-orientation.*
   In the virtual organizations, there is a hierarchical leadership coordinating the activities. Relevant groups are connected by the tasks of cross-organizational projects and therefore skills for networking, goal-setting and goal implementation, and result-orientation become more important, especially when face-to-face communication is limited and reduced. A trustful relationship between virtual leader-member dyads could be developed through a competence-based mentoring and leadership style (Wang 2001) and a result-oriented performance approach through the process of Chinese social interaction and

networking.

4.  *Virtual organizations emphasize interactive communication and knowledge sharing both at leader and member levels.* From the case analysis, it is evident that effective communication is a prerequisite for high virtual-team effectiveness. This was also noted in the previous work (e.g., Townsend, DeMarie and Hendrickson 1998). Although the computer network provides the teams with more communication channels and opportunities, the way of utilizing those channels and communicating information is very different. Traditionally, Chinese communication was largely characterized by implicit communication, listening-centeredness, politeness, focus on insiders, and face-directed communication strategies (Gao, Ting-Toomey and Gudykunst 1996). It is particularly true in the cross-organizational context emphasizing the instrumentality of face-concerns as a method of achieving business goals (Smith and Wang 1996). These cultural characteristics would certainly affect the teamwork behavior under the virtual organizational setting.

In general, the main features of virtual organizations are:

1.  Team objectives are more long-term oriented and strategic;
2.  Team coordination is in multi-phases and highly interactive;
3.  Team responsibility is more based upon trust, knowledge sharing and horizontally-distributed; and
4.  Team expertise includes skills of communication, coordination, strategic thinking, goal-setting and independent working.

These features of virtual teams create and promote the organizational climate and are crucial to enhancing virtual organizational performance.

## Conclusions:   Leadership   Strategies   and   Relationship Competence

Three conclusions could be drawn on the basis of discussions and review in this chapter.

First, relationship-based leadership competency modeling is an active area of research and has provided a general framework for understanding and developing various kinds of human resource management strategies and designs for Chinese organizations. Relationship management has become a core of implicit leadership and teamwork process in China. Specifically, there are three first order leadership competency factors: Emotional competence (moral quality, personality, job motivation), cognitive competence (strategic decision skills, empowerment skills and monitoring skills), and performance competence (behavioral, functional and organizational performance). Behind these leadership factors, there is a relationship-based higher order leadership competence factor.

Second, the most effective leadership and entrepreneurship strategy in the current Chinese business environment is the one based on leadership integration of various resources. There are two important implications. One implication is that the task-behavior integration is crucial for entrepreneurship and organizational changes such as joint-ventures, mergers and acquisitions. Another implication is that the transformational leadership emphasizes knowledge sharing and transfer and is most effective under the Third Culture principles. The effective leadership and entrepreneurship strategy has been also reflected in team conflict management and event management in which relationship competence and organizational norms play an important role.

Third, virtual team leadership has been a new area for strategic HRM practice and important for IT business development. Apparently, efforts need to be made for developing adaptive knowledge sharing mechanism and cross-functional teamwork mentoring programs. These principles and approaches are also most relevant to cross-regional business development and entrepreneurship.

With the above-mentioned three aspects of implications, more integrative research need to be carried out to test those models and more principles are expected to be applied in the practice of leadership in China.

# References

Bond, M. H., ed. (1996). *The Psychology of the Chinese People.* Hong

Kong: Oxford University Press.

Cascio, W. F. (2000). "Managing a virtual workplace". *Academy of Management Executive*, **14**(3), 81-90.

Chen, J. (1998) *Conflict Management in Chinese Enterprises*, Doctoral dissertation, Hangzhou University

Chen, L. 1989. "Organization development in China: Chinese version". *Chinese Journal Applied Psychology*, **1**,1-5 (in Chinese)

Chen, Z. X., Anne S. Tsui; Jiing-Lih Farh. (2002). "Loyalty to supervisor vs. organizational commitment: relationships to employee performance in China". *Journal of Occupational and Organizational Psychology*, **75**(3), 339-357

Dyer J. H. & Singh H. (1998): "the Relational view: Cooperative Strategy and Sources of Interorganizational Competitive Advantage". *Academy of Management Review*. **23**(4), 660-679.

Gao, G., S. Ting-Toomey and W. B. Gudykunst (1996) "Chinese communication processes", Chapter 18 in Michael H. Bond ed. *The Handbook of Chinese Psychology*, Hong Kong: Oxford University Press.

Graen. G & Schieman W. (1978): "Leader-member agreement: a vertical dyad linkage approach". *Journal of Applied Psychology*, **63**(2), 206-212.

Graen, G. B., & Uhl-Bien, M. (1995). "Relationship-based approach to leadership: Development of leader-member exchange (LMX) theory of leadership over 25 years: Applying a multi-level multi-domain perspective." *Leadership Quarterly*, **6**, 219-247.

Guzzo R. A.&. Shea. G. P (1992). "Group performance and intergroup relationship in organization". In: Marvin D. Dunnetter and Leaetta M. Hough ed. *Handbooks of Industrial and Organizational Psychology*, (3), 262-313.

Heneman, R. L. & David G. Greenberger, (2002). *Human Resource Management in Virtual Organizations,* Greenwich: Information Age Publishing

Ho, D. Y., & Chiu C. Y. (1996) "Component Ideas of Individualism, Collectivism, And Social Organization: An Application in the Study of Chinese Culture". In: M.Bond Ed. *The Psychology of the Chinese People*. Hong Kong: Oxford University Press, 143-181.

Huang, G. G. (1988), "Renqing and Face: The Chinese Power Game". In

Yang K.S. ed. *The Psychology of Chinese People*, Taipei: Laureate Book Ltd. (in Chinese)

Kenney, R. A., Schwartz-Kenney, B., & Blascovich, J. (1996). "Implicit leadership theories: Defining leaders described as worthy of influence." *Personality and Social Psychology Bulletin*, **22**, 1128-1143.

Laaksonen, O. (1988). *Management in China: During and after Mao in Enterprises, Government, and Party.* Berlin: Walter de Gruyter

Leung, K. (1997). "Negotiation and reward allocations across cultures". In P. C. Earley & M. Erez (Eds.). *New Perspectives on International Industrial and Organizational Psychology* (pp. 640-675). San Francisco: The New Lexington Press.

Leung, K., Bond, M. H. (1984). "The impact of cultural collectivism on reward allocation". *Journal of Personality and Social Psychology*, **54**,793-803

Leung, K., P. B. Smith, Z. M. Wang & H. F. Sun. (1996) "Job satisfaction in joint venture hotels in China: an organizational justice analysis". (Special Issue) *Journal of International Business Studies*, **27**(5), 947-963

Li, J. & Chalmer E. Labig Jr. (2001). "Negotiating with China: Exploratory study of relationship-building". *Journal of Managerial Issues*, **13**(3), 345-360

Li, J. T., A. Tsui; K. R. Xin, & D. C. Hambrick, (1999). "Building effective international joint venture leadership in China". *Journal of World Business*, **34**(1), 52-53

Lin, W. Q. (1989). "Pattern of leadership behavior assessment in China." *Psychologica Sinica*, **32**, 129-134.

Lin, W. Q., Chen, L. (Long), Wang, D. 1987. "The construction of the CPM scale for leadership assessment". *Acta Psychologica Sinica* **19**,199-207 (in Chinese)

Lin, W. Q., R. C. Chia, & L. L. Fang, (2000). "Chinese implicit leadership theory". *The Journal of Social Psychology*, **140**(6), 729-740

Luo Y. D. (1997): "Guanxi and performance of foreign-invested enterprises in China: An Empirical Inquiry". *Management International Review.* **37**, 51-70.

Markus, H. R. & S. Kitayama. (1991). "Culture and the self: Implications for cognition, emotion and motivation". *Psychological Review*, **98**,

224-53.

Miles, M. (2000). "Power and relationship: Two elements of the Chinese/Western divide". *Journal of Comparative International Management*, **3** (1), 39-51

Misumi J. (1985). *The Behavioral Science of Leadership*. Ann Arbor: Univ. Mich. Press

Nevis, E. C. (1983). "Using an American perspective in understanding another culture: toward a hierarchy of needs for the People's Republic of China." *Journal of Applied Behaviora. Science,* **19**,249-64

Pang, P. (1997). *The Chinese Confucianism*. Shanghai: Oriental Publishing Center, **4**, 57-73 (in Chinese)

Pervaiz K A. & Li X.K.(1996). "Chinese Culture and Its Implication for Sino-Western Joint Venture Management". *Strategic Change*, 1996(5), 275-286.

Peterson, M. F., P. B. Smith, J. Misumi & M. H. Bond. (1990). "Personal reliance on alternative event management processes". *Group and Organization Studies*, **15**, 75-91.

Redding, S. G., & Wong, G. Y. Y. (1996). "The social psychology of Chinese organizational behavior". In M. H. Bond (Ed.), *The Psychology of the Chinese People* (pp. 267-295). New York: Oxford University Press.

Smith, P.B., M. F. Peterson & J. Misumi. (1994) "Event management and work team effectiveness in Japan, Britain and USA". *Journal of Occupational and Organizational Psychology*, **67**(1), 33-44

Smith, P.B., M. F. Peterson & Z. M. Wang. (1996) "The manager as mediator of alternative meanings: a pilot study from China", the USA and U.K. *Journal of International Business Studies,* **27**(1), 115-138

Smith, P. B., Z.-M. Wang, & K. Leung (1997). "Leadership, decision-making and cultural context: Event management within Chinese joint ventures", *The Leadership Quarterly*, **8**(4), 413-432

Tjosvold; D., C. Hui, & K. S. Law, (1998). "Empowerment in the manager-employee relationship in Hong Kong: interdependence and controversy". *The Journal of Social Psychology*, **138** (5), 624-637

Tjosvold; D., C. Hui, & K. S. Law, (2001). "Constructive conflict in China: Cooperative conflict as a bridge between east and west". *Journal of World Business*, **36**(2), 166-173

Townsend, A. M., DeMarie, S. M., & Hendrickson, A. R. (1998), "Virtual teams: Technology and the workplace of the future". *Academy of Management Executive,* **12** (3),17-29

Tsui, A.S., & Farh, L.J. (1997). "Where guanxi matters: Relational demography and guanxi in the Chinese context". *Work and Occupations,* **24**, 56-79.

Tsui, A.S. & C.M. Lau, (2002). *The Management of Enterprises in the People's Republic of China,* Boston: Kluwer Academic Publisher.

Wang, Z. M. (1986). "Worker's attribution and its effects on performance under different responsibility systems". *Chinese Journal of Applied Psychology.* **2**, 6-10 (in Chinese)

Wang, Z. M. (1988). "The effects of responsibility system change and group attributional training on performance: a quasi-experiment in Chinese factories". *Chinese Journal of Applied Psychology.* **3**,7-11 (in Chinese)

Wang, Z. M. 1989a. "Human resource management in China: recent trends". In *Human Resource management: An International Comparison,* ed. R. Pieper, (pp. 195-210). Berlin: Walter de Gruyter

Wang, Z. M. (1989b). "Participation and skill utilization in organizational decision making in Chinese enterprises". In Fallon, B. J., Pfister, H. P., Brebner, J. *Advances in Industrial Organizational Psychology.* North-Holland: Elsevier

Wang, Z. M. (1990). "Action research and O. D. strategies in Chinese enterprises". *Organization Development Journal.* **8**(1), 66-70

Wang, Z. M. (1992). "Managerial psychological strategies for Sino-foreign joint-ventures". *Journal of Managerial Psychology.* **7**(3):10-16

Wang, Z.M. (1993). "Psychology in China: a review dedicated to Li Chen." *Annual Review of Psychology,* **44**, 87-117

Wang, Z. M. (1995). "Culture, economic reform and the role of industrial and organizational psychology in China". In *Handbook of Industrial and Organizational Psychology,* ed. M. D. Dunnette, L. M. Hough, Vol. 4. Palo Alto: Consulting Psychologists Press, Inc. 2nd ed. In press

Wang, Z. M. (1998). "Conflict management in China", In Jan Selmer Ed. *International Management in China,* London: Routledge

Wang, Z. M. (1999a). "Management in China", In *The IEBM Handbook of International Business,* ed. Rosalie L. Tung, London: International

Thomson Business Press

Wang, Z. M. (1999b). "Developing joint-venture leadership teams", In *Advances in Global Leadership*, Eds. William H. Mobley, M. Jocelyne Gessner and Val Arnold, Vol. 1. JAI Press Inc.

Wang, Z. M. (1999c). "Strategic human resource management for twenty-first-century China", In *Research in Personnel and Human Resources Management*, Supplement 4, (pp. 353-366), JAI Press Inc.

Wang, Z.M. (2000). *Managerial Psychology*, Beijing: People's Educational Press. (in Chinese).

Wang, Z.M. (2002a). "New perspectives and implicit managerial competency modeling in China." Chapter 8 in C. L. Cooper and I. T. Robertson ed. *International Review of Industrial and Organizational Psychology*, Vol. 17, John Wiley & Sons

Wang, Z.M. (2002b). HRM strategies in managing virtual organizations in China: A case analysis of banking E-commerce projects". In R. L. Heneman & D.B. Greenberger eds. *Human Resource Management in Virtual Organizations*, Greenwich: Information Age Publishing.

Wang, Z.M. (2003). *Advances in HR and OB Studies in China*, Shanghai: People's Publishing House (in press).

Wang, Z.M. & M.K. Chen, (2002). „Competency modeling for top managers in China", *Journal of Psychological Science,* 6, 1-6. (in Chinese)

Wang, Z.M. & J.M. Feng (2003). "Integration strategies for mergers and acquisitions in entrepreneurial firms". In Wang, Z.M. ed. *Advances in HR and OB Studies in China*, Shanghai: People's Publishing House (in press).

Wang, Z. M., & He, G. B. (1991). "The information structure and decision support strategies for hi-tech decision-making in Chinese enterprises." *Chinese Journal of Applied Psychology,* 2,22-29 (in Chinese)

Wang, Z.M. & B. Schneider, (2003). „Cross-cultural leadership team development and the Third Culture", In Wang, Z.M. ed. *Advances in HR and OB Studies in China*, Shanghai: People's Publishing House (in press).

Warner, M. (1987). *Management Reforms in China*. London: Frances Pinter

Xie, J. L. & G. Johns. (2000). "Interactive effects of absence culture salience and group cohesiveness: A multi-level and cross-level analysis of work absenteeism in the Chinese context." *Journal of Occupational and Organizational Psychology*, **73**(1), 31-47

Xu, L. C. (1986). "Development on organizational behavior study in China." *Acta Psychologica Sinica.* **18**,343-348 (in Chinese)

Xu, L. C. (1987). "Recent development in organizational psychology in China." In *Advances in Organizational Psychology: An International Review,* ed. B. Bass, (pp. 242-51). New York: Sage

Xu, L. C. (1989). "Comparative study of leadership between Chinese and Japanese managers based upon PM theory". In Fallon, B. J., Pfister, H. P., Brebner, J. *Advances in Industrial Organizational Psychology.* North-Holland: Elsevier

Yang G. S. (1995): "Chinese Social Orientation: An Integrative Analysis". In: T. Y. Lin, W. and S, Yen (eds.). *Chinese Societies and Mental Health.* (pp19-39) Hong Kong: Oxford. 1995..

Yang, K. S. (1986). "Chinese personality and its change". See Bond 1986, pp. 106-70

Zhang, L. H. (2003). *An Interactive Model of Transformational Leadership ad Organizational Change Process: Empirical and Case Analyses*, Doctoral dissertation, Dalian University of Science and Technology.

Zhu, R.L. (1989). "Face and Achievements: A Study on Socially-Oriented Motivation". *The Chinese Journal of Psychology*, **31** (2), 79-90. (in Chinese).

*Chapter 4*

# Leadership in Taiwanese Enterprises

Bor-Shiuan Cheng
Department of Psychology, National Taiwan University, Taiwan

Kuo Long Huang
Department of Management Sciences, Tamkang University, Taiwan

Hsin Chang Lu
Department of International Business, National Taiwan University, Taiwan

Min-Ping Huang
Department of Business Administration, Yuan Ze University, Taiwan

The study of leadership has varied in many ways over time. The main approach in the past has focused on a nomothetic approach. House, Wright and Aditya (1997) pointed out that the prevailing viewpoint by 1980 had been the universal leadership style, which was perceived as a general model to be beyond cultural and geographical bounds. However, this line of research has been modified recently. Cross-cultural studies and the synthesis of related theories since 1980 have indicated the impact of cultural factors on the content of leadership. Although the phenomenon of leadership is overwhelming worldwide, the details of leadership is embedded in culture, and there are cultural differences both in the content of leadership and in the relationship between leadership and organizational effectiveness (Chemers, 1993; Hofstede, 1980).

Most empirical studies indicate that Chinese societies are distinguished from the Western World mainly in the contrast of individualism to collectivism and the differences in power distance among hierarchical levels.  Be it research conducted in Taiwan, Hong Kong, Singapore, or Mainland China, the common theme is to observe the pattern that Chinese people are more collectivistic and have larger power distance than most people in the Western World (Birnbaum & Wong, 1985; Chong, Cragin & Scherling, 1983; Lai & Lam, 1986).

According to early studies (e.g. Hsu, 1953), the value system held among Chinese differs significantly from the Western World in many ways.  If the Western leadership models were imposed on the Chinese society directly without modification, it would result in unfavorable outcomes.  Not only would the uniqueness of Chinese leadership be ignored, but  it might also be distorted (Smith & Wang, 1996).  To construct a sound theoretical framework of leadership, researchers must appreciate the related cultural context.  Therefore, it does not seem to be a fruitful approach to overly address similarities between the Western and Chinese leadership styles.

**Familism and Leadership**

From the cross-cultural perspective, recent studies have switched to adopt the emic approach to investigate related topics such as organizational structures and managerial styles in Chinese enterprises (see Cheng, 1991; Redding, 1990; Whitley, 1992; Wong, 1985).  From studying Chinese enterprises based in Taiwan, Hong Kong, Singapore, Philippines, Indonesia, Thailand and Malaysia, one can conclude that the majority of Chinese enterprises were owned and run by core family members.  The central theme of the empirical findings is that familism matters.  The top managers in Chinese family enterprises have clear and vibrant leadership styles.  Their managerial style features paternalistic and hierarchical leadership as well as favoritism and nepotism towards employees with close relationships to the families.

Lin (1989) pointed out that the passage of family authority and responsibility across generations is the utmost priority so as to preserve the Chinese family heritage.

In general, the eldest son inherits the paternalistic authority while the family assets are divided equally among the sons with the following conditions:

1. a close-knit and bi-level structure with the father centered around the sons;
2. the definition of family membership based solely on the kinship tie of the father's side;
3. the family is run as a small social unit and dictated by the father's ruling;
4. a strong tendency to treat people differently on the basis of family membership.

Since the family-run business is simply an extension of the family, the employees in Chinese enterprises are further differentiated as either insiders or outsiders, solely based on their family relationship. The father has the highest authority in management and the final say in making decisions in the family business. The expansion of these family enterprises depend on whether the control by the core families is stable and solid, along with the premise that the well being of the family is more important than that of its enterprises.

Based on an in-depth observation of Taiwanese family enterprises, Cheng (1991) pointed out that familism contains a two-fold important value, namely paternalistic authority and differential guanxi. The first value says that the enterprise head exercises absolute authority under familism. The second value means that the insiders with kinship ties and the outsiders are taken as separate groups of employees and treated accordingly. The insiders can share more resources within the enterprises than the outsiders can. These values, evolved out of Chinese tradition, have strong influence on Chinese leadership styles and managerial practices. Redding (1990) also reached a similar conclusion after investigating overseas Chinese enterprises. He pinpointed that paternalism and personalism were key factors in describing and analyzing leadership in Chinese enterprises.

## Paternalistic Authority and Leadership

In Chinese enterprises, the relationship between paternalistic authority and leadership is mainly manifested in a large power distance between the leader and his subordinates. It features ruling by personal discretion such that the father figure holds the sole authority while the organization members all abide by a stringent set of rules and are governed by benevolent ethics and moral integrity.  This type of leadership style is labeled paternalistic leadership by most scholars (Cheng, 1995a; Farth & Cheng, 2000; Redding, 1999).

Recent research on paternalistic leadership in Chinese enterprises can be classified into three main types.  One type of research, including Silin (1976), Redding (1999), and Cheng (1995a), focused on qualitative study by using observation and in-depth interviews.  Another type of research was a theoretical investigation done by Westwood (1997).  The third one was an integrated research conducted by Farh and Cheng (2000).

## Cultural Values and Leadership

Silin (1976) is one of the pioneering researchers to study leadership in Chinese enterprises empirically.  In the late 1960s, Silin investigated one large Taiwanese private enterprise and documented the interactions among the CEO, managers and workers carefully.  He utilized the approach of comparative sociology to study the manager-subordinate relationships and the leadership styles.  Silin (1976) described the essential characteristics of paternalistic leadership as follows:

1. Moral leadership: In addition to documenting their management competencies, Chinese leaders have to be recognized by their subordinates as morally superior individuals.  Here, morality refers to the leader's ability to reject his egocentric impulses for the organizational goals and the ability to translate abstract ideas into concrete actions.
2. Didactic leadership: The leader is willing to share with subordinates his successful experience and to show them how to convert abstract theory into practical success.
3. Centralized authority: The management authority is highly centralized and the boss's power is not easily shared with the subordinates.
4. Maintaining social distance with subordinates: The leader purposely keeps distance from the subordinates and makes his intentions ill-defined in order to maintain his authority and be properly dignified.
5. Rigid control: The leader tends to use all possible resorts to strengthen his control over subordinates.  This includes using side rewards to encourage good deeds, making the subordinates divided and competing with one another, etc.

If possible, trustworthy subordinates will be assigned to monitor so as to make sure the boss is not fooled under any circumstance.

How do the subordinates respond to this type of leadership behavior and meet the leader's expectation? According to Silin, subordinates must obey and rely on the leader completely. They also have to show respect and appropriate fear toward their leaders. No second thought is allowed by the subordinates other than to trust their boss with a full heart.

## Chinese Capitalism and Leadership

Redding (1990) investigated the relationship between the organizational structure and management practice in Chinese enterprises. His continuous and systematic studies of family enterprises in Taiwan, Hong Kong, Singapore, the Philippines and Indonesia indicated that there exists a distinct pattern of economic culture labeled Chinese capitalism, of which paternalism is the key element. Through in-depth interviews, Redding found that the essential features of Chinese patriarchalism are as follows:

1. Subordinates rely on the leader mentally.
2. Subordinates totally accept the authoritative leader.
3. In the mind of subordinates, the leader is their role model as well as their mentor.
4. The leader will show personalized support to loyal subordinates, inducing them to conform to the leader more willingly.
5. The leader is willing to modify his authoritarianism by showing sensitivity to his subordinates' views.
6. In general, benevolently autocratic leadership is observed.

We have reasons to believe that Redding's findings are quite persuasive in many ways due to the use of a large sample size from those Chinese enterprises in various industries and countries. However, this sociological analysis is insufficient to address the dynamic interactions between the leader and his subordinates (Farh & Cheng, 2000).

*Paternalistic Headship*

Based on the study of overseas Chinese enterprises in Southeast Asia, Westwood (1997) proposed the concept of "paternalistic leadership" as contrastingwith the prevailing leadership construct used by most Western research.   According to Westwood, the emphasis of leadership instead of Western leadership is largely due to the prominent features in Chinese culture to stress social order and harmony, more so than individualism, freedom and justices, which are highly emphasized in the Western World.

The main features of paternalistic leadership include:

1.  The head shows didactic behavior toward subordinates.
2.  The head keeps his intentions ill-defined and maintains social distance with the subordinates.
3.  The head tries every way possible to build up authority and to request subordinates' complete obedience.
4.  The head tends to manipulate his subordinates in order to be in full control.
5.  The head shows favoritism toward close subordinates.
6.  The head allows for no conflict among subordinates.
7.  The head and his subordinates can share ideas together and dialogue ideal

Although Westwood (2000) reached similar findings as Silin (1976) and Redding (1997), the concepts of conflict diffusion and dialogue ideal are relatively new. According to Westwood, social harmony is the paramount value and belief held in the Chinese society.   The primary role of the head is to allow no conflicts in public and to prevent and diffuse conflicts within the organization.   As to dialogue ideal, it describes the process of the head's informal communication with his subordinates in order to maintain social harmony in the enterprises.   In this subtle way, the head can make sure that the subordinate's dignity is preserved fully and he can express his personal caring about the subordinates (Farh & Cheng, 2000).

The above discussions are based on the findings obtained by organizational sociologists from their studies of Chinese enterprises.   However, the details of leadership dynamics and interpersonal interactions between the leader and the subordinate are less emphasized.   Below we will review some studies with subordinates' responses taken into account.


## Paternalistic Leadership and Subordinates' Responses

In the late 80's, Cheng used the case study approach to investigate the leadership style of the CEOs as well as the top managers of many Taiwanese family businesses (Cheng; 1995a). Through in-depth interviews and extensive fieldwork, Cheng found that the leadership style in Taiwanese enterprises was quite similar to what was observed by Silin (1976) and Redding (1990). Cheng first termed this leadership style authoritative leadership and then switched its name to paternalistic leadership later on.

Between 1993 and 1994, Cheng interviewed 18 CEOs and 24 top managers of private enterprises in Taiwan. These family-owned businesses were composed of firms in various industries such as electronics, plastics, food processing, construction, the financial sector, managerial consulting and marketing. From his findings, Cheng concluded that the pattern of paternalistic leadership was quite common. Using the framework of a didactic relationship, Cheng described in great details this type of leadership and the corresponding subordinates' responses. In particular, he emphasized both authoritarian leadership and benevolent leadership.

As to authoritarian leadership, Cheng identified four major aspects of leader behavior, which includes asserting authority and control, underestimating subordinate competence, building a lofty image, and directing subordinates in a didactic style. The corresponding subordinate responses include compliance, obedience, respect, fear and shame. Cheng (1995a) also found that the attribution process of the subordinate's performance could be used to strengthen authoritarian leadership. For instance, the subordinate's success is usually attributed to the merit of the boss, while a failure would be attributed to the subordinate's personal responsibility. Since the boss will never share the blame, it further strengthens the superior status of the boss , while disqualifying the subordinates.

As to benevolent leadership, the leaders show individualized caring in private and avoid embarrassing subordinates in public even if some serious mistakes occur. In return, the subordinates will show gratitude and strive to reciprocate this favor. Furthermore, benevolent leadership is not equivalent to the concept of consideration (Fleishman, 1953; Stogdill, 1974) or supportive leadership (Bowers & Seashore, 1966; House & Mitchell, 1974). Consideration is the degree to which a leader acts in a friendly and supportive manner, shows concern for subordinates, and takes care of the welfare of his subordinates. Supportive leadership includes a variety of behaviors in which a leader shows consideration, acceptance, and concern for the needs and feelings of his subordinates (Yule, 1994). As to benevolent leadership, it means somewhat long-term caring and holistic concern for subordinates (Cheng, 1995a). Comparison of the above research on paternalistic leadership is summarized in Table 1.

**Table 1 Summary of Researches on Paternalistic Leadership in Chinese Enterprises**

| Research | Silin (1976) | Redding (1990) | Westwood(1997) | Cheng (1995a) |
|---|---|---|---|---|
| Field | Organizational Sociology | Organizational Sociology | Organizational Sociology | Organizational Psychology |
| Approach | Interview | Interview | Literature Review | Field & Case Study, Interview |
| Subjects Studied | Large Taiwanese Family Enterprise | Family Enterprises in Hong Kong, Taiwan and the Philippines | Overseas Chinese Family Enterprises in Southeast Asia | Taiwanese Private Enterprises |
| Cultural Root | Confucianism | Confucianism, Buddhism, & Taoism | Confucianism | Confucianism, Legalism |
| Value System | Paternalistic Authority | Paternalistic Authority | Compliance, Social Order & Harmony | Paternalistic Authority |
| Focus of Research | Describing Management Philosophy & Leadership Style of CEO | Investigating Relationship between Cultural Value and Leadershin in Family Enterprises, Constructing a Conceptual Framework | Exploring the Influence of Cultural Value on Leadership of CEOs in Family-owned Enterprises | Constructing Paternalistic Leadership Model in Chinese Organizations, Characterizing Dimensions of Leadership Style and Subordinates' Responses |

Source: Cheng & Huang (2000).

*Three Dimensions of Paternalistic Leadership*

After reviewing the studies conducted by Silin, Redding, Westwood, and Cheng, Farh and Cheng (2000) pointed out that moral leadership was another important element of Chinese paternalistic leadership in addition to authoritarian leadership and benevolent leadership. Farh and Cheng also noticed that there is quite a consensus among these researchers over authoritarian leadership and benevolent leadership while the exact content of moral leadership seemed to be less consistent. Silin (1976) argued that leaders' financial achievements and business accomplishments are major elements of moral leadership other than being fair in most circumstances. On the contrary, Westwood (1997) thought that leaders have to be morally superior in order to behave according to Confucian ethics such as Jen (human heartedness), Li (propriety), and Shao (filial piety). What these researchers tend to agree on is that leaders have to set good example by themselves. To motivate subordinates properly, leaders have to serve the public good, rather than behave purely for their own self-interest. They must always go first in any situation, and become role models for their subordinates. Certainly this viewpoint was not new. Cheng and Zhuang (1981) raised a similar argument but it did not get enough attention by other interested researchers.

Thus, Farh and Cheng (2000) argued that there are three major dimensions of leader behaviors and corresponding subordinate responses in paternalistic leadership. As to authoritarian leadership, leaders tend to assert authority and control, degrade subordinates' competence, make up a lofty image, and direct subordinates in a didactic style. Correspondingly, the subordinates tend to respond with full compliance, obedience, respect, fear and shame. As to benevolent leadership, leaders will show individualized care in private and avoid embarrassing subordinates in public. In return, subordinates will show gratitude and strive to return the favor. And finally as to moral leadership, leaders will act unselfishly and set a good example while subordinates will identify and imitate their behavior.

The empirical study by Cheng, Cho and Farh (2000) confirmed this paternalistic leadership model (PL model) proposed by Cheng and Farh. Cheng, Cho and Farh analyzed the data collected from 538 employees in 59 Taiwanese enterprises by using a structural equation model. The result showed good fitness to the PL model.

Next, the related question is what is the underlying psychological mechanism, which elicits subordinate responses to strengthen the paternalistic leadership? Farh and Cheng (2000) singled out emotional fear of the leader by subordinates as the main psychological mechanism for authoritarian leadership. This fear came from two possible sources of influence:

1.  The leaders have the right to exercise reward power and coercive power.
2.  The subordinates must obey the leaders in any case.

Were there no fear, it would be unlikely for subordinates to comply with authoritarian leadership.   As to benevolent leadership, the important psychological mechanism is the subordinate's feeling of indebtedness.   Subordinates feel obliged to reciprocate for the favor given by the leader.   Many researchers have noted the norm of reciprocity in Chinese culture (see Hwang, 1987; Yang 1957).   If the leader's benevolence does not lead to a response of indebtedness, then this leader behavior will be terminated immediately.

As to the moral leadership, the underlying psychological mechanism is the subordinates' identification with the leader.   Through this identification process, the subordinates will imitate the leader's behavior.   If leader's behavior does not meet reasonable expectation of subordinates, then the effectiveness of moral leadership will be downgraded accordingly.   Although this argument makes sense mostly, it is still in great need of more solid empirical support as yet.

*Differential Guanxi and Leadership*

Other than paternalistic leadership, *guanxi* is another important factor in analyzing Chinese leadership style.   As yet, only a few empirical studies have been conducted to investigate the relationship between *guanxi* and leadership.   Fortunately, the preliminary research in this front has been quite promising.   Although researchers are still in great dispute as to the meaning of *guanxi*, two sets of exploratory research deserve our special attention.

The first set of research investigates *guanxi* and its impact on Chinese business behavior.   The main focus was on the influence of *guanxi* on managerial performance (Farh, Tsui, Xin & Cheng, 1998; Tsui & Farh, 1997; Xin and Pearce, 1996).   Through investigating the issue of vertical dyadic *guanxi*, this research contributed to our better understanding of differentiated *guanxi* and leadership within Chinese organizations.

The second set of researchstudied the social cognition of CEOs with respect to their subordinates and the employee categorization process (Chang, 1995; Cheng, 1995; Cheng & Lin, 1999; Cheng, 1999).   These researchers found that *guanxi* including both objective social ties and subjective interpersonal affection is one of the most important criteria for the Chinese CEOs to categorize their employees into in-group or out-group members, and then the CEOs will manage them accordingly.

## *Guanxi and the Interactions between Superiors and Subordinates*

Studies of Western organizations suggest that demographic similarity is one of the key factors in explaining interpersonal relationships and work outcomes. Although the concept of relational demographics is well established in the Western world, the prevailing view in Chinese society tends to utilize *guanxi* as the key factor in explaining the effects of common background and shared experience among related individuals on interpersonal interactions and related work outcomes in Chinese enterprises (Tusi & Farh, 1997).

What exactly does it mean by *guanxi* when investigating the interactions between the superiors and the subordinates? There is no doubt that the term *guanxi* in the Chinese language is very complicated. It takes on multiple meanings. The consensus in the research field of Chinese organizational behavior is that *guanxi* refers to a certain type of interpersonal relationship, one that is personal and built upon particular criteria, rather than applicable to the general public (Tsui & Farh, 1997). Using the concept *lun* discussed in Confucian ideology, some researchers defined *guanxi* as "the existence of direct particularistic ties between an individual and others (Farh, Tsui, Xin & Cheng, 1996, p.471-73). Although this definition of *guanxi* is a bit narrow and ignores the richness in meaning of *guanxi* (Kim, 1991), it does help to differentiate *guanxi* from friendship or the superior-subordinate relationship. It also helps researchers to measure *guanxi* appropriately and to explore the relationship between *guanxi* and leadership.

Generally speaking, the bases of *guanxi* in Chinese society mainly derived from one's personal origin and social interactions at a later stage in life. Most *guanxi* is built up through some acquired or shared attributes rather than just an inherited relationship. The most common bases for *guanxi* can be kinship, locality (native place), coworkers, classmates, surname, brotherhood, teacher-student relationships and in-law relationships (Jacobs, 1979). Chiao (1982) categorized the types of *guanxi* similarly, although he did not define what constitutes the basis of *guanxi*. Generally speaking, *guanxi* refers not only to the objective existence of a common background or experience between people, but also to the actual interactions between people (Tsui & Farh, 1997).

Given this definition of *guanxi*, how does it affect the interactions between the superior and the subordinates?   Theoretically speaking, the subordinates who have particularistic *guanxi* with their superiors should maintain a better interpersonal relationship and a higher level of mutual trust between them (Tsui & Farh, 1997). This reasoning is further confirmed by two empirical   studies.

Farh, Tsui and Cheng (1998) surveyed 560 employees in one insurance company in Taiwan.   They investigated the effects of bases of *guanxi* and demographic similarities on such work outcomes as the level of subordinates' trust in their superiors, subordinates' performance ratings by their superiors, subordinates' commitment to the organization, subordinates' actual sales performance, and subordinates' invention to quit.   When demographic similarities between the superiors and the subordinates were properly controlled, the results indicated that the existence of *guanxi* helps to increase the level of the subordinates' trust in their superior.   Were there kinship or a neighborhood relationship among them, the level of the subordinates' trust in the superior tended to be higher.

In another   study, Xin, Farh, Cheng and Tsui (1999) compared sample observations from Taiwan and Mainland China to investigate the impacts of bases of *guanxi* and demographic similarity on the quality of relationships between subordinates and their superiors, organizational commitment, and performance evaluation.   The Taiwanese sample composed of 175 subordinate-superior dyads. The interesting finding was that the existence of a past relationship between the subordinate and the superior, either as colleague or being from the same hometown, made subordinates perceive a better quality of superior-subordinate relationship, and resulted in the subordinates' higher commitment to the organization.   In addition, the superiors who were past colleagues of the subordinates perceived a better quality of superior-subordinate relationship, and gave them higher performance ratings.

Thus we can conclude that some kind of *guanxi* or social ties between the superiors and the subordinates do contribute to better interpersonal relationships and stronger mutual trust between them.   In other words, the existence of particularistic ties, or *guanxi,* is a crucial factor   in influencing the chosen style and effectiveness of leadership.   However, this line of research simply explored the functions of *guanxi* within and between Chinese organizations.   It cannot tell us what the underlying mechanism of the effects that differential *guanxi* has on leadership effectiveness. Below we will introduce an employee categorization model to link *guanxi* to leadership directly.

## Employee Categorization Model and Leadership Style

Many researchers of Chinese social relations (e.g., Butterfield, 1983) have suggested that in comparison with Westerners, the Chinese have a much stronger tendency to divide people into categories and treat them accordingly (Farh, Tsui, Xin and Cheng, 1998). Coincidentally, Cheng (1991, 1995b, 1999) investigated the social interactions within Taiwanese enterprises and found that Taiwanese CEOs also tend to categorize employees. Both cultural traditions and the market force influence this social categorization process. Based on the *guanxi* between the CEOs and their subordinates, the subordinates' loyalty and competence, the CEOs assign employees into hierarchical groups and lead them accordingly, in order to promote organizational effectiveness.

This employee categorization model identifies *guanxi*, loyalty and competence as the three key elements in employee categorization. Loyalty is taken to mean self-sacrifice with no reservation for the organization, competence means the employee's ability to complete job assignment well, and *guanxi* means important social ties. Subordinates in different categories have different degrees of closeness with the CEOs. Those who are relatives will have a closer relationship with the CEOs. As pointed out by Cheng and Kao (1991), subordinates with quasi-kinship do also have a closer relationship with the CEOs. Due to the need of business operation, those who are recognized by the CEOs or meet some or all of the "nine sameness of affinity" requirements will be appraised and accepted as quasi-kinship.

Based on the closeness of *guanxi*, different degrees of loyalty and different levels of competence, leaders can categorize their subordinates accordingly. The rules of interactions between the leader and his subordinates constitute the basis of daily operations of Taiwanese enterprises. The leaders treat in-group and out-group members with different level of trust. Those who share a similar background with the leader will be taken as in-group members, while the rest will be taken as out-group members. The differentiated responses and treatments will be shown in various managerial styles and leadership behavior.

For instance, the leaders will correspond more often with in-group members and provide more opportunities for them to participate in decision-making.  The leaders also tend to be more considerate and delegate more authority to in-group members. The out-group members will be treated quite differently.  Accordingly the subordinates will respond with different work attitude under these differentiated treatments.  Due to being trusted more, in-group members will be much more obliged to the leaders.  Not only do they work harder and are more willing to contribute to the organization, but also do they have higher compliance, job satisfaction and organizational commitment.  Besides, they are more likely to talk positively about the organization, help others, and go beyond the normal expectations in their job.  Their turnover rate is also lower than out-group members.

Cheng and Lin (1999) did one qualitative study regarding to the employee categorization model.  The authors collected related information with respect to seven large Taiwanese enterprises and asked 13 top rank officials in these enterprises to describe the interactions between the CEOs and their subordinates.  The results validated the model quite well.  *Guanxi* does play an important role in the process of employee categorization, especially as the subordinates happen to be family members.  They are more likely to be categorized as in-group members.

Cheng, Farh and Chang (1999) conducted a quantitative study by selecting 173 superior-subordinate dyads from six private Taiwanese companies.  Their findings indicated that a close relationship between the superior and his subordinates would lead to more generous treatment.  The superior tended to be more considerate and concerned about the welfare of his subordinates with close ties contrary to those without this relationship.  However, this line of study is still at its early stage and more evidence is needed before we can fully understand the underlying mechanism concerning the effects of *guanxi* on leadership.

## Leader and Chin-Shin Relations in Taiwanese Organizations

In a series of empirical studies Chi (1994,1996,1997) examined an important leadership phenomenon in Taiwanese business organizations, the role of '*chin-shins*' (or confidants) of top managers, and the leader and *chin-shin* relations. The concept of *chin-shin* is composed of two subconcepts: *chin* and *shin*.  *Chin* has the meaning of closeness, while *shin* signifies trustworthiness. In other words, a *chin-shin* refers to a subordinate who is close and trustworthy to a superior. Often times, a *chin-shin* is more than an ordinary subordinate to a superior; in some cases there can be pseudo-kinship between them (Chi, 1999).

## The Five Roles of Chin-Shins in Taiwanese Organizations

Chi (1999) argued that there are five roles of *chin-shins* in Taiwanese organizations: (a) decision aide, (b) public relations agent, (c) black/white face (or nice guy/devil), (d) information gatekeeper, and (e) resource controller.

*Decision Aide* One of the most important roles of chin-shins is that they may serve as decision aids to superiors. In addition, chin-shins often serve as advisors, giving valuable suggestions to their superiors, coming up with ideas for their superiors, or acting as devil's advocates so their superiors do not rush too fast into decisions.

*Public Relations Agent* The second role of *chin-shins* is as 'public relations agents'. In Chinese societies, personal connections and relationships are very important. *Chin-shins* may help superiors maintain relationships with people outside the company, and superiors may use their *chin-shins'* *guanxi* to expand their own relational matrices.

*Chin-shins* may also help superiors establish closer relationships with other subordinates. In addition, *chin-shins* can serve as intermediary mechanisms to facilitate information flow and also help to maintain better human relations between superiors and their subordinates.

*Black/White Face* The third role of *chin-shins* is the 'black/white face'. Superiors and their *chin-shins* can work together taking varying parts in face-making play. In one situation, for instance, a superior may play the role of a nice guy (white face), while his/her *chin-shin* plays the devil (black face). In another situation, their roles may be reversed.

*Information Gatekeeper* The fourth role of a *chin-shin* is as the information gatekeeper. Information that is going to be passed to the superior may be reviewed by the *chin-shin*. The *chin-shin* screens and rules out unimportant communications so that superiors may spend more time on crucial decision-making.

Some possible unintended consequences may result from this role, however. A *chin-shin* may develop great power because he/she controls information channels.

*Resource Controller* The fifth role of a *chin-shin* is as a resource controller. *Chin-shins* do not have the formal authority to exercise power on behalf of superiors. However, since *chin-shins* are located close to the center of the superior's differential matrices, they are, informally speaking, a surrogate for their superiors. Thereby, *chin-shins* may gradually gain power over certain resource allocation.

## Perceptions of the Superior and Chin-Shin by Subordinates

In order to understand subordinates' perceptions of the superior and *chin-shin* relations, Chi (1995) has collected a sample of 137 managers in 137 different companies. These respondents were asked to respond to questions regarding a high-level manager and his/her *chin-shin*. The results showed that, when respondents rated the superior positively, they also rated the *chin-shin* positively, and vice versa. Hence, it seems that the superior and the *chin-shin* are perceived as a unit. Their joint leadership styles toward subordinates are inter-linked with each other. If subordinates hold good impressions of superiors, they also tend to view their *chin-shins* favorably. Likewise, if subordinates hold good impressions of the *chin-shins*, they see their superiors favorably as well (Chi, 1999).

## The Effects of Superior and Chin-shin Relationships on Performance Appraisal

Chu (2000) investigates the possible influence of trust in the subordinates by the superiors and the closeness between them on the evaluation of subordinates' work performance. His findings are as follows: as the superior trusts the subordinate more or as their relationship become closer, the superior tends to give a higher score on the subordinate's performance evaluation. That is to say, subordinates perceived as *chin-shin* receive the highest scores, other-in-group members the second, while the out-group members receive the lowest.

Furthermore, it seems that the *chin-shins'* performance scores are overestimated significantly while that of out-group members are underestimated significantly. From the above findings, one can conclude that relationships between the leaders and *chin-shins* do influence the attitudes and behaviors of the leaders toward his subordinates.

## Leadership Behavior and Employee Effectiveness

In addition to the investigation of the relationship between familism and leadership, other leadership research conducted in Taiwan during the past two decades has directed attention to the impact of leadership behavior on employee effectiveness. Two major aspects of leadership behavior investigated by these studies were task-oriented and relationship-oriented behaviors. As to the indicators of employee effectiveness, job satisfaction, organizational commitment and organizational citizenship behavior were most often used. The tools for the assessment of leadership behavior as well as employee effectiveness were mainly adapted from instruments originally designed for studies in the United States.

For example, Cheng and Zhuang (1981) studied effective leadership styles in Taiwanese military organizations. They asked soldiers to generate statements to describe leader behavior and then combined these statements with items adapted from Fleishman's Leadership Behavior Description Questionnaire (LBDQ) to construct their leadership scale. Factor analysis of the data collected from 1160 soldiers yielded three independent factors of leadership: consideration, initiating structure and *gong-si-fen-ming* (being scrupulous in separating public from private interests). The first two factors were identical to those typically found in LBDQ in the West. The third factor refers to certain aspects of a leader's moral character. Cheng and Zhuang found that this factor of moral character is an important predictor for leadership effectiveness in Taiwanese military organizations (Farh & Cheng, 2000).

Huang (1982) investigated the relationship of teachers' job satisfaction to their job characteristics, locus of control, achievement motivation, dogmatism and the leadership behavior of the principal. In sum, 178 secondary teachers and 247 elementary teachers were surveyed in this study. The results showed that, among all of 19 predictors investigated, consideration has the highest predictive validity for job satisfaction and intention to quit. In addition, the higher the principal scored on either consideration or initiating structure, the higher the teachers' job satisfaction and the lower the teachers' intention to quit. Furthermore, the leader scored high in both consideration and initiating structure (a "high-high" leader) tended to achieve the highest subordinate job satisfaction and the lowest intention to quit. Other related studies on leadership behavior and employee effectiveness (Cheng, 1977; Huang & Weng, 1980; Hsu, 1981; Huang, 1983) directed their focus on institutions such as businesses, schools and governmental bureaus. These studies also generated similar results to Huang (1982).

As to the impact of leadership on organizational commitment, most Taiwanese researches indicated that the more the superiors emphasized relationship-oriented behaviors, the more their subordinates would commit to the organizations. Similarly, the more the superiors emphasized task-oriented behaviors, the higher their subordinates scored on the scale of organizational commitment. Furthermore, among those predictors investigated in these studies, relationship-oriented behavior has the highest predictive validity for organizational commitment (Huang, 1984; Huang, 1986; Lee, 1986).

As far as the effects of leadership behaviors on organizational citizenship behaviors were concerned, Huang (1998) found that, the more the superiors placed importance on "consideration" and/or "initiating structure", the more likely the subordinates were to perform organizational citizenship behaviors. In addition, superiors' consideration had higher predictive validity than "initiating structure" with regard to organizational citizenship behavior.

From reviewing the above research findings regarding the impact of leadership behavior on employee effectiveness, we conclude that leadership behavior has a similar impact on job satisfaction, organizational commitment and organizational citizenship behaviors. The Chinese society has been well known for its emphasis on relationships and *guanxi*. As such, the relationship-oriented behavior seems to have more significant influence on employee effectiveness than that of task-oriented behavior (Huang, 1982; Huang, 1988). In addition, the relationship-oriented behavior has higher predictive validity for employee effectiveness than other predictors (such as work stress, job characteristics, achievement motivation, etc.)

These research findings seem to signify the importance of relationship-oriented behavior (i.e. care and consideration) in Taiwanese organizations and its positive influence on employee effectiveness.

## Transformational Leadership and Follower Performance

Transformational leadership is one of the most interesting research topics for contemporary researchers in leadership. Transformational leaders attempt to transform the values and attitudes of followers, activate their higher-order needs, reconstruct their self-perception, and motivate them to innovate.

Transformational leaders can also induce followers to transcend self-interest for the sake of the organization and to perform beyond the level of expectation (Bass, 1985; Podsakoff, et al., 1990; Yukl, 1998).

Podsakoff, et al. (1990) developed a scale to measure the six key dimensions of transformational leader behaviors: (a) identifying and articulating a vision, (b) providing an appropriate model, (c) fostering the acceptance of group goals, (d) high performance expectation, (e) providing individual support, and (f) intellectual stimulation. These six dimensions could be grouped into two main categories: (1) task-oriented transformational leader behaviors (which include identifying and articulating a vision, high performance expectation, and intellectual stimulation); and (2) relationship-oriented transformational leader behaviors (which include providing an appropriate model, fostering the acceptance of group goals, and providing individual support) (Chen & Farh, 2000).

Furthermore, Podsakoff, et al. (1990) investigated the impact of transformational leader behaviors on organizational citizenship behaviors, and the potential mediating role, played by follower's trust and satisfaction in that process. It was found that the effects of transformational leader behaviors on organizational citizenship behaviors are indirect, rather than direct, in the sense that these effects are mediated by followers' trust in their leaders (Podsakoff, et al., 1990).

In Taiwan, Cheng, et al. (2002) examined the relationships among principal's leadership, the quality of principal-teacher relations, and teachers' extra-role behaviors. They found that: (a) the principal's relationship-oriented transformational leader behaviors have significant positive effects on the teachers' extra-role behaviors, whereas the effects of task-oriented transformational leader behaviors and transactional leader behaviors are insignificant; (b) taking the effects of transformational leadership and paternalistic leadership on teachers' extra-role behaviors into account simultaneously, two dimensions of paternalistic leadership (i.e. benevolent leadership and moral leadership) have significant effects, while the effects of transformational leadership are negligible; (c) although both relationship-oriented and task-oriented transformational leader behaviors have positive impacts on principle-teacher relations, the impacts of the former are much higher than those of the latter.

The above findings pointed out the important role of paternalistic leadership in Chinese organizations and its significant impact on both followers' and group performance, which did not only exist in business organizations but also in nonprofit organizations, such as schools.   Through controlling the effects of the Western style transformational leadership, the authors still found the unique and significant effects of paternalistic leadership.   Further investigation of the impact of transformational leadership alone showed that relationship-oriented transformational leader behaviors, which are compatible with the Chinese cultural tradition, had a higher impact on follower performance than task-oriented transformational leader behaviors.   These findings also lend strong support to the emphasis of the idiographic approach in that leadership is bound to cultural influence and is effective only if leader behaviors match the distinctiveness of the underlying culture (Cheng, et al., 2002).

## Conclusion and Implication

Most Taiwanese business organizations are of small scales with relatively simple structures, and the core families have absolute control.   In retrospect to the Chinese cultural tradition, the impact of family structure and familism on business practices is profound.   On the one hand, the emphasis on paternalistic authority and duties of subordinates leads to paternalistic leadership.   On the other hand, the emphasis on differential *guanxi* leads to differential leadership.   These two features of leadership happen to be the very important characteristics of Taiwanese business management. Based on the findings of past research, we believe that the paternalistic and differential leadership can actually increase subordinates' compliance and commitment to the organization, and result in more efficient resource exchanges between the employees and the organization. Consequently, the effectiveness of leadership increases as shown in the graphical process of Figure 1. We also believe that the research findings and implications discussed in this paper can shed light on future research topics, such as Chinese leadership and organizational effectiveness, contingency leadership in Chinese enterprises, Chinese leadership and organizational changes. This paper will contribute to our better understanding of Chinese leadership, cross-cultural management and management of Chinese family enterprises.

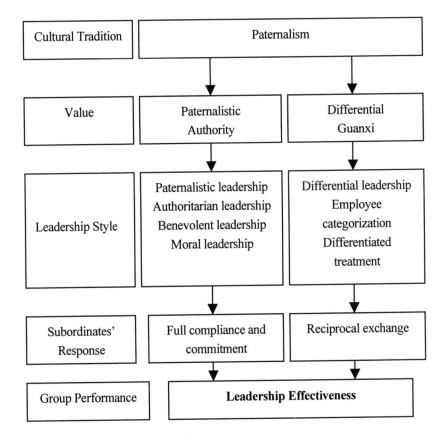

**Figure 1 The Relationship between Paternalism, Leadership Style and Leadership Effectiveness**

Source: Cheng & Hwang (2000)

# References

Bass, B. M. (1985). *Leadership and Performance beyond Expectations.* New York: Free Press.

Birnbaum, P. J. & Wong, G. Y. Y.(1985). *Cultural Values of Managers in the People's Republic of China and Hong Kong.* Paper presented at the Annual Meeting of the Academy of Management, San Diego.

Bowers, D. G. & Seashore, S. E.(1966). "Predicting organizational effectiveness with a four-factor theory of leadership". *Administrative Science Quarterly,* **11,** 238-263.

Butterfield, F.(1983). *China: Alive in a Bitter Sea.* London: Coronet Books.

Chemers, M. M.(1993). "An integrative theory of leadership". In M. Chemers & R. Ayman (eds.), *Leadership theory and research: Perspectives and directions.* New York: Academic Press.

Chen, C.S. & Kao, C. S. (1991). "Social order in the operation of Taiwan enterprises: renqing, guanxi and low". *The Tonghai University Journal,* **32,** 219-232.

Chen, X.P. & Farh., J.L. (2000). *The Effectiveness of Transactional and Transformational Leader Behaviors in Chinese Organizations: Evidence from Taiwan.* Working paper of Department of Organization and Management, Hong Kong University of Science and Technology.

Cheng, B.S., Hsieh, P.I., & Chou, L.F.(2002). *Principal's Leadership, Quality of Principal-teacher Relation and Teachers' Extra-role Behavior: The Effects of Transformational and Paternalistic Leadership.* Working paper of Department of Psychology, National Taiwan University.

Cheng, B. S & Huang, M. P.(2000). "Leadership in Chinese business organizations: A cultural value analysis." *Sun Yat-Sen Management Review,* **8**(4), 583-617.

Cheng, B. S. & Lin, C. W.(1999). "Differential mode of the association and Chinese organizational behavior : An exploratory study of Taiwan large-scale enterprises," *Bulletin of the Institute of Ethnology, Academia Sinica,* **86,** 29-72.

Cheng, B. S. & Zhuang, S. J.(1981). "Factor analysis of effective leader behaviors of rank-and-file military personnel in Taiwan: Relationships among leadership effectiveness, leader roles, and leadership styles", *Journal of Chinese Psychology,* **23,** 97-106.

Cheng, B. S., Chou, L. F., & Farh, J. L.(2000). "A triad model of paternalistic leadership: The constructs and measurement." *Indigenous Psychological*

*Research in Chinese Societies*, **14**, 3-64.

Cheng, B. S., Farh, J. L., & Chang, H.(1999). *Employee Categorization and Managerial Behavior in the Chinese Context: A Theoretical Model and Its Validation.* Working paper of Department of Psychology, National Taiwan University.

Cheng, B. S.(1995a). *Authoritarian Values and Executive Leadership: The Case of Taiwanese Family Enterprises.* Paper submitted to National Science Council, Taiwan.

Cheng, B. S.(1995b). "Differential guanxi and Chinese organizational behavior." *Indigenous Psychological Research in Chinese Societies*, **3**, 142-219. (In Chinese)

Cheng, B. S.(1977). *The Effects of Leadership Style, Situational Factors and Personality Traits on Employees' Job Satisfaction.* Master Thesis of Department of Psychology, National Taiwan University.

Cheng, B.S.(1991). "Familism and leadership behavior". In Z. F. Yang & H. S. R. Kao (eds.), *Chinese and Chinese Soul*, Taiwan: Yuan Liu (In Chinese).

Cheng, C. J.(1999). *Communication Media and Its Effectiveness : The Effects of Guanxi and Related Contingent Factors.* Master Thesis of Department of Psychology, National Taiwan University.

Chi, S. C.(1994). "The role of confidants of top managers in Chinese organization. Proceedings of the Management Functions and Applications Group". *The Association of Management 12th Annual International Conference*, **12**(2), 160-165.

Chi, S. C.(1996). "An empirical study on confidant roles in business organizations." *NTU Management Review.* **15**(1), 37-59.

Chi, S. C.(1997). "Perceptual differences between business chin-shins and other employees: an empirical study". *Journal of Management and Information.* **2**, 55-75.

Chi, S. C.(1999). "The role of chin-shins of top managers in Taiwanese organizations: Exploring Chinese leadership phenomena". In H. S. R. Kao, D. Sinha, & B. Wilpert (eds.), *Management and Cultural Values: The Indigenization of Organizations in Asia.* Thousand Oaks, CA: Sage Publications (India), 252-264.

Chong, L. E., Cragin, J. P. & Scherling, S. A.(1983). *Manager Work-related Values in a Chinese Corporation*. Paper presented at the Academy of International Business 1983 Annual Meeting, San Francisco.

Chu, C. M.. 2000. "The effects of confident relationship on performance appraisal: A differential matrices perspective", *Management Review*. **19**(3). 125-147. (In Chinese).

Farh, J. L. & Cheng, B. S.(2000). "A culture analysis of paternalistic leadership in Chinese organization". In A. S. Tsui & J. T. Li (eds.), *Management and Organizations in China*. London: McMillam.

Farh, J. L., Tsui, A. S., Xin, K. R., & Cheng, B. S.(1998). "The influence of relational demography and guanzi: The Chinese case". *Organization Science*, **9**(4). 471-488.

Fleishman, E. A.(1953). "The description of supervisory behavior". *Journal of Applied Psychology*, **37**, 1-6.

Hofstede, G.(1980). *Culture's Consequences: International Differences in Work-related Values*. Beverly Hill, CA: Sage.

House, R. J. & Mitchell, T. R.(1974). "Path-goal theory of leadership". *Contemporary Business*, **3**, 81-98.

House, R. J., Wright, N. S., & Aditya, R. N.(1997). "Cross-cultural research on organizational leadership: A critical analysis and proposed theory". In P. C. Earley and M. Erez (eds.), *New Perspectives on International Industrial/organizational Psychology*, 535-625.

Hsu, F. L. K.(1953). *American and Chinese: Two Ways of Life*. New York: Belard-Schuman.

Hsu, F. L. K.(1981). *Americans and Chinese: Passage to Differences*. Honolulu: University of Hawaii Press.

Huang, K. Y. & Wong, I. F.(1980). "The effects of leadership style and personality trait on workers' job satisfaction", *The National Chengchi University Journal*, **41**, 45-60.

Huang, K. L.(1982). "The relationship of teachers' job satisfaction to leadership style, job characteristics, locus of control, achievement motivation and dogmatism," *Research in Education & Psychology*, **5**, 47-76.

Huang, K.L.(1984). "Employees' job satisfaction in Taiwanese organization." *Proceedings of the Conference on Chinese Management*, Taipei, Taiwan, 316-334.

Huang, K.L.(1986). "Organizational and professional commitment of Taiwan middle school teachers". *The National Chengchi University Journal*, **53**, 55-84.

Hwang, K. K.(1987). "Face and favor: The Chinese power game". *American Journal of Sociology*, **92**, 944-974.

Huang, K.L. & Tsai, C.T.(1998). "The effects of work value and leadership behavior on employee effectiveness". *NTU Management Review*, **9**, 51-85.

Jacobs, J. B.(1979). "A preliminary model of particularistic ties in Chinese political alliances: Kan-ching and Kuan-hsi in a rural Taiwanese township". *China Quarterly*, **78**, 237-273.

King, A. Y.(1991). "Kuan-hsi and networking building: A sociological interpretation." *Daedalus*, **120**, 63-84.

Lee, S.C.(1986). *The Relationships among Job Characteristics, Organizational Structure, Leadership Style, Personal Characteristics and Work Attitude: Comparisons among Chines, Japanese and American Managers.* Unpublished master thesis of Chung Yuan Christian University.

Lin, N.(1989). "Chinese family structure and Chinese society". *Bulletin of the Institute of Ethnology, Academia Sinica*, **65**, 59-129.

Podsakoff, P.M., Mackenzie, S.B., Moorman, R,H. & Fetter, R. (1990). "Transformational behaviors and their effects on followers' trust in leader, satisfaction, and organizational citizenship behaviors". *Leadership Quarterly*, **1**(2), 107-142.

Redding, S. G.(1990). *The Spirit of Chinese Capitalism*. Berlin: Walter de Gruyter.

Silin, R. F.(1976). *Leadership and Values.* Cambridge, MA: Harvard University Press.

Smith, P. B. & Wang, Z. M.(1996). "Chinese leadership and organizational structures". In M.H. Bond (ed.), *The Handbook of Chinese Psychology*, 322-337.

Stogdill, R. M.(1974). *Handbook of Leadership: A Survey of Literature*. New York: Free Press.

Tsui, A. S. & Farh, J. L.(1997). "Where guanxi matters: Relational demography and guanxi in the Chinese context". *Work and Occupation*, **24**(1), 56-79.

Westwood, R.(1997). "Harmony and patriarchy: The cultural basis for "paternalistic headship" among the Overseas Chinese." *Organization Studies*, **18**(3), 445-480.

Whitley, R.(1992). *Business System in East Asia Firms, Markets, and Societies.* London: Sage.

Wong, S. L.(1985). "The Chinese family firm: A model". *British Journal of*

*Sociology*, **36**(1), 58-72.

Xin, K. R. & Pearce, J. L.(1996). "Guanxi: Connections as substitutes for structural support." *Academy of Management Journal*, **36**, 1641-1658.

Yang, L. S.(1957). "The concept of 'bao' as a basis for social relations in China", In J. K. Fairbank(ed.), *Chinese Thought and Institution* (pp.291-309). Chicage, IL: University of Chicago Press.

Yukl, G. A.(1994). *Leadership in Organizations.* (3rd ed.), Englewood Cliffs, NJ: Prentice-Hall.

Yukl, G.A. (1998). *Leadership in Organizations.* (4th ed.), Englewood Cliffs, NJ: Prentice-Hall.

Zhang, H. F.(1995). *The Determinants of Trust and the Implications of Trust for Leadership and Job-satisfaction.* Unpublished master thesis of Department of Psychology, National Taiwan University.

*Chapter 5*

# Organizational Leadership in the Malaysian Context[1]

Mahfooz A. Ansari

School of Management, University Science Malaysia, Malaysia

Zainal A. Ahmad

School of Management, University Science Malaysia, Malaysia

Rehana Aafaqi

School of Management, University Science Malaysia, Malaysia

## An Overview

Despite the centuries of armchair speculations and decades of empirical investigations, the issue of effective leadership still persists for professional experts in organizational behavior and industrial/organizational psychology. The fundamental debate centers round the universal versus specific nature of leadership. Recent researchers (see such reviews as those of Bass, 1990; Sinha,

[1] We are grateful to Zahid Mahmood and two editors, Dean Tjosvold and Kwok Leung, for their constructive comments on an earlier draft of this chapter. Correspondence concerning this article should be addressed to Mahfooz A. Ansari, School of Management, University Science Malaysia, 11800 USM, Penang, Malaysia; E-Mail: mahfooz@usm.my.

1994) seem to be favoring the latter position. The cultural perspective suggests that as each culture is relatively unique it may require specific kinds of leadership in order to be effective. Unfortunately, as will be clear a little later, not much is empirically known about leadership in Malaysia. The strategic challenges that Malaysian leaders face are how to maintain organizational growth and renewal; how to pursue excellence; and how to better prepare for the next millennium within the context of our multiracial and multi-religious society (Yeoh, 1998, p. 71). In other words, leadership in Malaysia must be discussed against the context of a multiracial and multi-religious society. Problems in Malaysia are complex in the sense that the country is peopled by distinct racial elements; various religious beliefs exist side by side, and various languages flourish. Such variety certainly adds color and vigor to Malaysia's historical canvas. Thus, it would be misleading to assume that there is only one Malaysian culture, or one leadership style, as there are distinct differences in the cultural attributes of the ethnic groups that determine the styles and practices of leadership (Kennedy & Mansor, 2000; Poon, 1998). Recent researches, however, suggest that the three ethnic groups; Malay, Chinese, and Malaysian Indiansdo not differ significantly on work-related values (Abdullah & Lim, 2001; Lim, 2001).

The present chapter addresses the issue of organizational leadership in the Malaysian context. We have divided the discussion into four major sections. First, we discuss the relevant literature on the Malaysian multicultural context. It is in this section that we present the views of different scholars by integrating them into two interwoven values, reference for relationship and preference for hierarchy, and their manifestations. The second section presents a brief orientation to the key elements relating to leadership studies conducted in Malaysia. Thus the first two sections set the stage for a model of leadership to be presented in the third section. The third section is an integration of socio-cultural values and a proposed leadership style. It is entirely devoted to a framework for studying leadership in Malaysian organizations. Our central thesis is that we need to adopt a two-stage model, nurturant-task (NT) to participative (P) style, of leadership effectiveness. The NT leader is a task-and-efficiency-oriented leader with a blend of nurturance. The notion of the NT$\rightarrow$P model has been empirically found to be successful in the Indian socio-cultural milieu. Given there are a great deal of similarities between Malaysian and Indian culture, we advocate in favor of NT leadership as a transitional style. Our final section sums up our arguments developed in the previous sections and spells out the implications and directions for upcoming investigations.

## The Malaysian Context

### The Backdrop

Malaysia is a multiracial and multiethnic country with a diverse population of 24.92 million (Key Statistics, Malaysia, 2003), of which the Malays and indigenous people (bumiputra, "Sons of the soil")? comprise about 60 percent, Chinese comprise 31 percent, and Indians comprise about 8 percent. A young independent nation of 46 years, Malaysians can trace their rich multiethnic origins in the annals of recorded history since the days when it was known by Greek sailors as the Golden Chersonese and popularized by Ptolemy'smap.

The work of Hashim (1992) on The Malaccan Sultanate of Malacca attests to the early accounts of the Malay leadership in the Malay Archipelago. As recorded in the Malay Annals, Malacca,the cradle of the Malay civilization,started as a small settlement in 1400 and evolved into a bustling metropolitan and multicultural entrepot (Kheng, 1998; Shellabear, 1994). The Malaccan Empire reached its zenith through a series of empire buildings even before America was discovered in 1492. The Malaccan Sultanate, characterized by a patriarchal feudal system,came to an abrupt end in 1511 when the Portuguese colonized Malacca in order to control the spice trade over the Straits of Malacca. In 1624, the Portuguese rescinded and handed Malacca over to the Dutch. The race for controlling the spice trade in Southeast Asia saw the Dutch and British parceling out territories, and they signed a treaty in 1784 to allow the British to colonize the Malay Peninsular with Penang, Malacca, and Singapore as the Strait's Settlements.

Under the British, the colonial divide-and-rule policies and migration of workers from India and China, the two world wars, the Japanese occupation, and the communist insurgencies shaped the socio-political and religious-cultural history of Malaya as it was known then. Malaysia gained independence in 1957 through a unique blend of leadership, the sharing of political and economic power among the indigenous Malays and the immigrant Chinese and Indians through a binding social contract. The Malaysian version of leadership is imbued with values from many subcultures and influences, namely the Malays, Chinese, Indians, and 446 years of foreign colonization which has left traces of Western and Japanese values.

As for the Chinese, Dato' Seri Dr. Ling Liong Sik (1995), past President of the Malaysian Chinese Association (MCA), in his book "The Malaysian Chinese", recounted the history of Chinese immigrants dating back as early as the 14th century. However, the major influx of Chinese immigrants was after the 1820's when they came as traders, shopkeepers, planters, and miners. They worked in tin mines and on pepper, rubber, gambier, coconut, and sugar cane plantations. In 1794 under the British regime, Sir Francis Light even acknowledged the economic contributions of the Chinese, calling them a "valuable acquisition". Ling adds that the Malaysian Chinese, often known as an overseas Chinese,has been described as follows by the chairman of the SGV Group of Manila, Washington Sycip: The Malaysian Chinese possess "the ability to smell profits and make decisions quickly; a penchant for eating well and preferring round tables for quicker exchange of information; generally avoiding politics but maintaining good relations with the government; and being good citizens in their host countries" (Ling, 1995, p. 3). Ling summed up Sycip's observation by saying that the modern overseas Chinese businessman wants to make money so he can eat and live well, steer out of trouble, and pay or his taxes. However, underneath this rather materialistic description of the Chinese "lies a deeply ingrained belief that one must work hard to achieve success", which requires "persistence, patience, tolerance, and stamina; qualities which Chinese stories and fables extol" (Ling, 1995, p. 4). The Malaysian Chinese have the freedom to and still do maintain the Chinese heritage, culture, education system, language, and religion. As such, the Confucian values and beliefs are intact and transcend cross-cultural boundaries.

For the Malaysian Indians, their heritage can be traced back as early as the 7th century with theHindu influence on the Malay Archipelago through the Sri Vijaya Empire and Indian traders that traded along the Straits of Malacca. Even during the heydays of the Malaccan Empire, there was a large population of Indian traders in the Malacca port headed by the Syahbandar. The influx of Indian migrants came during the British colonization through the "Kangany" system of indented labor for the rubber plantations in Malaya (Razak & Ahmad, 1999). For an excellent summary of the historical and political development of Malaysia, see Kennedy (2002).

## The Socio-Cultural Milieu

Given a brief sketch of the Malaysian ethnic backgrounds, let us have a look at the underlying work preferences and values found in the multicultural Malaysian society. Values are defined as the preferred modes of behavior or scale of preferences (Sinha, 1994). The following values and preferences among Malaysians have often been noted by Malaysian scholars as well as expatriate managers.

One of the earliest empirical researche studies on the differences in Malays and Chinese values was the MBA thesis of Ismail (1977, cited in Othman, 1993). Ismail found that Malays and Chinese do not differ significantly in terms of the importance they attach to money, profits, work, and company regulations. However they do differ markedly in terms of their views on loyalty, leadership, freedom at work, and big corporations. He found that for the Malays, loyalty had its limits, whereas the Chinese were more filial in their loyalty. On the other hand, Lim (1998), using the Hofstede (1980) model, argues that the Malays and Chinese differ in cultural attributes but share similarities in power distance and collectivism. He suggests that researchers interested in understanding Malaysian management should incorporate the cultural diversity of Malays and Chinese. In another Hofstede-based study, the GLOBE (Global Leadership and Organizational Behavior Effectiveness) Research Program, Malay middle managers placed higher values on decisiveness, team integration, diplomacy, modesty, and humane orientation compared to their counterparts in the worldwide study (Kennedy & Mansor, 2000). Autonomy was also rated high as well as performance orientation, thereby suggesting that Malays value leaders who can achieve results. Very recently, Othman (2001) pointed out that Malaysian ethnic groups have values that significantly overlap. There is a great deal of emphasis on collectivism in all three groupsMalays, Chinese, and Malaysian Indians (Rashid, Anantharaman, & Raveendaran, 1997).

The seminal works by Asma Abdullah, a Malaysian corporate anthropologist, suggest that the Malaysian work values are an amalgam of the Malays, Chinese, Indian, Anglo, and Japanese work values. Specifically, Abdullah (1992) identified several underlying values held by the Malaysia workforce as observed by Malaysian and expatriate managers. These underlying values include: non-assertiveness (extremely dedicated to do a good job, eager to please others), respect for senior/elderly people (will not argue with the boss, reluctant to ask for help or check for understanding), respect for loyalty (loyal to authority, act with deference and obedience), respect for authority (paternal), preserving face (avoid loss of face and self esteem, avoid public criticism, not expressive, uncomfortable in critically evaluating peers and subordinates, giving negative feedback), collectivism (performance orientation, teamwork, cooperation, strong sense of belonging, priority to group interest, satisfaction derived from respect from colleagues), harmony (compromise, consensus seeking, avoid overt display of anger and aggressive behavior), status, good manners, courtesy (elaborate forms of courtesy and standardized ritual), respect for hierarchy (social formality), non-aggressiveness (non-confrontational), trust and relationship building (relationship based orientation, developing trust and goodwill), third party intervention (deal with ambiguities via indirect approach of a third party or intermediary), and tolerance and respect for differences (religious sensitivities and observances). Abdullah also suggested that there are ethnic values that are deeply embedded in the Malaysian multi-ethnic and multicultural workforce that are supportive of productive business behaviors, namely trustworthiness, honesty, integrity, sincerity, hard work, participative decision-making, teamwork, and the desire for excellence.

In her later work, Abdullah (1994) identified the common culturally based value orientation of the Malaysian workplace as follows: collectivism, hierarchy, relationship-orientation, face, religion, and the pursuit of success. She (1996) also reported the results of a survey on Malaysian managerial values, and identified the following 10 managerial values: goal clarity, cooperation, decisiveness, commitment, high achievement, accountability, shared wisdom, performance merit, continuous improvement, and the meeting of deadlines.

How do all those values mentioned above relate to leadership in Malaysia? Our initial analysis of the values highlighted by Abdullah (1992, 1994, 1996), the GLOBE studies (Kennedy & Mansor, 2000), and other research indicates that values evolve around key elements that suggest the dynamic interaction between two or more individuals. We would group these key overlapping elements into two broad dominant values categories: Preference for Relationships (such as trust and relationship building, preserving face, "we" orientation, teamwork, cooperation, harmony, personalized relationships) and Preference for Hierarchy (such as respect for senior/elderly people, non-assertiveness, respect for loyalty, status, good manners, courtesy, respect for hierarchy, respect for differences, non-aggressiveness, status differential, and power distance). We next turn to elaborating these two work preferences with examples.

## The Two Interwoven Work Values

### *Preference for Relationships*

Leadership in Malaysia is about leading hierarchical relationships. Managers in a high context culture like Malaysia have to spend time in building personal relationships that may transcend the workplace (Abdullah, 1994). Abdullah asserts that there is an unwritten code governing relations and differentiating peers, superiors, and subordinates. Thus any manager, local or expatriate, will have to understand how to relate to other employees. Harmonious relationships are emphasized, hence many supervisors and managers shudder at giving negative feedback to their subordinates. Similarly, many employees hesitate to give negative information up the channel (Poon, 1998). This is further elaborated by what Dahlan (1991) refers to as the "polite system", which for the Malays is based on budi, or virtuous qualities such as generosity. In sum, the Malaysian culture is said to be collectivist (Hofstede, 1991), wherein maintaining relationships is much more important (Abdullah, 1994) than performing a task. Naturally, relationships assume a much greater significance in considering the appropriateness of a leadership style. It is not that relationships are unimportant in the West, but in Malaysia it has developed like an "obsession" Relationships are basically contractual in the West, whereas relationships are personalized in Malaysia. Thus work is performed as a favor to others (McClelland, 1975).

### *Preference for Hierarchy*

The preference for hierarchy manifests itself in a strong status orientation. Relationships are hierarchically arranged into superiors and subordinates (Abdullah, 1994). Seniors (superiors or elders) are respected and obeyed. They are the decision-makers and subordinates are obliged to implement. In general, societal norm dictates that juniors do not disagree with seniors. Thus anger and hostility against a superior are suppressed and displaced, and the tendency is to appease the superior. The superior in return is obliged to provide patronage. The superior must protect and guide the subordinates. In other words, hierarchical relationships are maintained through "affective reciprocity" (Roland, 1984). Preference for hierarchy thus fosters dependence. Lim (1998) reported that the Malays and Chinese differ in cultural attributes but share similarities in power distance and collectivism. He found that the Malays are slightly more hierarchy-oriented toward building relationships with a sense of responsibility to help friends, relatives, and neighbors through networks that are not necessarily business related. There is an obvious mismatch between the egalitarian Islamic values and the traditional Malay hierarchical social structure (Mansor & Mohd Ali, 1998). The Chinese, on the other hand, prefer to incorporate business dealings into hierarchical relationships. They do so by joining associations and guilds that link with the business community to provide mutual support and assistance.

## Manifestations of Interwoven Values

The above interwoven values manifest themselves in several ways. A sort of class-consciousness (hierarchical arrangement) inhibits productive activities. In general, work ethic needs drastic reorientation and regard for work, manual or otherwise, should be given top priority. One can readily notice that a mechanic needs a helper and a helper needs an assistant helper to hand over tools when a job is being done. In offices, one would be amazed to see that officers are averse to doing their own filing and look around for helpers to file papers and carry files on their behalf. This is an incredible arrangement and the cumulative result of all this makes an organization sluggish, overstaffed, and unproductive. The manifestations of poor work ethic can be readily noticed, such as long coffee breaks, loafing, and unwanted leisure (i.e., relaxation without being preceded by hard and exhausting work). Delays, buck-passing, and slowness at work are easily tolerated as normal in exchange for maintaining harmony. Obviously, there is low regard for the value of time (Abdullah, 1994, 1996; Hassan, 1994). Deadlines and punctuality can be sacrificed for maintaining relationships. Attribution of inefficiency and poor performance is reflected in the Tidak apa (never mind) attitude, which is very similar to chalega (an expression of ready acceptance of the status quo) type syndrome in India (Kanungo, 1990).

Even minor re-adjustments in the work-pattern are resisted. This is not to say that there is total rejection of any change, but, by and large, the status quo is preferred. Hassan (1994) highlights several socio-cultural hindrances of the contemporary Malay community that bear implications to work values and leadership. He suggests that the Malays have to deal with the phenomena of liberal vs. secularist mindset, conspicuous and ostentatious lifestyle, "money politics" syndrome, weak moral fiber syndrome, slave-master relationships, patron-client complex, lepak (loafing) syndrome, mediocrity syndrome, dependency syndrome, and many other negative influences. Whereas Hassan reiterated that his observations are not empirically proven, the impact of these negative influences on Malay leadership are worthy of further explorations. According to Kennedy (2002), there is obvious conflict between traditional values and international outlook among Malaysians. For example, Malaysians have strong preference for hierarchy and relationships (i.e., traditional values). Yet in the same vein they have strong future orientation and above-average level of performance orientation (i.e., international outlook).

*The Issue of Effective Leadership*

The previous section on the Malaysian socio-cultural milieu provides the backdrop to understanding the work values and preferences of the Malaysian workforce. As suggested by several authors (see the works of Abdullah, 1992, 1994, 1996; Dahlan, 1991; Kennedy & Mansor, 2000), these work values and preferences may have significant impact on the Malaysian conceptualization of what constitutes effective leadership and may differ from the Western thoughts and theories on leadership.

*Leadership Studies in Malaysia*

Malaysian researchers do not seem to be behind in digging up the leadership mines. But, in most cases, they have followed the Western models, thus evaluating leadership in Malaysia from an external perspective. Our aim is not to present a comprehensive review of the leadership literature in Malaysia. Instead, we provide a brief orientation to representative research in this area. Much of the published literature on this subject seems to capture four distinct, yet related, theoretical frameworks: leadership preferences, leadership behavior, leader-member exchange approach to leadership, and power-influence approach to leadership.


## Leadership Preferences

Let us first look at the preference for leadership of Malaysian workers. Following the implicit leadership paradigm, researchers have examined the preference for "ideal" bosses or leaders in work organizations. Implicit theories assume that individuals hold beliefs about the attributes consistent with effective leadership. Sulaiman, Arumugam, and Wafa (1999) defined the ideal boss as "an imaginary boss who possesses the most preferred behavior qualities" (p. 25). Drawing a sample of 230 managers from 50 multinational companies, they found that expatriate bosses are close to the ideal. The expatriate boss (a) acts as a better representative of workers, (b) makes effective use of rational persuasion, (c) allows followers greater scope for initiative, (d) acts as a more visible leader, and (e) places high importance on comfort and well-being of followers. Interestingly, relative to men, Malaysian women viewed American expatriates closer to the ideal. The Malays and the Chinese preferred the Japanese bosses most, whereas the Indians preferred the Americans most. It should be noted that in the Sulaiman et al.'s study, there was no attempt to measure the leadership style of expatriate managers.

In another leadership preference study (Saufi, Wafa, & Hamzah, 2002), a sample of 142 Malaysian managers preferred their leaders to lead using the participative and delegative styles. However, ethnic difference was apparent: Malay and Indian managers preferred to be led in the participative style, whereas Chinese managers preferred the delegative style. Saufi et al. concluded that the leadership preference of Malaysian managers seems to conform quite closely to the Western findings. In yet another study, Mansor and Kennedy (2000) found that Malaysian managers rated the dimensions of decisiveness, team integration, diplomacy, modesty, humane orientation, and autonomy as being more important contributors to effective leadership than did managers in most other countries.


### Effective Leadership Styles

Gill (1998) did a cross-cultural comparison of leadership behavior of managers in the UK, USA, and Southeast Asia. Among other findings, he reported that

Southeast Asian managers were more directive, less delegating, more transactional, and more laissez-faire in terms of leadership behavior than were the US and UK managers.

Saufi, Wafa, and Hamzah (2002) found a significant positive relationship between power distance and "telling" leadership style, thus supporting the earlier research by Gill (1998). But, contrary to Gill (1998), they reported a significant relationship between uncertainty avoidance and participative leadership style. In yet another study, Govindan (2000) reports that preferred styles of Malaysians are consultative and participative leadership. Finally, Nizam (1997) found greater endorsement for a relationship motivated (high LPC) leader.

## *Leader-Member Exchange (LMX) Approach to Leadership*

Given the Malaysian preference for relationships, the LMX Model espoused by Dansereau, Graen, and Haga (1975) is another Western model that may help explain leadership from the standpoint of relationships in the Malaysian context. The LMX model assumes that leaders treat different subordinates differently based on the quality of exchange between them (Bhal & Ansari, 2000). Most, perhaps all, studies reviewed under this heading were conducted on managerial groups in diverse manufacturing concerns located in northern Malaysia. LMX in most of the reported studies was conceptualized as a four-dimensional construct: affect, loyalty, contribution, and professional respect (Liden & Maslyn, 1998). As hypothesized, LMX was found to be a strong negative predictor of turnover intentions (Ansari, Daisy, & Aafaqi, 2000) and a strong positive predictor of organizational commitment (Daisy, Ansari, & Aafaqi, 2001; Farouk, 2002) and organizational citizenship behavior (Ruth, 2003). LMX has been studied as a consequent variable as well. Specifically, managerial roles congruence was found to be a strong predictor of LMX (Lim, 2001).

## *Power Influence Approach to Leadership*

The Malaysian preference for hierarchy can be understood from the perspective of power and influence, be it upward, downward, or lateral. A few interesting studies have been conducted to examine the power-influence approach to leadership. These studies were conducted in northern Malaysia with managerial samples from diverse multinational companies.

*Downward influence* Let us first report on a most recent study conducted by Liew (2003). Liew examined the impact of LMX and affectivity (positive and negative) on the leader's use of influence tactics (as rated by subordinates). She reported several important findings. (a) Liking, defined as affect and professional respect, dimension of LMX had a strong positive impact on rational persuasion and personalized exchange tactics, and a negative impact on hard tactics of influence, such as assertiveness. (b) The loyalty dimension of LMX had positive impact on all the above tactics but a negative impact on showing expertise tactic. (c) Positive affect had a strong positive impact on rational persuasion and showing expertise. (d) Negative affect correlated strongly with personalized exchange, instrumental dependency, showing expertise, upward appeal, and hard influence tactics. (e) Interestingly, personalized exchange and instrumental dependency tactics were used more often with the same-sex subordinates. (f) Some interactions between LMX and affectivity were also observed. In another study, Omar (2001) administered four measuresof downward influence tactics (as rated by subordinates), LMX, intention to quit, and job satisfaction. Her findings can be summarized as follows. (a) Ingratiation, personalized help, and exchange tactics of influence had a positive impact on job satisfaction. (b) Manipulation, Upward appeal, and assertiveness had a negative impact on satisfaction. (c) Surprisingly, use of rational persuasion and showing expertise also had a negative impact on satisfaction. (d) As expected, manipulation, showing expertise, and assertiveness led to greater intention to quit the organization. (e) Personalized help, ingratiation, rational persuasion, and upward appeal had a negative impact on turnover intentions. (f) LMX, conceptualized as a two-dimensional construct (affect and contribution) in this study, had a positive impact on job satisfaction and a negative impact on turnover intentions.

*Upward influence* We found a few studies conducted in an upward influence framework. Rohaida (2002), using experimental scenarios (vignettes), examined the impact of leadership style (participative and autocratic) and interactional justice (fair and unfair) on the use of influence tactics. Both factors impacted the use of upward influence, but the interaction between the two explained more variance in the use of influence. Kaur (2003), in a field experiment, examined the use of upward influence tactics by most and least successful managers. She found a significant interaction between gender and success of the manager. Her analysis indicated that most successful male managers were found to make more frequent use of the rational persuasion tactic than the successful women. But, least successful men and women were found to make the least frequent use of this influence tactic.

*Bases of power* Another group of field experimental studies were conducted on bases of power typology. Jayasingam (2001) examined entrepreneurial success in an attributional framework. She found that, compared to unsuccessful entrepreneurs, successful entrepreneurs were rated higher on personal power (referent, expert, and information) and connection power. But, ratings of the two groups were not significantly different in terms of position power (reward, coercion, and legitimate). In a second study, Alip (2003) examined the impact of several bases of power on subordinate compliance and commitment (commitment was conceptualized as internalization and identification with the supervisor). Specifically, she found that coercive, expert, legitimate, referent, reward, and connection power had relatively stronger impact on subordinates' compliance than information power. On the other hand, commitment was higher with the use of expert, referent, connection, and legitimate power than with reward, coercion, and information power. Another field experiment by Chaw (2003) is worthy of mention. Using the recent conceptualization of legitimate power (Raven, 1993), Chaw manipulated four legitimate bases of powerformal legitimacy, legitimacy of reciprocity, legitimacy of equity, and legitimacy of dependence, in order to examine the impact of this power on attribution. Her experiment demonstrated that the causality of compliant behavior derived from legitimacy of reciprocity and legitimacy of dependence was perceived as more internal and more controllable than that of the compliant behavior derived from formal legitimacy and legitimacy of equity. These perceptions, in turn, led to higher degrees of positive reactions in good outcome conditions.

## Knitting the Threads

An overall observation of the aforementioned studies suggests several conclusions. First, there are not enough studies conducted on organizational leadership. Second, different researchers have used different Western theoretical frameworks. Third, there is no systematic attempt to propose a leadership style around the Malaysian socio-cultural milieu. Finally, the study findings are not consistent with one another. Some studies (e.g., Gill, 1998) suggest that Malaysian managers are more directive, less delegating, and more transactional. On the other hand, other researchers (e.g., Govindan, 2000) found that the preferred styles of Malaysians are participative and consultative. Mansor and Kennedy (2000) reported that among other values, modesty and humane orientation contribute to effective Malaysian leadership.

However, the most interesting aspect of the above studies is the findings on power and influence. As is evident, two influence tactics that have emerged in those studies are not reflected in any Western studies. They are personalized help or exchange and instrumental dependency. Whenever the two tactics have been employed in conjunction with other influence tactics, they have explained a larger variance in the Malaysian organizational context (Liew, 2003; Omar, 2001). Also, the salience of connection power (Ansari, 1990) seems to be evident in the Malaysian context (Alip, 2003; Jayasingam, 2001). This observation is in tandem with the preferences for hierarchy and relationships discussed earlier.

The conflicting results reported above and some new insights into influence behavior thus emphasize the need to draw upon familial values in Malaysia to set up organizations (Abdullah, 1994; McLaren & Rashid, 2002) just as the Japanese (Misumi, 1985) and Indians (Ansari, 1990; Sinha, 1980) have been doing. Our literature search also directs us to understand the power dynamics of Malaysian organizations are slightly different from those of the West. Thus we next examine what kind of leadership will best suit the Malaysian culture, keeping in view the two interwoven values, preference for relationships and preference for hierarchy, and the empirical studies on leadership reviewed above.

## Organizational Leadership in Malaysia

What kind of leadership is needed to effectively run Malaysian organizations? Given the presence of the above work preferences, habits, and expectations of subordinates, Abdullah (1996) recommends a paternal style of leadership. According to her, paternalism would fit. The values of mutual obligation require the employer [leader] to give his [her] employees some form of protection in exchange for their loyalty and commitment (p. 72). McLaren and

Rashid (2002) and Ahmad (2001) appear to support the notion of paternalism in the Malaysian context. Kennedy (2002), while affirming the "paternalism" notion, denies that paternalistic and patronage relationships are valued in the Malaysian culture. Unfortunately, we are aware of no empirical research that has attempted to integrate leadership and underlying Malaysian work values.

The process of labeling the Malaysian culture authoritarian in terms of preference for directive leadership could be circumstantial. Malaysians do, to some extent, possess certain behavioral manifestations of authoritarianism. For example, they do manifest a certain amount of rigidity (resistant to change, preference for maintaining the status quo) in their interpersonal conduct. The proscriptive and prescriptive norms are well defined and conformity to these norms is demanded. Maintaining personalized relationships is desirable and a strong preference for hierarchy is relished. But, we are aware of no research, empirical or conceptual, that documents that Malaysians possess underlying psychodynamics of authoritarianism. For example, there is no evidence that Malaysians are highly anxious, insecure, cynical with ego-alien sexuality, or paranoid.

Does this mean a people-oriented leadership style (democratic, considerate, or participative) is universal? One line of argument would be that if it is effective in the West, it should also be effective in a developing country like Malaysia or India. Given that argument, Jeffersonian democracy can very well be imported to these countries. On the other hand, evidence exists (see Stogdill, 1974) that, even in the United States, an authoritarian style of leadership has produced member satisfaction in large, task-oriented groups. The crux of the issue is not the match between style and geographical location. The crux is that when will a particular style be more productive than other styles in terms of group performance and member satisfaction. Perhaps, part of the answer lies in the fit between the style of the leader and that of follower. Evidence comes from the United States (Stogdill, 1974) that authoritarian subordinates are more productive and feel more comfortable under directive, authoritarian leaders. The fit hypothesis implies that low authoritarian subordinates will be more satisfied under equalitarian leaders (Stogdill, 1974). Also, style-climate fit on authoritarianism has been found to be predictive of managerial success (Ansari & Rub, 1982).

Thus the answer to which style is more effective is neither autocratic nor completely participative. We believe that the answer is very much in line with a leadership style, which has recently been advocated as suitable for Indian organizations (see, for example, Ansari, 1986, 1990; Sinha, 1980, 1994). Although there are many differences in terms of population size and area, literacy and poverty rates, and import and export businesses, there are substantial similarities between India and Malaysia. Historically, the relations between the two countries have been cordial; there is a closecorrelation of views in issues of mutual interest. The two work closely in international and regional forums such as UNO, NAM, G-15, ASEAN, and IOP-ARC, and WTO. Both countries were under the British rule for years, both have announced the year 2020 as the year they will reach the status of developing nations, and both countries are truly multi-religious societies. These similarities are reflected in their corporate governance, work values and preferences. Hofstede (1980, 1991) identified five cultural dimensions along which different countries could be compared. Of which two dimensions, collectivism and power distance, were found to be on the higher side of the continuum for both India and Malaysia. Collectivism is characterized by a tight social framework (Hofstede, 1980) and suggests that Indians and Malaysians define themselves in terms of groups and collectives and yield to these over their own needs and interests. They are generally concerned with promoting and maintaining harmony in the workplace (Earley & Gibson, 1998). In both countries, the power differential is large and persons with greater, as well as less power, concede the higher status of the more powerful persons as a matter of fact (Sinha, 1994).

## Toward Nurturant-Task (NT) Leadership in Malaysia

### The Background

To answer the question we raised in the previous section, we propose the salience of the nurturant-task (NT) style as an alternative model suited to the Malaysian culture. Given the presence of work habits and preferences mentioned above, and a great deal of similarity in the typical expectations and characteristics of Malaysian and Indian subordinates, we wondered whether a task-oriented (with a blend of nurturance), discipline-minded, tough leadership style with a personalized approach would be effective in the Malaysian setting. This style was named nurturant-task (Sinha, 1980). The nurturant-task (NT) style of leadership was developed in India as a result of 25 years of research (see such reviews as those of Ansari, 1990; Bhal & Ansari, 2000; Sinha, 1980,

1994). We believe that the NT style can successfully lead Malaysian subordinates who also possess traditional values but have an international outlook (Kennedy, 2002).

Before we describe the proposed NT model, let us first look at the similarities between India and Malaysia in terms of observable factors. For example, subordinates in both countries tend to depend excessively on their superior, with whom they want to cultivate a personalized rather than contractual work relationship. They readily accept the authority of their superior and yield to his or her demands. Work is not valued in itself. Yet, the subordinates are willing to work extra hard as a part of their efforts to maintain a personalized relationship with the superior (Abdullah, 1996; Sinha, 1994). Under these circumstances, an NT leader is likely to be more effective than other leaders (Ansari, 1986, 1990; Sinha, 1980, 1994).

Just to strengthen our assertion, let us briefly describe a recently conducted field experiment (Daphne, Ansari, & Jantan, 2003). Daphne et al., in a mixed 3 (Delegation Styles: Advisory; Informational; Extreme) x 2 (Country: US; Malaysia) x 2 (leader gender: Male; Female) factorial design, compared the US and Malaysian managers on leadership perceptions of three different delegation styles: advisory (the subordinate makes the decision after first getting a recommendation from the leader), informational (the subordinate makes the decision after first getting needed information from the leader, and extreme (the subordinate makes the decision without any input from the leader) (Schriesheim & Neider, 1988). Delegation style (a repeated-measure factor) and manager gender (between-factor) were experimentally manipulated variables, while the country was as a non-manipulated variable. The experiment was conducted in a single US manufacturing concern, a widely known semi conductor company, by employing the US managers (n = 100) working in the US and Malaysian managers (n = 118) working in Malaysia. The two groups were matched in terms of demographic profiles. The dependent measure, leadership perceptions, was conceptualized as the extent to which the manager displays ideal leadership qualities and is effective in terms of present and future performance. Among other significant findings, Daphne et al. reported an interesting interaction between delegation and country on leadership perceptions. Both the US and Malaysian managers almost equally favored informational delegation style. But they differed significantly in terms of attributing extreme delegation style, the US managers outperformed Malaysian managers. But Malaysian managers outperformed the US managers on leadership perceptions under advisory delegation condition. In brief, Malaysian managers are not yet as ready for extreme delegation (i.e., participative management) as are US managers.

*Theoretical Assumptions*

One of the earliest and perhaps most influential study in the history of leadership is the one conducted under the leadership of Kurt Lewin. This was an experimental study designed to examine the relative effectiveness of democratic, laissez-faire, and authoritarian leadership styles (Lewin, Lippitt, & White, 1939). Lewin et al. found no significant difference in the amount of work done under democratic and authoritarian leaders. Yet, groups with democratic leaders were considered most effective: the members seemed to be group-minded, and they pronounced "we" rather than "I". Groups with authoritarian leaders tended to display hostility and aggression towards either the leader or scapegoat for the leader, and the atmosphere of the group was strained and tense. The least productive was the laissez-fair style.

Inspired by the classic Lewin et al. leadership study, study after study was added to the organizational literature (Ansari, 1990; Bass, 1990). For about three decades, the 1950's through the 1970's, researchers, mostly in the United States,attempted to identify different styles of leadership. Broadly speaking, their empirical search (mostly through factor analysis) identified two strikingly distinct styles of leadership: task-oriented and people-oriented. Different researchers labeled the two styles differently. Some of the variants in chronological order are as follows: initiating structure vs. consideration (Shartle, 1956), directive vs. participative (Likert, 1961), exploitative vs. consultative (Likert, 1961, 1967), 9, 1 vs. 1, 9 style (Blake & Mouton, 1964), low LPC (least preferred coworker) vs. high LPC (Fiedler, 1967), task vs. relationship (Hersey & Blanchard, 1977), and so on. Subsequently, transformational, transactional, and charismatic leadership styles came into existence (Bass, 1985). For each approach, trait, behavior, or contingency,volumes of research has been conducted across the globe.

The NT model, yet another contingency model of leadership, states that an effective leader is one who carries his or her subordinates toward a shared goal. Leading means more than serving. Before leading the leader must cater to the needs and expectations of the subordinates. Only then will the subordinates follow the directives. However he [she] must not stop at meeting the subordinates' needs and keeping them happy. He [she] must lead them. Only then can he [she] be called effective (Sinha, 1994, p. 102). That means "leading" part of the role requires the leader to be task-oriented. In the same vein, the NT leader cares for his or her subordinates, shows affection, takes personal interest in their well-being and, above all, is committed to their growth (Sinha, 1980, p. 55). The leader, however, makes his or her nurturance contingent on the subordinates' task accomplishment. Thus, the NT leader is effective for those subordinates who want to maintain dependency, a personalized relationship, and a status differential. The leader helps his or her subordinates grow up, mature, and assume greater responsibility. Once the subordinates reach a reasonable level of maturity, they generate pressure on the leader to shift to the participative (P) style. From this perspective, then, the NT style is considered to be a forerunner of the P style in the reciprocal influence processes between a leader and his or her subordinates. The uniqueness of the NT model is the priority attached to productivity over job satisfaction. It assumes that meaningful and lasting job satisfaction has a precondition, the productivity of the organization (Porter & Lawler, 1968).

Task orientation in this model is quite close to performance dimension in the Japanese PM leadership style (Misumi, 1985) and to the initiating structure dimension of Ohio State leadership studies (Shartle, 1956). The model assumes that neither nurturance nor task orientation alone is sufficient for leader effectiveness. Nurturance creates a good feeling of being comfortably dependent, secure, and relaxed, but work is likely to be neglected. Task orientation gets the work done but might cause resistance to build up. A blend of the two is more likely to render a leader effective (Sinha, 1994, p. 103). However, the leader is nurturant to those subordinates who are hardworking, sincere, and committed to task performance. In other words, nurturance serves as a positive reinforcer. Thus the NT model is based on watch-and-win principle and is interactive rather than additive. Nurturance facilitates task orientation and the latter creates conditions for more nurturance. The NT leader keeps his or her subordinates busy with clearly defined jobs. The leader frankly appreciates the subordinates successful task accomplishment. Then both leader and subordinates feel happy and enjoy their respective performance. It can be symbolized as productivity→prosperity→ happiness.

*Shift in Style (NT to P)*

The NT model overlaps with other existing contingency theories. First, the model is based on a dynamic view of leadership. Given that subordinates' behavior affects their leader's behavior (Farris & Lim, 1969; Lowin & Craig, 1968), the model assumes a dynamic reciprocal influence relationship. In other words, the leader and subordinates influence each other and together take the group on a growth path (Sinha, 1994). From this perspective, then, the NT model comes close to the life cycle model of leadership (Hersey & Blanchard, 1977). Both models consider subordinates' maturity as the basis of deciding which style is likely to be most effective. But the basic difference between the two is that there is an absence of nurturance in the Hersey and Blanchard model. Also, the two models define maturity in slightly different manners. Secondly, the NT model is close to the path-goal theory (House, 1971), where subordinate characteristics play an important moderator role in leadership effectiveness. Finally, the NT model is much closer to leader-member exchange theory (Dansereau, et al., 1975), where quality of exchange between leader and subordinate is critical for leadership effectiveness.

If the NT leader is more effective for subordinates with a specific set of expectations and characteristics, then wouldn't subordinates with different set of characteristics require a different kind of leadership? We are aware of the fact that a majority of subordinates in a collectivist country may prefer hierarchy, dependency, and personalized relationships, and may not be work-conscious. Yet, a group of subordinates who possess opposite characteristics should require a participative (P) leader. It has been argued that over time the same set of subordinates might change (Sinha, 1994). The rationale is that, following reinforcement principles, subordinates under NT leadership might grow up by working hard, showing sincerity, gaining expertise, and developing self-confidence. As a result of that preparation, they would need lessclose supervision, guidance and direction. This is the stage where the leader has to shift his or her style from nurturant-task (NT) to participative (P).

What is a participative (P) style of leadership? Likert (1961, 1967) views an organization as consisting of multiple overlapping groups. In such groups, each leader serves as a linking-pin for connecting his or her group with the higher level group of which the leader is a member. Overlapping groups have three important features: (a) maintaining supportive relationships with one another, (b) joint decision-making and group methods of supervision, and (c) setting high performance goals. The P leader acts as a facilitator of group interactions and a representative of the group to the higher level group of which he or she is a member. In such a group, communication is explicit and adequately understood. There is emphasis on high productivity, high quality, and low costs. Decisions are reached promptly. Clear-cut responsibilities are established, and tasks are performed rapidly and productively. Confidence and trust pervade all aspects of the relationship. The group's capacity for effective problem solving is maintained by examining and dealing with group processes when necessary (Likert, 1961, pp. 50-51).

## Empirical Evidence from India Supporting the NT Model

The NT style has received meaningful support from empirical studies conducted in India (for details, see such reviews as those of Ansari, 1986, 1987, 1990; Ansari & Shukla, 1987; Bhal & Ansari, 2000; Sinha, 1980; 1983; 1994). Some of the major findings are summarized as follows. (a) The NT style is perceived as distinctly different from other styles, such as autocratic, bureaucratic, or participative. (b) It has a positive impact on several indicators of effectiveness such as commitment, facets of job satisfaction, and perceived effectiveness. (c) NT leaders earn more favorable ratings on the evaluation of the leader and attributions of leadership than the autocratic one. Interestingly, on some occasions, they receive even higher ratings than participative leaders. (d) NT leaders are different from autocratic and participative leaders in the use of downward and upward influence tactics. It should be noted that different studies have employed different measures and different designs in reaching these conclusions.

## Empirical Evidence from Malaysai Supporting the NT Model

Although strong evidence in support of the model is still awaited, we now report a few experimental and survey studies that seem to be supportive of the NT model. We first present two field experiments conducted in an implicit leadership theoretical framework. The first study (Ansari, Jayasingam, & Aafaqi, 2000) examined the leadership attributions of successful and unsuccessful entrepreneurs. Entrepreneurial success was manipulated experimentally, using a critical incident method. A group of working managers (N = 305) in manufacturing concerns were randomly assigned to treatment conditions. They rated most and least successful entrepreneurs in terms of leadership behavior items. Among other findings, Ansari et al. reported that most successful entrepreneurs were rated significantly higher than the least successful entrepreneurs on NT and P leadership behavior. Interestingly, mean attribution score of NT was significantly higher than P leadership behavior for successful entrepreneurs. An interesting finding was the success by respondent gender interaction. Male participants rated the most successful entrepreneurs significantly higher on NT style than the female participants. But males and females were not significantly different in rating the least successful entrepreneurs.

In another attributional study, Chand (2001) manipulated two leadership effectiveness dimensions: managers performance and workers satisfaction. She used a 2 (manager performance: low performing; high performing) x 2 (workers satisfaction: dissatisfied workers; satisfied workers) between-subjects factorial design. Dependent measures were leadership behavior items: nurturant-task (NT), participative (P), and autocratic (F). She randomly assigned 382 managers, representing manufacturing sectors located in northern Malaysia, to four experimental treatments. Her analysis indicated that most effective leaders received significantly higher ratings on NT, followed by P leadership behavior.

We now report two survey research studies. Desa (2002) conducted the first study on a sample of 170 bank managers in northern Malaysia. She employed three leadership behaviors, autocratic (F), nurturant-task (NT), and participative (P)rated by direct reports and some outcome variables. Her analysis indicated that both NT and P styles were related to the measures of job satisfaction, but NT had stronger impact than P style. As expected, F style had negative impact on satisfaction measures.

Another correlational study that was conducted by Wahab is especially interesting (2001). Wahab administered three measures of leadership behavior, organizational commitment, and values. It should be noted that she included preference for hierarchy, preference for personalized relationships, and dependency as three value dimensions (described in the earlier section). Her hierarchical regression analysis supported the interaction hypothesis only for leadership by personalized relationship interaction. She found that the NT style led to more normative commitment to those subordinates who were high in maintaining personalized relationships than those who had low preference for personalized relationships.

However, the above studies are limited on five counts. (a) All four studies used the same leadership measure, psychometric properties of which are not well established. (b) Both correlational studies had a small sample size. (c) Participants (respondents) in all four studies were drawn from northern Malaysia, thus doubting the external validity of the findings. (d) A variety of effectiveness measures have not been employed in these studies. (e) Measures of subordinate characteristics and expectations were not strong. Despite inherent limitations in the reviewed studies, one thing is clear: the NT model receives significant support from the data.

## The Summing Up

### *Summary and Implications*

Participative management is trans-cultural and, hence, applicable to Malaysian organizations. Nonetheless, we believe that unless an organization passes through a phase of preparation in which employees understand and accept the normative structure and goals of the organization and thereby develop a fair amount of commitment to the organization, any attempt to introduce participative management is likely to be misunderstood. Thus drawing upon existing leadership theories and typical expectations and characteristics of Malaysian subordinates, we propose a transitional model of leadership that is based on the watch-and-win principle, called the nurturant-task style of leadership. This two-stage (NT-P) model of leadership effectiveness is more normative than descriptive. It suggests that the NT style should be considered a stage of preparation for immature subordinates. Once the subordinates are mature enough the leader should change his or her style to participative. An illustrative example is shown in Figure 1. The leader should adopt a cafeteria approach. In order to be effective, the leader has to use the NT style with Subordinate 1,the subordinate who is high on both preferences for relationship and hierarchy. For Subordinate 2, the leader has to go in for a blend of NT and P (i.e., NT/P). But, the leader has to use the P style with Subordinate 3,the one who is low on both preferences. In sum, subordinates 1, 2, and 3 may be different individuals working for the leader, or they may be the same person going through changes in his or her preferences over time (see Figure 1).

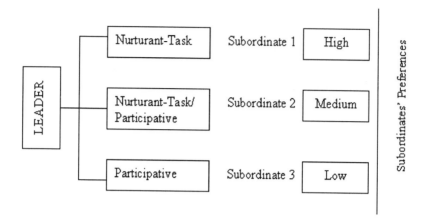

**Figure 1 NT to P style shift as a function of preferences for relationship and hierarchy (Adapted from Sinha, 1994)**

We are frequently asked by practicing managers a challenging question: if a manager can shift from NT to P, can he or she shift back to NT? The answer is a qualified "yes". The manager can drive one group of subordinates with the NT style and another group with the P style. Also, the manager can be NT and P with the same subordinates depending upon the circumstances (i.e., preparedness of the subordinates). However, reversal to either leadership style is not recommended at the cost of productivity.

*Directions for Future Research*

In sum, we have discussed sufficient studies conducted in India and Malaysia in support of the usefulness of the NT model. Even now there remain many more questions to be answered, many quests to be undertaken, and many webs to be unraveled in future research. First, multiple methodologies are required to see the relative impact of different styles of leadership effectiveness as moderated by Malaysian preferences for relationships and hierarchy.

Second, we have no solid experimental evidence in support of the shift from NT to P. Only can future longitudinal research tell us about the right time to shift from one style to the other. Third, experimental research is certainly needed to examine how a leader varies his or her style from subordinate to subordinate. However, leader-member exchange theory has provided enough support to this notion (Bhal & Ansari, 2000; Dansereau et al., 1975; Graen & Scandura, 1987).

Fourth, as mentioned in the previous section, psychometrically sound measures are definitely needed for assessing leadership styles and work values. Fifth, most of the previous studies conducted in India or Malaysia have used softer measures like satisfaction or perceived effectiveness. Future research should employ a variety of organizational effectiveness measures, such as objective in-role behavior (such as performance, progression, voluntary turnover, and promotability), extra-role behavior (such as organizational citizenship behavior), and attitudinal outcomes (organizational commitment and turnover intentions).

Finally, future research should be geared toward examining the tactics of influence adopted by NT leaders in comparison to participative leaders. It is hoped that these questions will keep the researchers interested in Malaysian leadership busy for quite some time.

## References

Abdullah, A, & Lim, L. (2001). "Cultural dimensions of Anglos, Australians and Malaysians". *Malaysian Management Review*, **36**, 9-17.

Abdullah, A. (1992). "The influence of ethnic values on managerial practices in Malaysia". *Malaysian Management Review*, **27**, 3-18.

Abdullah, A. (1994). "Leading and motivating the Malaysian workforce". *Malaysian Management Review*, **29**, 24-41.

Abdullah, A. (1996.) *Going Glocal: Cultural Dimensions in Malaysian Management.* Kuala Lumpur, Malaysia: Malaysian Institute of Management.

Ahmad, K. (2001). "Corporate leadership and workplace motivation in Malaysia". *International Journal of Commerce and Management*, **11**, 82-101.

Alip, R. S. (2003). *Supervisory Bases of Power and Subordinates' Compliance, Identification, and Internalization.* Unpublished MBA thesis. Penang: University Science Malaysia.

Ansari, M. A. (1986). "Need for nurturant-task leaders in India: Some empirical evidence". *Management and Labor Studies*, **11**, 26-36.

Ansari, M. A. (1987). "Effects of leader persistence and leader behavior on leadership perceptions". *Pakistan Journal of Psychological Research*, **2**, 1-10.

Ansari, M. A. (1990). *Managing People at Work: Leadership Styles and Influence Strategies.* New Delhi: Sage Publications.

Ansari, M. A., & Rub, M. (1982). "Executive success as a function of leadership style-organizational climate fit". *Managerial Psychology*, **3**, 56-68.

Ansari, M. A., Daisy, K. M. H., & Aafaqi, R. (2000). "Fairness of human resource management practices, leader-member exchange, and intention to quit." *Journal of International Business and Entrepreneurship*, **8**, 1-19.

Ansari, M. A., Jayasingam, S., & Aafaqi, R. (2000). "Entrepreneurial success, gender, and leadership behavior". *Journal of International Business and Entrepreneurship*, **8**, 33-46.

Ansari, M. A., Shukla, R. (1987). "Effects of group performance and leader behavior on leadership perceptions". *Psychological Studies*, **32**, 111-118.

Bass, B. M. (1985). *Leadership Performance beyond Expectations.* New York: Academic Press.

Bass, B. M. (1990). *Bass & Stogdill's Handbook of Leadership: Theory, Research, and Managerial Applications.* New York: Free Press.

Bhal, K. T. (2000). *Managing dyadic interactions in organizational leadership.* New Delhi: Sage Publications.

Blake, R. R., & Mouton, J. S. (1964). *The Managerial Grid.* Houston, TX: Gulf Publishing Company.

Chand, R. S. (2001). *Leadership Effectiveness and Attributions of Leadership Behavior.* Unpublished MBA thesis. University of Bath.

Chaw, S. F. (2003). *Forms of Legitimate Power from an Attributional Perspective.* Unpublished MBA thesis. Penang:   University Science Malaysia.

Dahlan, H. M. (1991). "Local values in intercultural management". *Malaysian Management Review*, **26**, 45-50.

Daisy, K. M. H., Ansari, M. A., & Aafaqi, R. (2001, October). *Fairness of Human Resource Management Practices, Leader-member Exchange, and Organizational Commitment.* Paper presented at the Fourth Annual Meeting of the Asian Academy of Management, Johor Bahru, Malaysia.

Dansereau, F., Graen, G., & Haga, W. J. (1975). "A vertical dyad linkage approach to leadership within formal organizations." *Organizational Behavior and Human Performance*, **13**, 46-78.

Daphne, L. H. S., Ansari, M. A., & Jantan, M. (2003). *Styles of Delegation and Leadership Perceptions: The Impact of Gender and National Culture.* Unpublished Paper. Penang: University Science Malaysia.

Desa, N. M. (2002). *Leadership Behavior and Job Satisfaction among Bank Officers: The Impact of Task Characteristics.* Unpublished MBA thesis. Penang: University Science Malaysia.

Earley, P. C., & Gibson, C. B. (1998). "Taking stock in our progress on individualism-collectivism: 100 years of solidarity and community." *Journal of Management,* **24**, 265-304.

Farouk, A. M. (2002). *Elements of Justice and Organizational Commitment: The Impact of Leader-member Exchange.* Unpublished MBA thesis. Penang: University Science Malaysia.

Farris, G. F., & Lim, F. G. (1969). "Effect of performance on leadership, cohesiveness, influence, satisfaction, and subordinates' performance". *Journal of Applied Psychology,* **53**, 485-497.

Fiedler, F. E. (1967). *A Theory of Leadership Effectiveness.* New York: McGraw-Hill.

Gill, R. (1998). "Cross-cultural comparison of the leadership styles and behavior of managers in the UK, USA and Southeast Asia." *Asian Academy of Management Journal,* **3**, 19-32.

Govindan, J. T. (2000). *The Influence of SocialValue Orientations and Demographic Factors on Leadership Preference among Malaysians.* Unpublished MBA thesis. Penang: University Science Malaysia.

Graen, G. B., & Scandura, T. A. (1987). "Toward a psychology of dyadic organizing". *Research in Organizational Behavior,* **9**, 175-208.

Hashim, M. Y. (1992). *The Malay Sultanate of Malacca.* Kuala Lumpur: Dewan Bahasa dan Pustaka.

Hassan, M. K. (1994). "The Malay community facing the 21st century: Socio-cultural hindrances to overall progress". *Intellectual Discourse,* **2**, 177-208.

Hersey, P., & Blanchard, K. H. (1977). *Management of Organizational Behavior.* Englewood Cliffs, NJ: Prentice Hall.

Hofstede, G. (1980). *Culture Consequences.* Beverley Hills, CA: Sage Publications.

Hofstede, G. (1991). "Management in a multicultural society". *Malaysian Management Review,* **26**, 3-12.

House, R. J. (1971). "A path goal theory of leadership effectiveness".

*Administrative Science Quarterly*, **16**, 321-338.

Ismail, N. A. R. (1977). *Work value system of Malaysian managers: An exploratory study*. Unpublished MBA Thesis. University of Kentucky, KY: Lexington.

Jayasingam, S. (2001). *Entrepreneurial Success, Gender, and Bases of Power*. Unpublished MBA thesis. Penang: University Science Malaysia.

Kanungo, R. N. (1990). "Work alienation in developing countries: Western models and eastern realities". In A. M. Jaeger & R. N. Kanungo (Eds.), *Management in Developing Countries* (pp. 193-208). London: Rutledge.

Kaur, G. (2003). *Attribution and Influence Perceptions of Success among Male and Female Managers: An Experimental Study*. Unpublished MBA thesis. Penang:   University Science Malaysia.

Kennedy, J. C. (2002). "Leadership in Malaysia: Traditional values, international outlook". *Academy of Management Executive*, **16**, 15-26.

Kennedy, J. C., & Mansor, N. (2000). "Malaysian culture and the leadership of organizations: A global study". *Malaysian Management Review*, **35**, 44-53.

Key Statistics, Malaysia (2003, June 11). Retrieved June 16, 2003, from "http://www.statistics.gov.my/Bahasa/framesetKeystats.htm"

Kheng, C. B. (1998). *Sejarah Melayu [The Malay Annals]*. Kuala Lumpur: Malaysian Branch of the Royal Asiatic Society.

Lewin, K., Lippitt, R., & White, R. K. (1939). "Patterns of aggressive behavior in experimentally created social climates". *Journal of Social Psychology*, **10**, 271-299.

Liden, R. C., & Maslyn, J. M. (1998). "Multidimensionality of leader-member exchange: An empirical assessment through scale development". *Journal of Management*, **24**, 43-73.

Liew, L. L. (2003). "Downward influence tactics: The impact of positive/negative affect, leader-member exchange, and gender". Unpublished doctoral dissertation. Penang: University Science Malaysia.

Likert, R. (1961). *New Patterns of Management*. New York: McGraw-Hill.

Likert, R. (1967). *The Human Organization*. New York: McGraw-Hill.

Lim, J. C. (2001). *Managerial Roles Congruence and Leader-member Exchange*. Unpublished MBA thesis. Penang: University Science Malaysia.

Lim, L. (1998). "Cultural attributes of Malays and Malaysian Chinese: Implications for research and practice". *Malaysian Management Review*, **33**, 81-88.

Lim, L. (2001). "Work-related values of Malays and Chinese Malaysians."

*International Journal of Cross Cultural Management*, **1**, 229-246.

Ling, L. S. (1995). *The Malaysian Chinese*. Petaling Jaya: Pelanduk Publications.

Lowin, A., & Craig, J. R. (1968). "The influence of level of performance on managerial style: An experimental object lesson in the ambiguity of correlational data". *Organizational Behavior and Human Performance*, **3**, 440-458.

Mansor, N., & Mohd Ali, M. A. (1998). "An exploratory study of organizational flexibility in Malaysia: A research note". *International Journal of Human Resource Management*, **9**, 506-515.

McClelland, D. C. (1975). *Power: The Inner Experience*. New York: Free Press.

McLaren, M. C., & Rashid, M. Z. A. (2002). *Issues and Cases in Cross-cultural Management*. Petaling Jaya, Malaysia: Prentice Hall.

Misumi, J. (1985). *The Behavioral Science of Leadership: An Interdisciplinary Japanese Research*. Ann Arbor, MI: The University of Michigan Press.

Nizam, M. (1997). *The Leadership Style and Situational Variables of Malaysian Managers*. Unpublished MBA thesis. Penang: University Science Malaysia.

Omar, F. (2001). *Downward Influence Tactics, Leader-member Exchange, and Job Attitudes*. Unpublished MBA thesis. Penang: University Science Malaysia.

Othman, A. H. (1993). *Psikologi Melayu [Malaysian psychology]*. Kuala Lumpur: Dewan Bahasa dan Pustaka.

Othman, R. (2001). "The Malaysian balik kampong". In M. J. Gannon (Ed.), *Understanding Global Cultures: Metaphorical Journeys through 23 Nations* (pp. 251-263). Thousand Oaks, CA: Sage Publications.

Poon, J. M. L. (1998). "The Malay wedding". *Asian Thought and Society*, **23**, 221-237.

Porter, L. W., & Lawler, E. E. (1968). *Managerial Attitudes and Performance*. Homewood, IL: Richard D. Irwin.

Rashid, M. Z. A., Anantharaman, R. N., & Raveendran, J. (1997). "Corporate cultures and work values in dominant ethnic organizations in Malaysia." *Journal of Transnational Management Development*, **2**, 51-65.

Raven, B. H. (1993). "The bases of power: Origins and recent developments." *Journal of Social Issue*, **49**, 227-251.

Razak, O. A., & Ahmad, Z. A. (1999). *Perhubungan Industri di Malaysia*

*(Industrial Relations in Malaysia).* Kota Kinabalu, Sabah: Universiti Malaysia Sabah.

Rohaida, S. (2002). *Effects of Leadership Styles and Interactional Justice on the Use of Upward Influence Tactics: An Experimental Study.* Unpublished MBA thesis. Penang:   University Science Malaysia.

Roland, A. (1984). *The Self in Indian and America.* In V. Kavolis (Ed.), In designs of selfhood (pp. 170-191). Princeton, NJ: Associated University Press.

Ruth, F. L. H. (2003). *Affect, Leader-member Exchange, and Organizational Citizenship Behavior: The Impact of Sex.* Unpublished MBA thesis. Penang: University Science Malaysia.

Saufi, R. A., Wafa, S. A., & Hamzah, Y. Z. (2002). "Leadership style preference of Malaysian managers". *Malaysian Management Review,* **37**, 1-10.

Schriesheim, C. A., & Neider, L. L. (1988). *Distinctions among Subtypes of Perceived Delegation and Leadership Decision-making: A Theoretical and Empirical Analysis.* Paper presented at the meeting of the Society for Industrial and Organizational Psychology, Atlanta, Georgia.

Shartle, C. L. (1956). *Executive Performance and Leadership.* Englewood Cliffs, NJ: Prentice Hall.

Shellabear, W. G. (1994). *Sejarah Melayu [The Malay Annals].* Kuala Lumpur: Penerbit Fajar Bakti Sdn. Bhd.

Sinha, J. B. P. (1980). *The Nurturant-task Leader: A Model of the Effective Executive.* New Delhi: Concept.

Sinha, J. B. P. (1983). "Further testing of a model of leadership effectiveness." *Indian Journal of Industrial Relations,* **19**, 143-160.

Sinha, J. B. P. (1994). *The Cultural Context of Leadership and Power.* New Delhi: Sage Publications.

Stogdill, R. M. (1974). *Handbook of Leadership: A Survey of Theory and Research.* New York: Free Press.

Sulaiman, M., Arumugam, S., & Wafa, S. A. (1999). "Subordinates? preference in leadership behavior: Expatriate or local bosses --The case of Malaysia." *Malaysian Management Review,* **34**, 24-31.

Wahab, N. Z. (2001). *Leadership Styles, Socio-cultural Values, and Organizational Outcomes.* Unpublished MBA thesis, Penang: University Science Malaysia.

Yeoh, M. (1998). *Management Challenges for Malaysian Companies.* Subang Jaya: Pelanduk Publications.

*Chapter 6*

# Leadership Challenges and Excellence in Singapore

Koh Lok Kiang William
Department of Management and Organisation, School of
Business, National University of Singapore

and

Wong Wee Siok
Department of Management and Organisation, School of Business,
National University of Singapore

*Today's organisations, more than ever, need effective leaders who understand the complexities of our ever-changing global environment and have the intelligence, sensitivity, and ability to empathize with others necessary to motivate their followers to strive to achieve excellence.*

Nahavandi, in The Art and Science of Leadership

## Introduction

In this chapter, the author will lay out the major leadership challenges in Singapore brought about by global changes. Major obstacles to leadership success in Singapore will also be discussed. These obstacles have been labelled mindsets, in that they reflect deep-seated beliefs that obstruct leadership effectiveness in Singapore. Next, varied examples of successful leaders in Singapore who have been able to overcome these leadership "traps" are also provided. These examples are chosen from leaders from different walks of life to illustrate how leadership talents are not in short supply in Singapore. Finally, the author presents some personal thoughts on how leaders in Singapore can improve, ending with a section providing guidance for the novice leaders in Singapore, in particular, expatriate leaders.

The main focus of this chapter will be on organisational leadership in Singapore rather than its political leadership.

## New Leadership Challenges for the New Age

As we enter the new millennium, many corporate leaders in Singapore must be wondering, "What must I do to help my organisation move ahead in this age of hyper-competition brought about by forces of globalisation, rapid and vast advances in information technology, and heightened employee expectations?"

The new economy competes on human talents, on ideas, and on change. Kanungo and Mendonca (1996) suggested that it is precisely in a situation like this that the element of leadership will be crucial in bringing about a nation's advancement onto the next level, a view first suggested by Kotter (1992). What is crucial at the national level will be just as crucial at the organizational level.

Like it or not, corporate Singapore has plugged itself into the new world order and the new economy where change will be a constant. Competition for creative talents will not be limited to the domestic market, but extended to the wide open international labour market. Already, we are feeling the impact of having hospitals from the United Kingdom coming to Singapore and luring away nurses from an already limited pool (Lee, 2000a). While they failed to lure local nurses, their success in attracting foreign nurses from local hospitals to make the move to the UK is a cause for concern, as many of the hospitals rely on these nurses to compensate for the general shortage of healthcare workers in Singapore.

Our teachers are next on the headhunters' list (Lee, 2000b). Needless to say, IT workers will be the next prime targets.

The next major leadership challenge is to have leaders who are change masters: leaders who are not afraid of change, and who are able to initiate and implement changes successfully, and are able to remain in control in the unpredictable environment of change and not be overcome by the extent of uncertainty. Intense competition brought about by global forces will mean that organizations have to change the way they provide service to or develop products for their customers. Even before the September 11 attacks on the USA, the world was teetering on the economic edge. Singapore was on the verge of recession. With the attacks, which plunged the US into recession, Singapore is now also going through a full-blown recession. We can expect more and more companies to restructure the size of their workforce.

Also affected will be the way organisations structure their human relations with employees, and the way they handle diversity in order to harness the human capital within their organisations. Hence there is a need for leaders who capable of handling change, in order to help their organizations navigate in such tumultuous terrain.

Finally, organizations will also need leaders with not only action, but passion. They need passion for their work, and the passion to excel in their work. In a recent interview with the local press, Gary Hamel mentioned that to compete in the new economy, organisations must adopt an 'innovation' agenda to succeed in the new economy, and that organisations should turn individuals into "activists", "heretics" and "revolutionaries" with a passion for what they want to achieve (Hamel, 2000). For this to happen, we will need more leaders who are seen as passionate activists and heretics by their followers. They need to lead, set examples, and create corporate cultures that will not only accommodate revolutionaries, but actively promote the emergence of followers who are "activists" and "heretics."

Finally, we will need leaders who are developers of people. Such leaders will be able to lead in a way that will enable them to retain creative talents in their organisations and prevent the infamous brain drain from Singapore. To take another quotation from Hamel, "The way to keep people with you is to realize their dreams, fund their ideas and help them accomplish what they want to accomplish" (Hamel, 2000). This view is certainly in line with employee comments in a recent employee survey. During the survey, employees expressed the desire for opportunities to learn, to do interesting and challenging work, and to be able to 'go places' within an organisation (Batacan, 2000).

To retain talents and to compete effectively, old mindsets and ways of working must be unlearned and destroyed before new mental models can be accepted. Many expressed concerns that these tasks will not be easy and that it will be an uphill struggle to change the way workers work, and relate to each other and the organisation. The author suggests that change must first come from senior managers themselves before it can cascade to lower levels of the organisation.

### The Current Situation: What Do Singaporean Employees Expect Out of Their Organizations' Leaders?

In a recent survey by Steve Morris Associates conducted in May 1999, 2505 employees from 29 companies were asked about their organisations and their organisational leaders in a 159-question survey (Batacan, 2000). The results? The main motivators for work were teamwork, conducive culture, trust and autonomy, commitment, clarity, collegiality, credibility, capability, and pride.

While 48% of respondents indicated that they were satisfied with their colleagues to a great extent, only 28.7% of them were satisfied with their management to a great extent, and only 27% thought that their companies were one of the best to work in. Commenting on the survey results, Ms Lorraine Peh, the project manager, mentioned that Singaporean workers have very high expectations of their leaders and would want their leaders to dare to do the unexpected, not hide anything from them, treat them as a team member, and to know how the employees really feel. Employees also expect a leader to be a visionary, a role model, to have integrity, and to mix and mingle, in short, to be a friend (Batacan, 2000).

With these survey results in mind, we will now move on to discuss some of the key mindsets, which hinder a leader from harnessing the creative energies in their followers. These include the lack of trust, which keeps them from sharing information with followers; the heroic leader mindset, which causes them to have a superior attitude towards their followers. The mindset that humour and business do not mix prevents leaders from using a friendly and approachable disposition. Finally, the fear of failure prevents them from trying to do things differently.

## Mindsets that Need to be Changed

### Fear of Failure

If there is any mindset of corporate culture that needs changing, it must surely be the 'fear of failure'. The general impression one gets from talking to many employees is that Singaporean managers and leaders have a low tolerance for failure. People who make mistakes often get their careers derailed. A Hokkien dialect term 'Kiasu', which literally means 'scared to lose', has entered the national vocabulary. And the fear of failure is something that most organisations in Singapore must grapple with. It is this fear that prevents organisations and leaders from experimenting with new ideas, revolutionary organisational management styles, and new ways of managing relationships within and across organisations. According to Peter Vaill, ultimately it is this very fear of failure that could result in stagnation as a result of the fear of change and the unknown, and this could possibly be the major stumbling block that prevents one, in this case the leader, from being a life-long learner (Tee, 1999).

A good example of how this fear is manifested in employment relations is the low rate of usage of part timers in Singapore. While this ratio is particularly high in the USA, Europe and even the rather conservative and traditional Japan, it is relatively low in Singapore. One suspects that the fear of failure prevents organisations from experimenting with new work ideas. A variant of this fear of failure stems from the fact that managers are answerable to higher authority when subordinates fail. Hence they rationalize, "No one else is capable of doing the job as well as I can, and so if I have to be held accountable for my unit's performance and results, I had better do as many things as best as I can by myself!"

*The Heroic Leader*

Another mindset that needs to be changed is that of the one-person heroic leader who knows all. As we move toward the knowledge-based economy, increasingly more emphasis will be placed on teams. Work will be crafted around teams instead of individuals. As such, leadership must be seen not in the context of one super-leader who leads a bunch of followers with sub-standard IQ, but leaders with followers who might have higher IQs than the leader himself!

In short, it is leadership in the context of knowledge and workers in the context of teams. This is a form of leadership that does not see ignorance in some areas as a threat to the leader's intelligence, credibility or ability to lead. In the new economy, the followers' knowledge in many technical areas is likely to be superior to the leaders'. The new age leader cannot be threatened by such followers, but must learn to work with them as a team in a shared leadership, which effectively draws on the talents and maximises the potential of each and every team member.

The fact that some followers might have technical knowledge superior to the leader's need not lower the leader's self-confidence. The leader's job is to guide a group toward accomplishing its goal (Roach & Behling, 1984), and not to be the technical master in every area. Acceptance of this fact will lead to greater empowerment and help make team or shared leadership a reality.

*Leaders Are Born*

> *Contrary to the opinion of many people, leaders are not born. Leaders are made, and they are made by effort and hard work.*

> Vince T. Lombardi

In many of the leadership seminars and workshops conducted in Singapore by the author or those that he has had the pleasure of attending, one question always pops up: Are leaders born or made? Just last week, at an orientation program for freshmen taking a leadership course offered by the author, students milled around and the very first question that was posed was, "How do you teach leadership?" These questions reflect a deep-seated belief among many that leaders are born. At a diploma level executive course, a survey of 150 participants revealed that nearly a quarter still believe that leaders are born. The comforting thing is that the greater majority believes that leaders are both born and made.

Avolio (1999) made the humourous observation that he has yet to find a leader who is not born. If you are not born, you cannot be around, let alone be a leader. The question is, can leaders and leadership be trained? The best respond to the question is to look at twin studies, which show that genes account for 50% of the variance in leadership style (Avolio, 1999). In short, there is still the other 50% that can be developed! If leaders do not move away from this mindset that leaders and leadership skills can be trained or developed, they are likely to sub-optimise their human resource potential by focusing their attention on merely training and developing a small group of individuals in their organisations. Or they may well ignore leadership development altogether and merely use selection instruments to pick out great leaders. This will lead to gross under-utilization of leadership talents within their organisations, something which they can ill afford to do in these turbulent times!

The opposing view, that leaders and leadership skills can be trained, will lead to greater motivation to train every single possible individual to excel in leadership. While it is true that not everyone can be trained to be a great leader, it is equally true that all can be trained to be better leaders than they are!

### Humour and Good Leadership Do not Mix

Having conducted countless executive courses at the NUS Business School for managers from various countries and different hierarchical levels in this region, as well as leadership courses for many large Singapore organizations, the author has found something rather interesting. When these middle to higher level executives were shown a videotape on the fun and humourous behaviours of Herb Kelleher, the ex-CEO of Southwest Airlines, the overwhelming response one receives is that if a manager leads a company this way in Singapore or even in this region, it will never be successful. Or they will say that, "Well, you could perhaps lead an airline company this way, but certainly not a bank!" Or, "If a leader is too humourous, followers will climb on top of him."

Yet, that was the very advice given by an American academic and management consultant, Richard Boyatzis, in a recent press interview in Singapore. Citing examples of world renowned corporate leaders like Herb Kelleher of Southwest Airlines, Anita Roddick of The Body Shop, Mary Kay of Mary Kay Cosmetics, and John Chambers of Cisco Systems, Boyatzis mentioned that such leaders are able to display a sense of playfulness because they have a deep sense of passion about their vision and their organisations. Mind you, he mentioned, these are people who have made lots and lots of money! (Teo, 2000). So, who says fun and good business do not mix?

Interestingly, in a management course that the author has been conducting for junior executives over the last few years, whenever the very same videotape on Herb Kelleher was screened and participants asked if they are ready for a leader like this, the answer is always a resounding yes! The author gets this same response showing it to secondary school and junior college students and even undergraduates. They all mentioned that they would never climb over the leader's head should he/she behave in a humourous way, and that humour is functional in relieving stress and tension in the work place and helps the leader come across as being more approachable to followers.

These contrasting views on the role of humour clearly reflect age and generational differences. It is clear that older leaders see no role for humour in the workplace, while younger followers feel otherwise. Narrowing this gap will be a challenge. Who should make the change?

The author strongly feels that it is time that leaders in Singapore learn from the world-class executives mentioned by Professor Boyatzis. Anecdotal evidence shows that humour clearly has a role to play in organisations (Avolio & Howell, 1999). Corporate leaders therefore should change their mindset about injecting fun and humour into the workplace. Their followers are ready for a completely new leadership model and, in fact, have probably been ready for the change for quite some time now. Perhaps it is time for corporate leadership in Singapore to change its age-old mentality that fun and business do not mix.

*Need for Physical Presence*

A final mindset that needs changing is the insistence for the physical presence of followers. It is perhaps a reflection of the Oriental culture that we can only trust people when we can see them, touch them and feel them (in some cases, we might even have to smell them!). However, the advent of IT makes it possible for people to work together from remote corners of the world.

Globalisation leads to geographic expansion into foreign markets. This means organisations must learn to operate in the virtual environment quickly or risk losing out to competitors who do. This new leadership mindset says, "I can trust my people to do the things that we have agreed on even when they could be miles away from me and we cannot be together physically." We can work and communicate using emails, faxes, video and teleconferencing.

Trust is the cornerstone of this new work relationship. And trust calls for the displacement of the current mindset of command and control, a mindset that demands physical interaction in order to get a job done.

The reality is far from this ideal. From the data gathered through numerous feedback exercises from executives who work with bosses in Singapore, a great majority find their bosses unwilling to trust their followers. Perhaps the greatest symbol of this lack of trust is the unwillingness to let employees telecommute.

While almost 20% of the American workforce and 15% of the European workforce telecommutes, in Singapore, the figure is a mere 2%. In a recent local current affairs programme on television, Talking Point, many viewers called in to express the view that this is because their bosses simply do not trust them.

If we can move away from this mindset of requiring the followers' physical presence, the usage of virtual teams could be enhanced and the productive capacities and capabilities of our employees could be increased many folds from their current levels. The number of people involved in telecommuting and part-time work will rise and help solve our labour shortage. An additional bonus would be the easing of the perennial traffic jams in many parts of Singapore during peak hours! The quality of work life for many workers will also improve.

## *Examples of Effective Leadership in Singapore*

While many organisations in Singapore are more than willing to spend millions of dollars investing in new computer hardware and software to update their organisations, it appears that many are simply not willing to embrace new managerial "heartware" and software like empowerment and trust. The new age brings with it new organisation forms like flexible organisation, boundaryless organisation, network organisation, virtual organisation and learning organisation. For these organisational forms and culture to be successful, corporate leaders must learn to empower and trust their subordinates. And they must learn to do it quickly in order to have a head start or even just to try and keep pace with the competition.

Singaporean managers may cite many reasons for not empowering their followers, but one perennial favourite often recanted is that their employees are simply not ready for empowerment and trust, and that employees want to be led and spoon-fed, and hence their reluctance to relinquish control. The Theory X leader lives!

So, who should make the first move to start the virtuous cycle? Must employees show that they can be trusted before bosses trust them? Or should the bosses start the positive spiral by making the first move? If no one takes the initiative, the relationship will end in caution and suspicion (Kouzes & Posner, 1997). Both Kouzes and Posner (1997) and Avolio (1999) have suggested that leaders should dare to allow themselves to be vulnerable. Perhaps they can display this vulnerability best by taking the first step to trust their followers, even if things do not work out or this results in mistakes being made. After all, is this not what being a leader is all about? A leader leads by making the first move. So, leaders should take the lead in trusting their followers. If employees fail to perform due of lack of skill, training can be provided.

Will this new style of leadership that   emphasizes trust, employee empowerment, and development work in Singapore?

## *Effective Leadership from the Educational Sector*

In a study that the author conducted more than 10 years ago in secondary schools in Singapore (Koh, Steers & Terborg, 1995), it was found that a transformational style of leadership, which uses vision, role models, and mission as a 'style' of leadership, would be more effective than mere transactional style, which relies on quid pro quo and focusing on the mistakes made by subordinates. Teachers who were led by these transformational principals reported greater commitment to their schools, were happier with the principals, and showed greater citizenship behaviour. Indirectly, these factors were subsequently found to have an impact on students' results.

The impact of good school principalship on school effectiveness also found much support when we looked at anecdotal evidence. Take Mr Lee Hak Boon of Xinmin Secondary School, for instance.

One of the two schools to be granted autonomous status[1] in January 2001 (Quek, 2000), Xinmin Secondary ranked 134 among 160 secondary schools in 1993. When Mr Lee took over the school principalship in 1997, the percentage of students with O level distinctions was 40%. In a merely one year, it soared to 70% (Nirmala & Koh, 1999). For the last three consecutive years it won sustained achievement awards, and also the value added award for the past consecutive eight years (Davie & Ariff, 2001). Recently, it bagged the Best Practice Awards, a distinction it shares with other big name schools like Raffles Institution, River Valley High, Anglo-Chinese School (Independent) and Paya Lebar Methodist Girls' Secondary. It bagged the award for excelling in areas such as teaching and learning, as well as staff welfare (Davie & Ariff, 2001).

---

[1] In Singapore when a school is granted autonomous status, it is a signal of success. Autonomous schools have sustained good academic results, well-rounded education programme and good community ties (Nirmala, 1999). They get more say in the way they are run and receive an extra grant of $ 300 per student each year from the Ministry of Education (Quek, 2000).

When the school ranking exercise was completed in 2001, Xinmin had climbed into the list of the top 20 schools in Singapore. (For these and other achievements, you can refer to Xinmin's website: http://schools.moe.edu.sg/xinmin/).

What exactly did he do to achieve such results? With the money collected from a student walkathon, Mr Lee set up a $ 20,000 welfare fund for needy students. The rest of the money was used to install air-conditioning in the school hall. As an act of appreciation to the school's teachers, $ 6000 from the $ 40,000 won by the school for giving value-added education to its students was spent on decorating the staff lounge. One student who used to recruit members for illegal activities became a member of the school lion dance troop and improved his class attendance when the school showed that him that he was loved and important. Students' suggestions were taken seriously, with approximately 15 suggestions boxes all over the school (The Straits Times, 2000a). One interesting outcome of the student suggestion scheme was the setting up of a coffee joint in the school. As a result, instead of having to pay $ 4-5 at designer coffee joints like Starbucks, students got to enjoy good coffee at about $1!

Very often, while his students pack their bags and head for home, Mr Lee would be spending time in the neighbourhood coffee shop, chatting with residents who live around the area to find out what they think of the school. This practice of getting feedback spreads to other avenues such as getting feedback from parents, and holding informal tea sessions with students, etc. (Quek, 2001).

In the recent GCE 'O' Level examinations in 2000, the school took extra steps to ensure that graduating students received all the help they needed, including granting them exclusive use of the air-conditioned rooms for them to study in, extra coaching from teachers, engaging students in de-stressing activities, and hanging up encouraging banners around the school (The Straits Times, 2000).

His vision for the school is best embodied in his message to his teachers, "Your job is to dream, dream big. Leave the problems to me." (Nirmala & Koh, 1999). It is a vision to challenge his teachers to dare to do the impossible. The challenge was followed up by a working retreat at Shangri La's Rasa Sentosa Resort to review school programmes in an informal and relaxed setting. For 2001, after gaining autonomous status, the school plans to build up niche areas in the arts and in the area of character development to produce more student leaders via activities such as the dance club, school band and choir.

Looking at what the school has achieved over the past few years, one cannot help but feel that something right must have happened at Xinmin Secondary School, and that Mr Lee has had a big part to play in that success.

Mr Lee attributed his success to his parents. Being dedicated teachers in a small school in Kluang, Johor, his parents were a source of inspiration for him (Nirmala & Koh, 1999). And Mr Lee is hardly alone in such a seemingly superhuman feat. Another well-known case is that of Mrs Lim Yen Ching, who led Zhonghua Secondary from nowhere to become an autonomous school in one year (Nirmala, 1999).

At Dunman Secondary School, the second school that was granted autonomous status in 2001, school principal Gan Chin Huat got students to dish out hot meals to the elderly, read to children, help run a community library, and organize activities for residents in the community. In 1999, about 163 Secondary 1 students from the school were given eduPAD, a portable and wireless hand-held computer to enable them to read electronic versions of their textbooks, surf the Internet, and e-mail questions to their teachers (The Straits Times, 2000b). The school has plans to develop student leaders in the near future.

If one were to point to one single source that has made our schools as vibrant as they are today, most of the credit must surely go to the top leaders at the Ministry of Education: Education Minister Rear-Admiral Teo Chee Hean and the Permanent Secretary for Education Mr Lim Siong Guan. Apart from the success stories mentioned above, what is telling of their abilities is how these top leaders in education handled mistakes committed at the school level. Two recent incidents are highly illustrative.

The first involves a misadventure in which two girls from Raffles Junior College drowned in Pulau Ubin in February of 1999, one of whom was a daughter of the author's colleague at the National University of Singapore. The second involved a 'mock attack' exercise in February 1999 in Jin Tai Secondary School, which left four studentshospitalized and 14 others needing medical treatment at a local hospital. Instead of using these negative incidents to discourage other schools from engaging in outside-classroom learning lessons, the Education Minister in parliament strongly defended the need for schools to engage in outside-classroom learning activities and urged for greater tolerance of mistakes. Mistakes committed in both incidents were carefully analysed in order to learn from them and not to justify public decapitation of the offenders or to discourage risk taking. To quote Rear-Admiral Teo, "Schools and the Ministry of Education must be prepared for some unstructured experiments and perhaps even a mistake or two." (Nirmala, 1999).

Again, at a graduation ceremony for principals in 1999, Admiral Teo asked principals to inspire those they work with, including teachers and students. Tolerance for mistakes and having no fear of failure were once again highlighted in his speech (Nirmala, 1999).

Under their joint leadership, school achievement took on new definitions. The focus is no longer just on narrowly defined academic results like the O and A level examination results. Community service involvement and a focus on the development of the whole person are just as important (Davie, 1999). In the words of the Rear-Admiral Teo, "Excellence means providing each student with the opportunity to be educated, to be the best he can be, doing the best he can under all circumstances, according to his combination of talents and abilities" (Nirmala, Kaur & Ho, 1999). Again under their leadership, schools have been given more freedom and autonomy. For instance, school principals now have the autonomy to decide on class size, which allows them the freedom to handle students separately according to their academic ability. School principals mentioned that academically weaker students would be placed in smaller classes, while the stronger ones in bigger classes (Nirmala, 1999). The Ministry's message to schools seems to be very clear: do not depend on directions from the top all the time; learn to chart your own destiny!

In a more recent study, we showed that transformational leadership in the healthcare sector leads to greater empowerment and members' satisfaction with the leader, and empowerment in turn leads to greater commitment and group cohesiveness among team members (Puja, 2000). A further study in the child-care sector in Singapore showed that supervisors who maintain a trusting relationship with their teachers resulted in teachers who were more satisfied and students who were happier with the child-care provider (Ong, 2000). Finally, another study shows that leaders who listen to their subordinates' opinions and allow for greater employee involvement in decision making, receive higher trust, motivation and commitment from their followers (Li, Koh & Heng, 1997).

Taken together, all the evidence suggests that employees in Singapore are ready to move from being lead by leaders who merely initiate structure or show consideration. They want leaders with a sense of mission; leaders who are visionary; leaders who are passionate about what they want for their followers and their organisations; leaders who lead by example; and leaders who are able to build a trusting relationship with them and allow for significant involvement by the staff in decision making. Leaders who view each subordinate as unique in his/her own right, and do not treat each person as a number. Certainly, they are quite ready for a style completely different from the traditional and authoritarian top-down leadership. Singaporean followers have been ready for years. It is simply a case of corporate leaders  not being  able to catch up with the masses!

## *Successful Leadership in Statutory Board*

Ko Kheng Hwa, formerly the Chief Executive Officer of Jurong Town Corporation (JTC), provides another example of effective leadership in Singapore. Despite the fact that JTC is a statutory board, which conjures up images of conservatism and risk aversion, Ko recently took a bold step toward change by offering Singapore $2 million to any two staff who could develop an Internet portal to link its 7000 companies in Singapore so that they can do business on-line among themselves and with their customers worldwide (Tan, 2000). Mind you, the scheme allows them to do so while JTC provides them with the safety net of a full salary! What was amazing was the origin of the idea - from a coffee break at its architecture unit, and not from the IT department!

Apparently, the seed of building such an innovative new economic culture was first planted by its previous CEO, Maj-General Lim Neo Chian (now JTC's current chairman), and was further nurtured into reality by Mr Ko Kheng Hwa. Ko built a culture of change and innovation at JTC, a culture where experimentation is encouraged, a culture where it is okay to fail, if in doing so an employee learns to do things better. And Ko did it because he is fully aware of the fact that the external environment is changing rapidly. In his own words, Ko said, "If the environment is changing so rapidly and our rate of change is slower than the rate of change out there, then it will be a matter of time before we become dinosaurs" (Ko, 2000). As a symbolic gesture of discarding the old and moving on to the new, at the opening of their new premises on 29 July 2000, Ko led JTC's 1,500 employees on a long march from its old premises to the new tower.  Not quite the same distance compared to the famous long march that Mao Ze Dong took, but the symbolism of the gesture was not lost on employees nor his superiors.

In August 2000, during the National Day Awards, Ko was given the Public Administration Award (Gold Medal) (Business Times, 2000). One wonders, if the CEO of a government statutory board could come up with such a radical idea, what excuse does a private sector CEO have for doing anything less?

Ko's style of leadership brings to mind the brilliant former-CEO of Oticon Holdings of Denmark, Mr Lars Kolind, who transformed the stodgy Danish company into one of the most formidable companies in the hearing aid business, good enough to compete against the might of giants such as Sony, Philips and Siemens. Kolind took a tremendous risk by transforming Oticon from a conservative organisation to one that is fast and innovative. He took away paper from the office (all important documents were scanned; unimportant ones were immediately shredded); build coffee bars all over the company premises to encourage informal communication; put all office furniture , such asfiling cabinets and chairs, on wheels to encourage greater employee networking; and formed myriads of self managed project teams to get things done. In 5 short years, Lars Kolind doubled the revenue of Oticon and increased its operating profit 10 fold! (for more details on Lars Kolind and Oticon please refer to the website: http://www.fastcompany.com/online/03/oticon.html)

At JTC, Ko had a fantastic team member in the form of deputy CEO, Ms Chong Siak Ching, who openly declared that she was all for empowerment, having a clear common vision, openly sharing ideas and meeting challenges (Ang, 2000). Incidentally, Ms Chong is also the Managing Director of Arcasia Land, the property development arm of JTC.

*Successful Woman Leadership*

We should now take a look at women who are successful in organisational leadership. One person who comes to mind immediately is Dr Jennifer Lee, the CEO of Kandang Kerbau Women's and Children's Hospital (KKH). She took over as the CEO in 1992. In 1999, all 1,200 nurses were divided into three groups and a flexible work arrangement was devised. Although everyone worked 42 hours a week, there was sufficient flexibility for some to work 6-day weeks, 5-day weeks or even 4-day weeks (Tee, 2000a). Since her selection as a Nominated Member of Parliament in 2000, Lee has been championing the cause of the family to improve the quality of family life in Singapore (Tee, 2000b). She has also made it her vision to turn KKH into a family friendly workplace (Tan, 2001).

Although she did not put it in so many words, the transcript of a newspaper interview reveals that she has a passion for women's issues, particularly that of older women, and children, one of her main concerns is how the hospital could provide affordable quality healthcare for the elderly (Tan, 1998). To do her part for a menopause support group formed by patients, Lee made available hospital space for the group's meeting, as well as administrative and expert support from the hospital staff. In 1999, the hospital, together with the Tsao Foundation, organized an international conference on older women in Asia. In decision-making, she stresses decentralization and empowerment, and believes that the hospital's major asset is its people, technical expertise and teamwork (Tan, 1998). She is known to be supportive and understanding, yet firm and not afraid of making difficult decisions (Tan, 2001).

As we progress into the knowledge-based economy, women leaders and women CEOs like Jennifer Lee will surely become more and more commonplace. Particularly in labour-scarce Singapore, we need even more women leaders like Jennifer, ex-Nominated MP and surgeon Dr Kanwaljit Soin, and Standard Chartered's Managing Director Theresa Foo to act as good role models, to blaze the trail and encourage more women in Singapore to take on prominent leadership roles. Recently, Hewlett-Packard announced that the new head of its Asia Pacific business would be Siaou-Sze Lien, a lady. Singapore Technologies has a female president, as does the construction firm Lim Kah Ngam, along with the famous Raffles Hotel. American multinational Motorola is determined that within a period of five to seven years (from) beginning 1999, half of its top management will be women (Teh, 1999). The glass ceiling looks set to be broken in Singapore!

## Successful Leadership in the Private Sector

In the private sector, perhaps the best example of the kind of corporate leadership that Singapore needs is found in Mr Sim Wong Hoo, the founder and chairman of Creative Technology. Creative Technology is arguably Singapore's greatest corporate success story, apart from Singapore Airlines. Its brand name is well known around the world, and it is the undisputed leader in the PC audio business (Tan, 2000). In a candid interview conducted recently, Sim revealed a style of leadership that best fits the new economy. It is one characterized by dialogue with subordinates (and one might even debate if the term subordinates should be replaced   with the more egalitarian "associates").   In Sim's leadership, even as the chairman of the company, he might still be overruled by his team members. Such an open and even humble style of leadership may just be what more and more Singaporean firms need in order to navigate the digital age. It is a style that indirectly admits that the leader may not have all the answers all the time and that others could be right and the leader could be wrong. By his own reckoning, the style of leadership used has encouraged more ideas from team members and is well worth the occasional chaos that it engenders.

Apart from being consultative, he is also known to be a good risk-taker (Tan, 2000). As with all risk-taking ventures, that comes with a price. The company "gambled" on CD-ROM drive manufacturing business during 1995-1996 and failed; stock price plummeted from a high of $36 to a low of $5. But this same spirit of risk taking has also taken it right back to the top in recent years. In a recent financial reporting, the full year result till June 2000 resulted in earnings going up by a whopping 57%, with investment gains of 589% and shareholder equity increasing by 42%. Over the last few years, it went back to focus on it's key strength: PC audio business. It also diversified successfully into personal digital entertainment (PDE) and started an investment fund to drive growth by investing in innovative start-ups such as Catcha.com, ChainCast, and DiMagic, among many others (Divyanathan, 2000).

While it might be debatable to say that his style of leadership was the key factor in accounting for the sort of sterling performance shown by the recent reporting results, we can certainly say that the leadership recipe of risk taking and democratic consultation must be one of the most important contributing factors. Like they say, it is difficult to argue with success!

The success of Creative Technology is indicative of Singaporean employees' readiness for a new paradigm of leadership that eschews open functional conflict in order to find the best solutions for organisational challenges. It is an environment where leaders need not feel threatened by subordinates who speak up and openly challenge their ideas and decisions. It is one where opposing and different views are eagerly sought, debated and discussed in order to find the best solutions to a problem. In this kind of environment, fun can be part of the corporate culture without any negative impact on the bottom line. One might well speculate that it is this spirit of fun in the company that has contributed to its success! (Dawson, 2000).

Another corporate success that owes a great deal to its CEO is Just-in-Time (JIT) Electronics. Its Chief Executive Officer, Mr Tommie Goh, won the businessman of the year award in 2000. When asked what was the most important thing in life, he responded, 'passion'. It was passion that brought him to start up the company with a friend, Mr William Goh. The company was listed on the main board of the stock exchange in November 1997 and its sales volume crossed the $1 billion dollar mark by March 2000. What can we glean about his leadership style? Leadership, passion, risk-taking, belief in teamwork, self-confidence and hard work (Tan, 2000).

A final corporate example of successful leadership comes from Dr Cheong Choong Kong, the Deputy Chairman and Chief Executive Officer of Singapore Airlines (SIA), Singapore's best-known brand name. He was named Asia's Businessman of the Year for 1998 by Fortune Magazine who cited Dr Cheong for his coolness, savvy and expansive outlook at a time of rude change (Fernandez, 1999). His long-term vision for sharpening SIA's international competitiveness through rigorous cost control and product expansion did not go unnoticed. As an indicator of the airlines success under his leadership, Fortune noted that SIA was the only Asian carrier to report significant earnings in 1998. Its staff writer Louis Kraar also noted that Dr Cheong and his top level managers gave up a pay raise in 1998, inspiring other employees to do likewise (Kraar, 1999).

Apart from financial performance, Fortune also looked at skilful people management, a penchant for risk, a feel for technology, and a clear vision for the future. On all these accounts, Dr Cheong excelled and continues to do so. By buying into Virgin Atlantic in December 1999, bringing SIA into the STAR alliance in April 2000 (Velloor, 2000) and the multi-billion dollar B2B online exchange Aeroxchange to trade in airframes, avionics, engine components and maintenance services (Chee, 2000), Cheong has displayed all those good qualities that the people at Fortune were looking for. And these qualities are certainly in line with what all the leadership experts are saying that leaders in the 21$^{st}$ Century should possess (e.g., see Conger, 1999). When SIA became an indirect victim of the recent September 11 attacks on the United States of America, Dr Cheong took the lead by taking a pay cut to rein in costs. As a matter of fact, among all the directors, he took the heftiest cut of 15% from his basic salary, to lead by example (Fang, 2001).

## Successful Leadership in Non Government Organisations

This segment concludes with a final example from charitable organizations, the

Youth Challenge. Mr Vincent Lam started the Youth Challenge in Singapore in 1985 when he and a group of acquaintances saw many young school children hanging out at the McDonalds' outlet at the Centrepoint Shopping Complex and not engaging in anything meaningful. These kids became popularly known as the Centrepoint Kids and in the 1980s they were infamous for making a nuisance of themselves at the shopping complex. He thought if he could get them involved in meaningful activities, they would grow up to be much better young people and adults. With 5 other concerned citizens, he set up Youth Challenge, a non-profit organisation, to provide alternative outlets for these restless youths to channel their boundless energies.

Today, Youth Challenge has about 2000 student volunteers and the movement is involved in many charitable deeds locally and internationally and has produced many outstanding student leaders. Two recent excellent examples come to mind. Serene Woon, a National Junior College student and a Youth Challenge volunteer who raised more than $ 17,000 selling bookmarks over 12 days! The money was used to finance the medic-on wheels programme for old folks who stay at the Redhill Housing district. Serene's achievement caught the attention of the then US ambassador to Singapore, Mr Steven Green, who promptly wrote her a letter of commendation for her personal sacrifice and outstanding spirit of volunteerism. A letter of recommendation was also penned for Serene to be admitted into Harvard University! Right now, Serene is waiting to finish her GCE "A" level examinations before applying for admission into Harvard University.

Another outstanding Youth Challenge leader is Jasmine Lee Mei Hua, 16, a Secondary Four student from Anderson Secondary School, who flew to Calcutta with a team of 15 students in July 2000 to help distribute clothes, toiletries, toys and medical supplies to the poor in Calcutta at a mission started by the late Mother Teresa. The end result? Jasmine received a Certificate of High Commendation from Mr Prem Singh, India's High Commissioner to Singapore (Poon, 2000), and it has been reported that both the Singapore Chinese Girls' School and the National University of Singapore students' union have approached Youth Challenge to help organize similar trips to Calcutta next year (Straits Times, 2000e). The author met Jasmine recently at a function she organized. My impression? She is a young lady full of energy and ideas, both of which were productively channelled in the right direction because of Youth Challenge.

Serene and Jasmine did not take part in Youth Challenge in expectation of those commendations. They merely wanted to use whatever spare time they could find to help the less fortunate. The commendations were just icing on the cake!

On August 20, 2000, the author attended a gala dinner organized by the Youth Challenge to honour Jasmine, Serene, and many other Youth Challenge leaders like them, and was amazed at Vincent's ability to mobilize resources and network with corporate sponsors. He is not a scholar by any imagination; he is not even a university graduate. Yet, guests invited to the dinner were some of the most prominent people in Singapore. Top bankers, University Administrators, and even the US Ambassador to Singapore were on the guest list. He was able to mobilize major institutions to donate money or offer other forms of support to Youth Challenge so that Jasmine and her team could make that trip to India, medical aid could be given to the poor staying in the housing estates in Singapore, and support could be given to many other Youth Challenge Activities. Vincent mentioned that in 2001, he would be enlisting superstars from the Hong Kong entertainment industry to help Youth Challenge in its recruitment exercise. At a talk that he gave to a class of students who were taking a course on leadership, some of his first words were, "Whatever you do, do it with love and passion."

The Centrepoint Kids have come a long way. If leadership is about "infecting" others with your vision, passion and enthusiasm, and setting good examples for others to follow, one will find no better example than what Vincent has done for the youths in Singapore. Sometimes, one person can and does make a difference.

When Vincent was told over a telephone interview that the author was writing a chapter about leadership in Singapore and would need a paragraph or two concerning the work that he has done at Youth Challenge, he replied instinctively, "But I am not a politician!" Leadership in Singapore cannot just be about our political leaders. Leadership in Singapore must be about leaders everywhere in Singapore who have touched the lives of Singaporeans and beyond, leaders who have made a difference in the lives of their followers and more.

Take the poor children of India who were brought new clothing and toys by the volunteers from Youth Challenge as an example. Not many of these children know who the Prime Minister of Singapore is. But, when they saw Jasmine Lee with her team, changing diapers for the sick, dancing to bring smiles into their lives, and bringing new and clean clothes which they could never afford, they saw the face of leadership in Singapore: compassionate, caring, sacrificial.

What is the common thread that runs through these successful leaders in Singapore? They are men and women of passion, vision and action. They see the challenges around them and instead of retreating into their shells, they move out to meet those challenges head on. They dare to make bold moves. With their vision and energy, they are able to harness the energy of those around them, build good teamwork and trusting relationships with their followers, empower their followers (which in the case of school principals, include not just the teachers but also students and parents) and lead their organizations to greater heights of achievement and adventure.

These leaders obviously enjoy what they do and view their work not just as tasks to be completed, but a mission to be fulfilled. This explains the passion, fun and enjoyment they bring to their workplace. They do not get trapped by many of the mindsets mentioned previously, such as the fear of failure, the heroic leader, and born leaders. They are enemies of the status quo and mediocrity and will not take no for answer; risk takers who take bold initiatives and dare to fail, full of boundless energy and drive. And finally, they are team players who acknowledge the contribution of their peers and subordinates. They do not feel uneasy when the spotlight falls on people other than themselves. These are the kind of entrepreneurial leaders that Singapore need in order to navigate the new economy and the new millennium!

Are there many of these leaders around? Are there other leaders whose leadership capabilities are even better than those mentioned above? There should be. But until they speak up, we can only guess. Judging from the responses the author gets teaching middle to lower level executives, such exemplary leaders could be the exception rather than the rule. This observation is borne out by the fact that in the Steve Morris Associates survey, only 28.7% of employees said that they were happy with management to a great extent (Batacan, 2000).

*The Future of Corporate Leadership in Singapore*

What would it take for Singapore leaders to change their leadership style? What would it take for weak leaders to realize that they must change? My guess is that nothing works quite as well as a good dose of competition. Competition will cause them to realize that they need to move fast and satisfy customers' needs in order to survive. And this need to move fast and meet customers' needs will gravitate them towards using a more empowering style than they would inherently like to. The example of schools in Singapore illustrates the usefulness of open competition. Schools that are badly led will lose good students and good teachers. In time to come, grades will fall, student learning will come to a standstill and the principals' inadequacies will be brought into the open. If they fail to make adjustments to their leadership style and improve school effectiveness, the Ministry of Education will take action. Hence the press, through its frequent highlighting of excellent schools and excellent school principals, is doing other school principals a great service by blazing the path for them and helping them to overcome resistance to change among their own teachers and students to build excellent schools.

What is done in the press to highlight excellent principals should also be done to highlight the leadership style of exemplary corporate leaders. If we see more and more leaders like Mr Sim Wong Hoo, Mr Tommie Goh, Mr Kho Kheng Hwa, Dr Cheong Choong Kong, and Dr Jennifer Lee, making public statements about their leadership styles and philosophies, and that these leaders are extremely successful in what they do, others will be convinced that they too need to do the same thing.

In short, increasingly more of our organisational leaders from various organisations should open up. Let others see their lives, their leadership and management styles and philosophies. Let others dare to be vulnerable. Only then can those lacking in leadership learn from the more competent and successful. Education Minister Rear-Admiral Teo had openly called for principals to learn from success stories of others and adapt their ideas (Nirmala, 1999). The same can apply in the private sector. Corporate leaders in the private sector can surely learn from the leadership successes of their counterparts if only more of such success stories were to be made public. There must be many good leaders in Singapore. How else could we have made it this far? What we need is for more corporate leaders in Singapore to speak up and share their success stories, like the way their counterparts in the USA share their recipes for success, such as the likes of Jack Welch, Lee Iacoca, Steve Jobs, and Bill Gates. This will help to educate, teach, and inspire other organisational leaders to excel and push Singapore into greater organisational excellence!

Finally, corporate leaders should make a trip to visit countries that experience open and hyper competition. They should make a trip to the USA to see what it means to compete in the Internet age, where if you do not innovate, you evaporate. This might convince them to take on a whole new perspective of what leadership is all about in the new economy.

## What Should a Non-Singaporean Do in a Leadership Situation in Singapore?

*If you believe something should change, then you must try to change it, no matter if there are risks.*

Jose Luis Guerrero, Local leader, Union Nacional Sinarquista, Mexico

In many of the executive courses that I taught at the National University of Singapore, one of the most frequent complaints by expatriate managers is that many of our graduate employees do not have initiative and do not want to take risks. This is what makes this section so relevant for someone who has just received a managerial posting in Singapore.

For a non-Singaporean who has just been posted to take up a managerial or leadership position and is wondering, "What should I do," my best advice would be to first size up the organisational culture in general and the type of followers in particular. Are they ready to take responsibility? What kind of leadership culture did the previous leader leave behind? A good first step would be to ascertain answers to these and other important questions before one decides which leadership style to use.

If the corporate culture of an organisation is geared toward the reward of risk aversive behaviours rather than risk taking behaviours, the whole reward structure might have to be changed in order to reward people for engaging in risk taking behaviour rather than maintaining the status quo. In short, people who try new things, who experiment, must be rewarded. When they are successful in risk taking, they must be rewarded. If they fail, they might be rewarded less, but in no case should they be penalized (unless it is a case of uncalculated and unnecessary risk), as this would send a very strong and clear message to others not to take risks.

Concerning employees, if they are used to following orders, the manager will have to engage in activities to modify their mindset before implementing any programmes in empowerment. For instance, the manager could carry out extensive education, communication, and training programmes to teach followers how to shoulder responsibility before embarking on a radically different leadership style. An effective empowerment program takes training, trust, and time (Offerman, 1996). If it is carried out too quickly, that is, when people are given more than they can handle and forced to change before they are even ready for it, the adverse result could be stress and burnout (Xie & Johns, 1995).

In addition, leaders at all levels in the organisation have to model risk taking behaviour and let people know that it is alright to take risks (Kouzes & Posner, 1997). Sylvia Yee, the senior program officer at Evelyn and Walter Hass Jr Fund said, "You have to be a role model for others. You cannot ask others to do anything you would not be willing to do yourself", and that certainly includes risk taking! If we need empirical case studies, look at what Walt Disney did for his organisation and followers. He was constantly taking risks with new techniques in film making, even buying up the rights to the Technicolour process in film making in its infancy (Thomas, 1976). How about slain political leaders like Gandhi and Martin Luther King, Jr., who stuck to their beliefs, even in the face of great risk and danger, to the extent of eventually loosing their lives. When Singaporean employees/followers see that risk taking can be a rewarding form of activity, there is little doubt that they will jump on the bandwagon. As Albert Einstein used to say, "Setting an example is not the main means of influencing others; it is the only means."

## References

Ang, L. (2000). "Focused on taking JTC into a new era". *Business Times*, **3** April, p. 2.

Avolio, B.J. 1999. *Full Development Leadership*. Sage Publications.

Batacan, F. 2000. "Workers here value human touch". *The Straits Times*, 30 July, p. 43.

Business Times. 2000. "NWC chief and NUS don to get Distinguished Service Order", 9 August, p. 6, *Straits Times Press*.

Chee, J. P. 2000. "SIA part of massive B2B venture". *The Straits Times*, 25 July, p. 65.

Davie, S, and Ariff, S 2001. "Neighbourhood school stands out." *The Straits Times*, 16 August.

Davie, S. 2000. "3 levels of awards with new appraisal." *The Straits Times*, 20 March, p.51.

Dawson, S. 2000. "Creative goes for 'out-of-the-box' fun". *The Straits Times*, 1 August, p. 57.

Divyanathan, D. 2000. "Creative turns in record $ 314 m profits". *The Straits Times*, 4 August, p. 74.

Fang, N. 2001. "Pay cut for SIA management", *The Straits Times*, 9 October, p. H2.

Fernandez, W. 1999. "SIA chief exec is Asia's Businessman of the Year", *The Straits Times*, 14 Jan., p. 42.

Gary Hamel, 2000, cited in Ng, I. 2000. "Scholarship bond? That's 'indentured servitude!'" *The Straits Times*, 13 July, p. 43.

Kanungo, R. and Mendonca, M (1996). *Ethical Dimensions of Leadership*, Sage Publications, Thousand Oaks, California.

Ko, Keng Hwa, cited in Tan, C. 2000. "JTC dangles $ 2m dot.com carrot", *The Straits Times*, July 31, p.50.

Kouzes, J.M and Posner, B.Z. 1997. *The Leadership Challenge*. Jossey-Bass, San Francisco.

Kraar, L. 1999. "Asian businessman of the year", *Fortune*, Vol. 139, Issue 2, p.27.

Lee, A. 2000. "British schools want teachers from Singapore". *The Straits Times*, 5 August. p.4.

Lee, A. 2000. "Leeds lures 100 nurses, all Filipinos", *The Straits Times*, 21 July, p. 3.

Nirmala, 2000. M. "More autonomous school to come", *The Straits Times*, 13 January, p.40-41.

Nirmala, M, and Koh, Y. 1999. "Your job is to dream, dream big", *The Straits Times*, 13 April, p.26.

Nirmala, M. 1999. "Who's afraid of school autonomy?" *The Straits Times*, 3 April, p.38.

Nirmala, M., Kaur, K, and Ho, A.L., 1999. "Schools among world's best", *The Straits Times*, 17 July, p.40.

Offerman, L.R. (1997) "Leading and empowering diverse followers" in *The Balance of Leadership and Followership*, Kellogg Leadership studies Project, ed. E.P. Hollander, and LR. Offerman, College Park, MD: University of Maryland, 31-46.

Quek, T. 2000. "Two more schools to go autonomous". *The Straits Times*, 22 July, p.64.

Tan, A. 2000. "Boundless energy and a passion for business". *Business Times*, 11 March SS1, SS5.

Tan, R 2001. "Woman of the year", *Her World*, April, p.212-218.

Tee, H.C. 2000. "Don't be thrown off-balance at work". *The Straits Times*, 1 July, Life, L7.

Teh, H.L. 1999. "Gender parity in the works", *The Straits Times*, 2 August, p. 4.

Teo, A. 2000 "These corporate bosses are playful - and they rock". *Business Times*, 5 August, p.1-2.

The Straits Times (*a*), 1999. "Students reach out to community", p.54, 27 March, *Straits Times Press.*

The Straits Times (*c*), 2000. "A café, thanks to suggestions from students", p. 64, 22 July, *Straits Times Press.*

The Straits Times, 2000. "Excellence in both studies and service", p.64, 22 July, *Straits Times Press.*

Thomas, B. 1976. *Walt Disney.* New York: Simon & Schuster.

Velloor, R. 2000. "Star alliance welcomes SIA to the constellation", *The Straits Times*, 8 April, p.89.

Xie, J.L. and G. Johns. 1995. "Job Scope and Stress: Can job scope be too high?" *Academy of Management Journal*, 38 (5), p.1288-1309.

*Chapter 7*

# Leadership Effectiveness in Thailand

Dr. Duangduen Bhanthumnavin
Professor of social psychology and Director of the principal project on
R & D of Thai behavioral system,
National Research Council of Thailand.

and

Duchduen Bhanthumnavin
Instructor of HRD and Psychology,
Graduate School of Social Development, National Institute of
Development Administration, Bangkok, Thailand.

## Introduction

"Sawaddee" to all of you. This is the greeting word when Thai people meet both strangers as well as old acquaintances. Therefore, it is mostly true that Thais are friendly and warm. More than others, Thais believe that life is to be enjoyed. However, moderation between work and play is a wiser viewpoint for both leaders and followers alike.

Since the 1950's, Thailand has prepared for rapid growth and development by sending promising young learners abroad to get higher education and training. Consequently, Thailand is now recognized as having some reliable research results, especially in behavioral sciences, produced by local Thai researchers to supplement international knowledge for local use.

The purpose of this paper is to employ cross-cultural, as well as local research findings in psycho-behavioral science, together with a touch of local wisdom, as a basis for making recommendations for international management in Thailand. By reading this paper, the future leaders and managers from abroad can get to know different types of Thai workers. A leader is considered by local people to be the most important in a work-unit. Leaders' behaviors and leadership styles are considered to be a winning step into the heart of Thai subordinates. Leaders' creation and modification of work-group climate and group environment can lead to successful management. In Thailand, at least five types of training are recommended for the making of outstanding management and leadership in this new century.

## Diversity of Thai Workforce

From ancient time, until 70 years ago, Thailand could be thought of as having two distinct types of citizens, namely, the ruling class, with more advanced education and opportunities; and the agricultural class, with little or no technology, resources, and education.

In 1921, compulsory education of 4 years was offered for all Thai citizens, and increased to 6 years by 1969, and 9 years in some locations in 1998. At present, all Thais have at least some education, but only half of the 66 millions people have more than 6 years of education. Familial and economic backgrounds strongly determine how much education a youth will receive. More than in other cultures though, poorer Thai parents value education rather highly and try to pay for at least one of their children to go on in school. Many of these children receive at least 2 to 4 years of college education.

### Educational and Psychological Diversities

Thai working personnel can be classified into at least 4 levels of education, i.e., (1) 6 years of compulsory education, (2) 7 to 9 years of education (completion of junior high school), (3) 10 to 14 years of education (finishing junior college), and (4) bachelor's degree or higher.

The lowest educated group remains farmers and laborers. The persons with 7 to 9 years of education usually occupy the lowest positions in private and public organizations. The ones with 10 to 14 years of education become health workers and clerical workers in governmental and private organizations. Bachelor's degree holders become teachers and governmental officials, as well as personnel in international organizations. First level leaders or supervisors are usually Master's degree holders.

Unlike in the United States and some other countries where people receive at least 12 years of education, Thai people have a wider range of education level. Research results have shown that, Thai people with different levels of education (especially the first three levels mentioned above) have different degrees of psychological traits and behaviors. In an important Thai study (Leowarin, 1991), 300 workers in Bangkok, whose ages ranged from 25 to 40 years old, were investigated. The more educated people are more capable of thinking far head, they also show a stronger belief in their ability to predict and control future outcomes and they agree to the fact that more appropriate health behaviors can lead to desirable health goals. In addition, this study revealed that two health behaviors namely, hygienic behavior and avoidant behavior of unhealthy intakes, were accordingly higher among high school graduates as well.

Somewhat similar to Thailand, a study of 175 workers in Singapore revealed that the high education group (with diplomas or degrees) scored higher in intrinsic work values than the low education group (with high school certificates or less) (Putti, Aryee, & Liang, 1989). Therefore, level of education is a good indicator for differentiating Thai workers.

## Cross-Cultural Values Comparisons

Thailand and Singapore had been grouped together with six other countries and termed "Far Eastern" (Ronen & Shenkar, 1985), when they were found to have similar patterns of work related values and attitudes. The other countries in this group were Hong Kong, Indonesia, Malaysia, Philippines, South Vietnam, and Taiwan.

Cultural values have been related to organizational concepts in four value dimensions: individualism vs. collectivism, masculinity vs. femininity, power distance and uncertainty avoidance. Thailand was found to be collectivistic, feminine, high power distance, and moderate on uncertainty avoidance

(Chemers, 1997; Hofstede, 1980). These predictions were mostly supported in a study of Thai managers who worked either in Thai companies or in American companies in Thailand (Sorod, 1991). In addition, it was also found that the work related values of these Thai managers in those two types of organizations were somewhat influenced by the culture of their organizations.

With this specific pattern of values and attitudes, Thai situations in comparison to those in other countries are as follows. First, organizations are rather highly centralized with taller structures. Second, interpersonal relations are in the form of harmonious relationships with high in-group loyalty. Followers see their leader as "good father" and leaders perceive their followers as "members of one's family". They also emphasize service to others. Third, they are less task-oriented and value quality of life rather than work achievement. Finally, they are tolerant of differences and feel more comfortable under informal rather than strict rules (Soonthornvipart, 1989).

Later, an eminent cross-cultural study of 22 nations discovered a Chinese value dimension called "Confucian Dynamism", which is composed of future-oriented concepts, such as thrift and perseverance, acceptance of status inequality, saving face and respect for tradition. Thai university students were found to endorse these values to a lesser degree than the students in the five Chinese societies, including Taiwan and Singapore, but more than European and American students (The Chinese Culture Connection, headed by M. Bond, 1987).

In conclusion, people in Thai society may seem to be highly homogeneous. However, there is now a common acceptance of the saying that foreign theories and practices are usually not well fitted to countries like Thailand. Hofstede (1988) was once asked to suggest elements of a management theory that could be more suitable to the Indonesian situation. He then offered "Theory T+" (T = traditional) in place of Theory X-Y proposed by McGregor for use in the USA in 1960. However, with advanced research techniques and local wisdom, Thailand is fortunate to have a modern psychological theory of Thai behavior, based on Thai research findings.

## Thai Psychological Theory of Moral and Work Behaviors

Followers in a work-unit form an important social environment for the leader. The followers can stimulate and elicit certain reactions from the leader, depending on the followers' behaviors and their inner quality perceived by their leader.

It is true that to get the same amount of work done, the leader should behave differently toward different types of followers. Both McGregor (1960) and Hofstede (1988) are partially correct in their theory X vs. Y, and theory T vs. T+, respectively, when applied to Thai people.

In 1974, a twin study headed by the first author of this chapter, supported by the National Research Council of Thailand, was conducted. The first part was an experimental study aimed at manipulating some modeling situations to produce honest behavior in 300 school adolescents who were playing games in a laboratory. It was found that both situational and psychological factors were necessary for honest behavior. In the second part of the study 1,500 school adolescents were examined to find the social antecedents of these psychological characteristics, namely, moral reasoning ability, future orientation, and self control, and favorable attitude towards honesty, and other virtues of honest actors (Bhanthumnavin & Prachunpachanuk, 1977).

Ten years afterwards, at least 20 empirical studies employing highly qualified measurements and well controlled research methodologies have been reviewed and conceptualized to form a theory entitled, "Psychological theory of moral and work behaviors" (Bhanthumnavin, 1988; 1995). Since then the hypotheses from this theory have been confirmed in more than 30 correlational and experimental studies in Thailand. In 1998 the Thai theory, research, studies, and its applications in Thailand, was presented as an invited paper at the 24th International Congress of Applied Psychology in San Francisco, USA (Bhanthumnavin, 1998).

In the studies mentioned above, Thai people, homogeneous in ages and situations, but displaying different behaviors, were investigated to find their related psychological characteristics. The behaviors studied were of a wide variety, from moral behavior (honest, etc.), health behavior to religious practices, and work effectiveness. The ages of the participants ranged from 7 to 70. These behaviors later become the objectives for human development of the country and were termed "good, competent and happy individuals", in various circumstances, including work situations.

At least three to four psychological characteristics are found to be responsible for each major type of behavior of Thai people. In order to cover a wide variety of behaviors of each individual, at least eight psychological characteristics are specified in this theory, which are (1) Future orientation and self- control, (2) Moral reasoning ability, (3) (Belief in internal locus of control of reinforcement), (4) Need for achievement, (5) Mental health, (6) Intelligence, (7) Social perspective taking, and (8) Attitudes, values, or virtues, relating to the behavior in question (see Figure 1). These psychological characteristics are found to be the antecedents of most pro-social behaviors of the Thais from adolescence to old age.

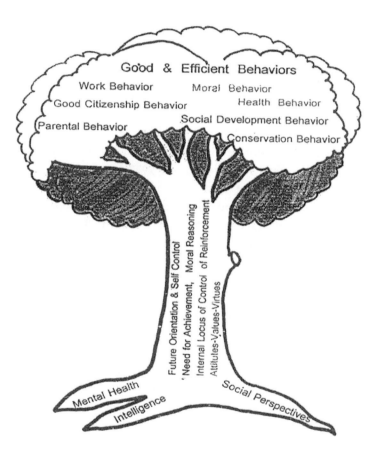

**Figure 1.   Psychological Theory of Moral and Work Behaviors**

More recently, several Thai studies have revealed that, many or all of the eight psychological characteristics are the necessary qualities of the "fittest" that will "survive" in this complicated and dangerous world. In more detailed, one award winning study showed that attitudes towards drugs, belief in internal locus of control relating to health, mental health, future orientation,  self-control, moral reasoning ability, and negative attitude towards risky peers, among other variables were important predictors of avoidant behavior of drug addiction in 560 high-school students in provincial Thailand (Juntasorn, 1998).

Also, in another award winning study, four of these psychological characteristics were found to be highly related to more appropriate behaviors in peer groups necessary for AIDS prevention of 325 male university students in Bangkok (Wannachart, 1998).

Another recent correlational study on 1,160 pupils from 12 high schools in provincial Thailand found that, more happiness and less suicide attempts were found among the adolescents with better mental health and higher belief in internal locus of control of reinforcement (Sukhanan, 2001).

Furthermore, an experimental study employing 405 male students from 3 major universities in Thailand, found that the ones who received the most training on five psychological characteristics, namely, knowledge on AIDS prevention, favorable attitude towards AIDS prevention behaviors, future orientation and self control, and belief in internal locus of control of reinforcement, four months after training were more highly qualified than their less trained and their control peers. In addition, most trained students reported having carried out behaviors such as knowledge seeking, diffusion of the message and campaigning behaviors for AIDS prevention on campus, more than the less trained or the control students (Ma-Oon, 2001).

In conclusion, Thai studies repeatedly show that Thai people, who are in similar situations, but display different behaviors, do so because they possess different degrees of certain important psychological characteristics. These characteristics consist of belief in internal locus of control of reinforcement, future orientation and self-control, moral reasoning ability, mental health, and favorable attitude towards the target behaviors.

Moreover, the "fittest for survival" in Thai organizations seem to possess similar characteristics. Research findings from many important Thai studies concerning a wide variety of personnel, from policemen, nurses and school teachers to bankers, are reviewed here as follows.

In a correlational study employing 203 commissioned police officers from 51 police stations in the northeastern provinces of Thailand, it was found that, psychological characteristics are better predictors of self-reported work behavior than situational variables, which accounted for 38% and 14% of the variance respectively. The three important psychological characteristics found to be strongly related to the self-report of general work behavior of these police officers were, need for achievement, favorable attitude towards work, and future orientation. Furthermore, for the policemen involved in investigations, moral reasoning ability was also found to be among the strong psychological predictors (Pinpradit, 2001).

At present, work behavior in Thailand has been examined, not solely on a dimension of effectiveness, but also on other more important dimensions as well, such as the dimension of morality at work. In one interesting study, 330 IPD nurses, in 6 general hospitals from five major provinces in Thailand, were studied (Tamavong, 2001). Their adherence to human rights behavior and ethical work behavior accounted for 51% and 56%, respectively, by six psychological characteristics (favorable attitude towards work, altruistic virtue, perceived human rights norms, future orientation and self-control, and low stress at work).

Moral reasoning ability training was given to low scorers among elementary school teachers in another experiment (Meekun, 2001). Three months after training, these 276 teachers who were randomly assigned to a 12 or 24-hour training session or the control group, showed different amounts of moral reasoning ability and moral behavior at work as predicted. Four psychological characteristics of these teachers were further found to account for 62% of the variance of moral behavior at work in the total sample, and even higher (70%) in male teachers. The four psychological characteristics were, in order of importance, favorable attitude towards moral behavior, and moral reasoning ability (both measured three months after training), professional value, future orientation and self-control.

The Psychological Theory of Moral and Work Behavior established in Thailand (Bhanthumnavin, 1988; 1998) found supportive evidence, not only among group members or subordinates, but among leaders as well. In the following two studies, leaders' behaviors while working and interacting with their subordinates were explained by many psychological characteristics predicted from the theory mentioned above.

Research findings from a study of 607 unit-leaders from the largest bank in Thailand showed that 59% of the self-reported effectiveness of these Thai bank branch leaders could be accounted by four psychological variables together with one situational variable. The four psychological variables were, need for achievement, moral reasoning ability, attitude towards work, and belief in internal locus of control of reinforcement (Sorod, 2001). The situational variable was leader-member relationship.

Another study on social support behavior of 509 supervisors of rural health centers from six major provinces in Thailand hypothesized that "all six psychological characteristics (from the Thai theory mentioned above) account for more variation of the social support behavior of supervisors than can the first entering psychological predictor alone" (Bhanthumnavin, 2002). The data in the total sample, as well as in some subsamples, supported this prediction. It was found that supervisors' need for achievement was the first and most important predictor of their social support behavior. However, more and better explanations of social support behavior can be developed by knowing the magnitude of three other psychological characteristics of the supervisors, namely, social perspective taking ability, future orientation, and work stress.

In conclusion, in order to be the "fittest for survival" at work, Thai leaders and followers alike need to possess a highly favorable attitude towards work in their respective professions, high need for achievement, high future orientation and self-control, high level of moral reasoning ability or strong virtues or values relating to the targeted behavior, as well as, better mental health with low work stress.

As for being the "fittest for survival" in the society at large, for both Thai adolescents and adults, so that they can successfully restrain themselves from undesirable and self-harming behaviors, the above mentioned psychological characteristics are also important, with the addition of belief in internal locus of control of reinforcement.

In this section, Thai studies have been cited to show that more than in other societies, (actor's) psychological characteristics are important predictors of his (or her) behavior. One should not overlook or underestimate the roles played by various psychological traits and states in the successful living of Thai people.

Many theories and development programs from abroad, which place more emphasis on modifying work and group situations, rather than incorporating psychological characteristics of working personnel, usually yield less success or event failure in Thailand. For example, the reengineering programs that came to Thailand about seven years ago are now considered a failure. A major part of it may be due to the empowerment of workers to increase work effectiveness.   Unfortunately, the program attempted to give more responsibility to the working personnel who originally had less favorable attitudes towards work and a low need for achievement. Therefore, for the developmental programs to be more successful, both psychological and situational factors have to be equally taken into account.

## Leadership Styles in Thai Organizations

Besides their own psychological characteristics, working people are also influenced by their social environment, in order for them to be effective at work. Social, more than physical, environment is important for the workers' situation. There is an old Thai saying that, "a crowded environment is livable, but an uneasy relationship is unbearable". The leader of the workgroup plays a more important role for building good group atmosphere. "A good father" type of leader is usually high in consideration, and at the same time, demands some work from the low educated followers (Triandis, 1993). However, if the leader and his or her followers are at the same high level of education (college graduates), the leader should be warm, but nondirective, to be regarded as more effective and highly satisfactory for their boss and followers alike (Soonthornvipart, 1989).

  This section will highlight two important leadership styles and behaviors that have been present in Thai history and continue into the present era. Theories and consonant research findings can give the readers the levels of assurance of their being true and their scope for areas of operations. The first topic deals with the characteristics of most desirable leader in Thailand and the second topic deals with how they should behave.

## Transformational-Moral Leader as Ideal

"A leader is a member of a work group who tries to get the rest of the members to do the group work, and to prevent them from doing wrong in the process." This is at present accepted as a definition of leading behavior in Thailand.

  A "Moral leader" unites leading behavior with moral behavior in one act. Moral behavior is defined as an action based on a virtue, value, or religious principles. In addition, interaction with other people is usually in the form of giving rewards or punishment, especially in a leader's roles. Moral behavior is to be fair and just in issuing rewards or punishment. The aims of working are high work performance, social well-being and long-term outcomes (Vilegas de Posada, 1994).

At present the world economic crisis, which has been caused largely by unethical business leaders and organizations, has demanded a reversal process for survival. Transformational leadership style is seen as the most compatible with this requirement both abroad (Carlson & Perrewe, 1995) and in Thailand.

The Office of the Thai Civil Service Commission reported on the ideal type of Thai leader by asking 178 executives of the civil service departments to respond to questionnaires. Afterwards, sixty other executives from private, governmental and university organizations gave their endorsement to the final list of 10 attributes most needed in Thai "new wave" leaders. Four of these attributes are: accountability, vision, creativity, and team building, which are the special characteristics of transformational leader. Three other attributes are honesty, sacrifice, and justice, which represent the moral behavior of leaders. Two other personal characteristics are leadership and psychological maturity. The last attribute is managerial skills of planning (Punnitamai, 1996).

The fact that Thai personnel valued transformational leaders was reported by a recent study on 588 teachers from 200 public schools in Thailand (Saetang, 1999). The results from the teachers, whose average age was 39 years old and 89 percent of which were Bachelor's degree holders, indicated that the more they perceived their school principal as being transformational, the more effective the leader and the more satisfied they reported being.

In 1997, Bass clearly differentiated transformational leader from transactional leader in five aspects as shown in Table 1. He then went on to indicate that leader-member interaction might start with a simple transactional relationship. But for work effectiveness, the interaction needs to become transformational. Thus, it can be understood that transformational leadership behavior can be used to differentiate this type of leader from the transactional leader, but not vice versa. In addition, Bass stated that transformational leaders can be found in both eastern and western cultures. However, it can be expected that, there should be more transformational leaders in collective societies such as in Asia.

Table 1  Comparing transactional and transformational leaders

| Characteristics of leaders | |
|---|---|
| Transactional | Transformational |
| 1) Leadership as exchanges of reinforcement by the leader that are contingent on followers' performance | 1) Enlarge and elevate followers' motivation, understanding, maturity and sense of self-worth for the good of their society |
| 2) Rules and regulations dominate the organization | 2) Adaptability is a characteristic of the organization. |
| 3) Leader works within the constraints of the organization | 3) Leader changes the organization |
| 4) Leadership depends on the leader's power to reinforce subordinates for their work-success. | 4) Addressing the follower's sense of self-worth to engage and commit them to work |
| 5) Emphasizing the importance of immediate self-interest of acquiring income, reward and security | 5) To do what is right and good in consonant with followers' self-worth and for the good of the group, organization or country. |

In Thailand, local research and the theory mentioned in the earlier section have indicated that "good, competent and happy leaders (as well as followers)", are the ones most likely to possess most or all of the eight psychological characteristics mentioned in the Thai theory.  In 1993, the first author of this chapter wrote a handbook for encouraging Thai governmental leaders to increase self-development and also to acquire techniques for eliciting most of these psychological characteristics from their followers in their everyday interactions (Bhanthumnavin, 1993).

At present (2002), Bass and other research psychologists have come to expect that the transformational leaders should posses three types of intelligence, namely, cognitive, emotional, and social. These intelligence traits can be measured via many psychological characteristics closely resembling some of the eight psychological traits and states mentioned in the Thai theory.

Consonant with the above observation, in one study (Turner, et al., 2002), 132 managers were classified as transformational or transactional by their 407 subordinates. The managers with high moral reasoning ability (measured by Defining Issue Test) were perceived by their followers to be more transformational than the managers with lower moral reasoning ability.

In conclusion, this section has identified a moral leader to be similar to a transformational leader. Furthermore, the Thai psychological theory of moral and work behaviors, consonant with Bass's research review (2002), clearly offers eight psychological characteristics which can be used to identify the authentic and universal type of transformational leader.

## Socially Supportive Leaders

The leadership styles mentioned in the above section are at a macro level, when compared to leader's behaviors. In the psychological literature on leadership behavior one can repeatedly find that there are two major types of leader behavior, namely, task related behavior and emotionally related behavior. Good examples of the two types of leader behavior suggested by Tjosvold (1984) are directive vs. nondirective behavior and warm vs. cold behavior. In an experimental study on 56 college students, it was found that among the subordinates with warm leaders, if their leaders were directive, the subordinates performed better than those with nondirective leaders.

In Thailand, a correlational study employed 81 first level leaders from the corruption office (Soonthornvipart, 1989). The finding was opposite to that of Tjosvold (1984). In this study, the nondirective and warm leaders were rated by their subordinates as more effective than other types of leaders, especially the nondirective and cold. Therefore, it can be interpreted that how a leader should behave in order to lead to work effectiveness depends on many other human and situational factors. There is no hard and fast rule of how an effective leader should behave to all subordinates, in all situations. Therefore, a great deal of research is needed to disentangle such a complicated phenomenon.

Originally, interest in social support behavior between two individuals came from two areas of research in Thai Psychology and Behavioral Science. The first and most important social support behavior was found between parent and child. It is called "love oriented child rearing practice". It has been found to be the basis for good parent-child relationships and an origin of many desirable psychological and behavioral characteristics of Thai youths (Bhanthumnavin & Prachonpachanuk, 1977; Bhanthumnavin & Vanintananda, 1997; Boonchit, 2001; Vanintananda, 1992; Sukhanon, 2001).

The second area of research in Thailand concentrates on the antecedents and consequences of "psychological alienation". This term signifies the feelings of normlessness, helplessness, hopelessness, and powerlessness of a person in the society at large, or in work environment. The first Thai study which investigated the reverse concept of "alienation", employed "perceived social support received from significant others" as the opposite of "helplessness". This study on 504 Thai elementary school teachers found strong relationships between "perceived social support" and teacher's effectiveness (Nirunthawee, 1989). At present, leader's social support behavior, and perceived social support received at work by group members have become a useful and more integrated area of knowledge and practice.

Definition of Socially Supportive Leader.   The term "social support" is defined as an interpersonal behavior between a supervisor and a subordinate in a working situation, in which the supervisor provides one or more dimensions of social support (Cohen & Wills, 1985; House, 1981). Bhanthumnavin (2001) has reclassified supervisory social support into three major dimensions, which are emotional, informational, and material, and has made separate assessments, and these behaviors of leaders assessed from both the actor and the receiver.

Emotionally-supportive leaders usually generate good feelings and reduce the anxiety of their subordinates, for example, cheering up the subordinate when he or she is facing work difficulty, showing appreciation of the subordinate's extra work efforts or valuing the subordinate's important contributions. Informationally-supportive leaders are concerned about the knowledge and skills of their subordinates. These leaders provide advice and suggestions relating to work, for example, explaining work procedures and methods, providing feedback, showing how the subordinates can do the task better, or clarifying the given assignment. Materially-supportive leaders plan, search, prepare, and provide equipment and materials necessary for ensuring their subordinate's success, for example, asking whether the subordinate has sufficient equipment to get the job done, allocating appropriate budget and labor, responding promptly to requests from the subordinates on this matter.

Social support in work situations had been studied in Thailand since 1989. Seven studies on its importance were reviewed by the second author of this paper. She then pointed out its important implications for leadership training in Thailand (Bhanthumnavin, 2000).

Importance of a Leader's Social Support at Work.   Research outside Thailand on a leader's social support has revealed its positive consequences. It was found that support from a leader increases members' job satisfaction (e.g., Mayfield, Mayfield, & Kopf, 1998; Rauktis & Koeske, 1994), organization assimilation at the entering stage and/or job transferring stage (e.g., Major, Kozlowski, Chao, & Gardner,1995), organizational and work commitment (e.g., Littrell, Billingsley, & Cross, 1994; Thacker, Fields, & Braclay,1990; Xiaodony, 1992), and transfer of training (e.g., Brinkerhoff & Montesino, 1995; Gregoire, Propp, & Poetner, 1998; Wexley & Latham, 2002) . Support from a leader also reduces many negative outcomes at work, for example, job stress/burnout (e.g., Etzion & Westman, 1994; Greenglass, Fiksenbaum, & Burke, 1994) and strain (e.g., Blau, 1981), accidents relating to work (e.g., Iverson & Erwin, 1997; Sherry, 1991), and work-family conflict (e.g., Goff, Mount, & Jamison, 1990; Thomas & Ganster, 1992).

Similarly, research findings in Thailand also revealed many advantages of a leader's social support at work. For example, a study on the antecedents and consequences of stress at work was conducted by Sorod and Wongwattanamongkol (1996). This study employed 174 Thai government officials in first level leadership positions in five ministries. Social support at work, including that from second level leaders, was found as one of the important antecedents of several consequences, such as, low stress, high job satisfaction, and low strain on these first level leaders. As can be expected, these researchers found that, the respondents reporting the least perceived social support at work had higher scores on the stress scale than those reporting moderate and high social support at work. Furthermore, those who reported higher social support at work also reported higher job satisfaction, less job strain (e.g., headache, stomach-ache, drowsiness), and less psychological strain (e.g., depression, emotional exhaustion). Social support at work, was also found to be associated with the self-reporting of work effectiveness. In other words, the Thai officials receiving the highest degree of social support rated themselves as more effective than those receiving moderate and low support. Researchers, moreover, found that social support from a leader was the most important predictor of job stress (9%) and even more on job satisfaction (34%) of these Thai officials.

A recent study of 355 pairs of matched supervisor-subordinate in community health centers in Thailand found strong relationships between the amount of supervisory social support and the amount of success of both individual subordinates and the whole centers (Bhanthumnavin, 2001). These relationships were found to differ in different types of subordinates as follows. Among the less educated subordinates (with only 9 to 14 years of education), the ones who received high material support from their supervisors reported themselves as more successful than did their opposites. This result on material support was not found in the high education workers, but informational support played more important role. It was further found that the highly educated subordinates (15 to18 years of education), if they perceived themselves as receiving high informational support from their supervisors, their group was rated by the supervisor as more effective than that of their opposites. This result was not found in the less educated workers.

## Group Situations for Successful Management

It is now evident from modern research findings that one can become a successful workgroup leader, if "the situation is right for him or her", or "if he or she makes the group situation right for himself or herself" (Fiedler, 1967; Fiedler & Garcia, 1987).

How can one know "the right group situation" or "what and how" can one make the group right for oneself? In order to learn this, a leader must read textbooks or papers written by researchers in social and organizational psychology.

In any multi-cultural organization, it can be expected that good leader-member relations may be more difficult to establish than in single culture work groups. In Fiedler's Contingency theory of Leadership Effectiveness (1967), leader-member relations variable is the most important factor necessary for high situational control for leaders. The other two factors are task structure, or being skillful on the group's task, and the leader's power to evaluate and reward his followers. Situational control has been found in most Thai studies, under this theory, to be the best predictor of group effectiveness and leader satisfaction with their work, in various types of Thai civil service groups (Bhanthumnavin, 1991; Sorod & Wongwattanamongkol, 1996), as well as, in both Thai and American banks (Sorod, 2001).

However, in this empirically based theory, Fiedler points out that high situational control is not generally beneficial to all leaders, but only for leaders who are low scorers on the LPC test. The low LPC scorers are the ones who accept their coworkers only on the merit of their success at work. On the other hand, high LPC scorers are the ones who accept their coworkers on other grounds, even though they fail in their work.

Fiedler says that if you are high LPC scorers, your "right" group is moderate in situational control. But, if you are low LPC scorers, you will be more successful when working in groups with either low or high situational control (see Figure 2).

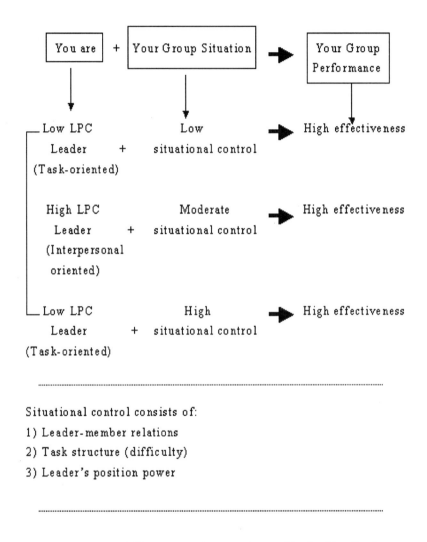

**Figure 2 Interpretation of Fiedler's contingency theory of leadership effectiveness showing the "right" group for two types of leaders**

After reviewing ten Thai studies based on Fiedler's theory (Bhanthumnavin, 1991; 1999), it was found that the above hypotheses from Fiedler's theory were supported in Thailand only under two conditions.

The first condition concerns the existence of low situational control groups among the work units being studied. The second condition, which offers good support of Fiedler's theory in Thailand, and probably in other similar countries, is that the theory is applicable only to leaders with high qualifications, be it educational or psychological.

For the first condition mentioned above, the data from two studies showed that the "in match-groups" (between LPC of the leader and the level of situational control of his/her group) were more effective than the "out of match-groups" only in organizations in which low situational control groups existed (6% in counter corruption agency, and 16% in teachers' colleges, respectively) (Soonthornvipart, 1988; Surakitbowon, 1989). While other studies had only moderate and high situational control groups. Therefore, it can be concluded that, Fiedler's theory may be more applicable in groups with low situational control, which were rarely found in Thai organizations.

The second condition which partially shows the universality of Fiedler's Contingency Theory of Leadership Effectiveness (Fiedler, 1967; Fiedler & Chermers, 1984), at least in Thai society, is the hypothesis concerning "in match-groups" versus "out of match-groups" and their differential effectiveness.

In one study on 80 rice farmers who were heads of cooperatives for rice selling (Bhanthumnavin, 1994), "in match-groups" were evaluated as more effective by a governmental office than the "out of match-groups", only when the group leaders were strong believers of internal locus of control of reinforcemen. The weaker believers' groups showed the opposite results from Fiedler's theory as will be mentioned below.

Stronger research evidence was found in a more recent study on Thai leaders in local branches of the largest bank in Thailand (Sorod, 2001). In this study 603 leaders were classified as being in an "in match-group" or "out of match-group". Fifty-three percent of these leaders were classified as being in "in match-group". They also were classified as either having more of the five psychological traits (from the Thai Psychological Theory of Moral and Work Behavior, Bhanthumnavin, 1991; 1998). Then the researcher proceeded to find that the leaders from "in match-groups" rated themselves as more effective at work than the leaders from "out of match-groups". This result was evident only among highly psychological leaders. Records show that only a few studies outside North America and Europe have tested Fiedler's model (Ayman, Chemers, & Fiedler, 1998). Thus, Thailand is an exception in this case.

Fiedler would be surprised to find that the "out of match-groups" are sometimes more effective than the "in match-groups". Such research results have only been reported in Thailand (Bhanthumnavin, 1999)

It was found in three Thai studies, one on rice farmers' cooperative leaders (Bhanthumnavin, 1994), another on school administrators (Chaumthong, 1993), and the third on department heads of Thai public universities (Soonthornvipart, 1992), that in the groups with less qualified leaders, the "out of match-groups" performed significantly better than the "in match-groups" (Bhanthumnavin, 1991; 1999). These results can signify that the "out of match-condition" can prevent leaders from influencing group performance, while the "in match-condition" let the leaders do so more easily. Therefore, the less qualified leaders (who had lower levels of education, showed less favorable attitudes towards work, or had a weaker belief in internal locus of control, in "out of match-groups" were put into an inactive position. If they happened to be in an "in match-group", they could be detrimental to their group work. On the contrary, highly qualified leaders in "in match-conditions" can be greatly beneficial to their group effectiveness as predicted by Fiedler's theory. Recently, this has been continuously confirmed by research data in and outside of Thailand

In Thailand, a study 607 heads of bank-branches (Sorod, 2001) revealed that Fiedler's theory was supported only in Thai leaders with high scores on 3 to 5 psychological characteristics (those from the Thai psychological theory, especially need for achievement), but not in the low scorers. However, in this study, American bank leaders were also examined, but similar result was found.

The fact that Fiedler's model works better for certain types of leaders also found support in a study on 70 Mexican managers (Ayman & Chemers, 1991). Fiedler's model worked well among the low self-monitoring leaders, but not so well among the leaders with high self-monitoring personalities.

Such research results signify that Fiedler's theory should be extended to incorporate some more psychological characteristics of leaders which are relevant to work behavior (Bhanthumnavin, 1999). The Thai Psychological Theory of Moral and Work Behavior seems to be a good choice for this job. The unification of Fiedler's Contingency Theory and the Thai Psychological Theory can lead to a more fruitful approach to leadership effectiveness and leadership training, especially in Thailand, as will be described in the following section.

## Leadership Training in Thailand

Most frequently, leadership training aims at two goals. One is to increase the leader's skills on the task assigned to the group. Another is for improving human relations. These two types of leadership training are obviously relevant to two of the three dimensions of Fiedler's group-situational control. However, these two types of training cannot be used to assure the leaders that they can improve group effectiveness. On the contrary, this training can even reduce group effectiveness if applied to the leaders indiscriminately. This can be explained based on Fiedler's theory ( 1969), that after the leaders received training, the groups changed from low to moderate situational control. These groups can become "out of match" for the low LPC leaders. Also due to the effect of leadership training, the groups may change from moderate to high situational control, and the high LPC leaders will become less effective. Therefore, the traditional training of leaders may yield overall "zero" improvement because half of the trained leaders may increase in performance, while the other half faces decreased performance.

Fortunately, Fiedler's theory and research come with an excellent training package for leaders, which can be used as a group or through self-instruction (Fiedler & Chemers, 1984). The technique is flexible and tailored to fit different types of leaders and different group-situations. The authors of this chapter can offer this "Leadership Match Training" in Thailand.

In preparation for going to work in a different culture or subculture from one's own, cross-cultural training is a good answer (Ayman , 1993, Mai-Dalton, 1993). In this type of training, one can learn about different ways of thinking, believing, perceiving, and behaving in the same situation by people from different cultures. The trainees can come to accept and understand people different from themselves with greater self-confidence and more readiness to mix. The cross-cultural training can be used to improve leader-member relations in multi-cultural task groups and thus lead to increase group-situational control for the leader (Chemers, 1969).

One famous cross-cultural training package called " The Culture Assimilator" was constructed at the University of Illinois beginning in 1965

(Fiedler, Mitchell, & Triandis, 1971) to be used for training Peace Corps Volunteers from the United States of America to developing countries in Southeast Asia and other parts of the world. The first author of this paper was fortunate to be one of the social psychologists to construct " The Culture Assimilator" and to carry out an experimental study for the successful demonstration of the use of this technique (Chemers, Fiedler, Lekhyananda, & Stolurow, 1966).

"The Culture Assimilator" traveled to the East-West Center in Hawaii, where some modifications were made and the applications widened. In 1990, the new version of "The Culture Assimilator" was translated and modified to be used for training Thai police cadets before their first practicum in rural areas. An experimental study was carried out and was able to demonstrate the effectiveness of this sub-cultural training package (Supapol, 1990).

Two other types of training are recommended for cross-cultural managers in Thailand. First is the "Buddhist ceremony training" which may become handy for foreign executives in Thailand. They need to learn to initiate a commencement ceremony for their company's birthday cerebration, establishment of a new work branch, or expansions into new service areas. Furthermore, they may be invited by their Thai subordinates to attend various social functions where the highest honor may be given to the supervisors to conduct a short religious ceremony. Together with religious training, Thai language training is another necessary acquisition for the foreign leaders to be accepted as an in-group member of their coworkers.

At present, transformational-moral leadership skills have become a new requirement for rapid promotion in the supervisory career. Psychological and behavioral training of the leaders are necessary for leaders' own sake. They also need to acquire new techniques for psychological development and behavioral modification of their subordinates. From 1985 on, the first author has directed her team to construct training packages for the five out of eight psychological characteristics mentioned in the "psychological theory of moral and work behaviors" for use with the civil service officials (Bhanthumnavin & Meekun, 1987). The training packages aim at developing and stimulating one of the four traits of the working personnel, i.e., need for achievement, future orientation and self-control, moral reasoning ability and favorable attitudes towards civil service work. Later the fifth training package on believe in internal locus of control of reinforcement was constructed and experimentally evaluated on Thai teachers (Sodmanee, 1993).

These five training packages, each consists of nine activities, requiring 15 hours of training. This training aims at improving psychological characteristics used both in working as well as in everyday life situations. An experimental study on the effect of future orientation and self-control training on the Thai civil service officials (Sukmanee, 1988), yields similar results to the ones carried out in the USA (Latham & Frayne, 1989). These five psychological training packages are now used as prototypes of many new training packages for various types of trainees, for a wide variety of objectives, i.e., from AIDS prevention in male university students (Ma-Oon, et. al., 2001) to moral-work effectiveness in elementary school teachers (Meekun, et. al., 2001). Many of these newer training packages in Thailand integrate several important psychological traits for promoting one type of trainees' behavior.

In Thailand, leaders can obtain at least two types of psycho-behavioral training. The first type is the five psychological training packages mentioned above. The second type is a training of leaders for enhancing their followers' psycho-behavioral characteristics necessary for work and quality of life in general. The first author has published a self-instructional handbook (Bhanthumnavin, 1993) as a response to the request from the Office of the Civil Service Training in Thailand. The book consists of 20 questions and easy-reading answers. In this book, the leaders learn about the necessity for them to promote the psychological health, morality and effectiveness of their followers. Afterwards, the leaders are informed of the "appropriate" behaviors and social environments they should create at work. Finally, the leaders are given several types of evaluative techniques they can easily use as feedback and for future management.

The Civil Service Training Center reported that the self-instructional handbooks have been sent to first level leaders in governmental units all over Thailand. The feedback from the leaders in rural work units has been very encouraging (personal communication with the director of the distant learning department, 1995).

## Conclusion

This chapter is based on research mostly gathered in Thailand. The empirical results demonstrate the diversities in levels of education and the psychological characteristics of Thai workforce, which call for three major types of leader behaviors, i.e., (1) "good father" managing style, (2) the ideal type of "transformational-moral leader", and also (3) altering group situation to fit one's psychological type.

In order to prepare oneself for a future position in Thailand, an executive may be more equipped if he considers getting one or more of the training packages available in Thailand. These are (1) leadership match training, (2) cross-cultural training, (3) Buddhist ceremony and language training, (4) psychological-behavioral training, and (5) training to become trainers of their subordinates. Only with such various trainings, the executive can expect to be more effective in his new position and also produce a better quality of life for himself (herself), the family and their employees.

# Reference

Ayman, R. (1993). "Leadership perception: The role of gender and culture". In M.M. Chemers, & R. Ayman (Eds.), *Leadership theory and research: Perspectives and directions* (pp. 137-166). San Diego, CA: Academic Press.

Ayman, R., & Chemers, M.M. (1991). "The effect of leadership match on subordinate satisfaction in Mexican organization: Some moderating influences of self-monitoring". *International Review of Applied Psychology*, **40**, 299-314.

Ayman, R., Chemers, M.M, & Fiedler, F.E. (1998). "The contingency model of leadership effectiveness: Its levels of analysis." In F. Dansereau, & F.J. Yammarino (Eds)., *Leadership: The multilevel approaches* (pp. 73-96). Connecticut: JAI Press, Inc.

Bass, B.M. (1997). "Does the transactional-transformational leadership transcend organizational and national boundaries?" *American Psychologist*, **52**(2), 130-139.

Bass, B.M. (2002). "Cognitive, social, and emotional intelligence of transformational leaders." In R.E. Riggio, S.E. Murphy, and F.J. Pirozzolo (Eds.), *Multiple intelligence and leadership* (pp. 105-118). New Jersey: LEA Publishers.

Bhanthumnavin, D. (1988). *Theory of morality for Thai people: Research and applications.* Special Monograph for the 33rd Anniversary of the Behavioral Science Research Institute. Srinakharinwirot University, Bangkok, Thailand.

Bhanthumnavin, D. (1991). "Leadership effectiveness: Development according to Fiedler's theory." *Yearbook of the Civil Service Training Institute* (pp. 137-158). Bangkok, Thailand.

Bhanthumnavin, D. (1993). *Leader's handbook for moral development of employees.* Training Center, Office of the Civil Service Commission, Bangkok, Thailand.

Bhanthumnavin, D. (1995). *Psychological theory of moral and work behaviors: Research and applications.* Graduate School of Social Development, National Institute of Development Administration, Bangkok, Thailand.

Bhanthumnavin, D. (1998). "A new model of socialization for improving work performance and quality of life in Thailand". Invited paper at the 24th International Congress of Applied Psychology, International Association of Applied Psychology, San Francisco, California, USA. August 13, 1998. (also published in 1999 in *Thai Journal of Development Administration,* **39**(1), 7-17).

Bhanthumnavin, D. (1999). "Discovering important assumptions underlying Fiedler's contingency theory of leadership effectiveness in empirical studies from Thailand." Presented at the third conference of the Asian Association of Social Psychology, Taipei, Taiwan. (also published in 2000, in *Thai Journal of Development Administration,* **39**(4), 99-114.).

Bhanthumnavin, D., & Meekun, K. (1987). *Academic background for the construction of four psychological training packages for Thai civil service officials,* Training Center, Office of the Civil Service Commission, Bangkok, Thailand.

Bhanthumnavin, D., & Prachonpachanuk, P. (1977). "Morality in Thai youth. Research report", Behavioral Science Research Institute, Srinakharinwirot University, Bangkok, Thailand.

Bhanthumnavin, D., & Vanintananda, N. (1997). *Religious belief and practice of Thai Buddhists: Socialization and quality of life.* Research report. Supported by National Research Council of Thailand.

Bhanthumnavin, Duchduen. (2000). "Importance of supervisory social support and its implications for HRD in Thailand". *Psychology and Developing Societies: A Journal,* **12**(2), 155-166.

Bhanthumnavin, Duchduen. (2001). *Supervisory social support and the multi-level performance in Thai health centers.* Unpublished doctoral dissertation, University of Minnesota, Minnesota, USA.

Bhanthumnavin, Duchduen. (2002). "Psychological and situational antecedents of supervisory social support in Thailand". Presented at the 25th International Congress of Applied Psychology (7-12 July, 2002), Singapore.

Bhanthumnavin, N. (1994). *An analysis of the effectiveness of rice farmers' associations in central Thailand using Contingency Model.* Research report, Office of Extension and Training, Kasetsart University, Bangkok, Thailand.

Black, J.S., & Mendenhall, M. (1990). "Cross-cultural training effectiveness: A review and a theoretical framework for future research". *Academy of Management Review*, **15**(1), 113-136.

Blau, G. (1981). "An empirical investigation of job stress, social support, service length, and job strain". *Organizational Behavior and Human Performance*, **27**, 279-302.

Boonchit, T. (2001). *Relationship between democratic experiences and psycho-behavioral characteristics of Thai school adolescents.* Research report. Supported by the National Committee on the Research and Development of Thai Behavioral System, National Research Council of Thailand.

Brinkerhoff, R.O., & Montesino, M.U. (1995). "Partnerships for training transfer: Lessons from a corporate study". *Human Resource Development Quarterly*, **6**(3), 263-274.

Carlson, D.S., & Perrewe, P.L. (1995). "Institutionalization of organizational ethics through transformational leadership". *Journal of Business Ethics*, **14**, 829-838.

Chaumthong, P. (1993). *Psychological characteristics of leaders and group situation relating to school success.* Doctoral dissertation in Development Education, Srinakharinwirot University (Prasarnmitr), Bangkok, Thailand.

Chemers, M.M. (1969). "Cross-cultural training as a means for improving situational favorableness". *Human Relations*, **22**(3), 531-546.

Chemers, M.M. (1997). *An integrative theory of leadership.* New York: LEA publishers.

Chemers, M.M., Fiedler, F.E., Lekhayananda, D., & Stolurow, L.M. (1966). "Some effects of cultural training on leadership in heterocultural task group." *International Journal of Psychology*, **1**(4), 301-314.

Chemers, M.M., Oskamp, S., & Costanzo, M.A. (Eds). (1995), *Diversity in organizations*: *New perspectives for a changing workplace.* London: Sage

Publication.

Cohen, S., & Wills, T. A. (1985). "Stress, social support, and the buffering hypothesis". *Psychological Bulletin*, **98**(2), 310-357.

Etzion, D., & Westman, M. (1994). "Social support and sense of control as moderators of stress-burnout relationship in military career". *Journal of Social Behavior and Personality*, **9**(4), 639-659.

Fiedler, F.E. (1967). *A theory of leadership effectiveness*. New York: McGraw Hill.

Fiedler, F.E. (1969). "Style or circumstance: The leadership enigma". *Psychology Today*.

Fiedler, F.E. (2002). "The curious role of cognitive resources in leadership". In R.E. Riggio, S.E. Murphy, and F.J. Pirozzolo (Eds.), *Multiple intelligence and leadership* (pp. 91-104). New Jersey: LEA Publishers.

Fiedler, F.E., & Chemers, M.M. (1984). *Improving leadership effectiveness: The leader match concept (2nd ed.)*. New York: John Wiley & Sons.

Fiedler, F.E., & Garcia, J.E. (1987). *New approaches to effective leadership: Cognitive resources and organizational performance*. New York: John Wiley and Sons.

Fiedler, F.E., Mitchell, T., & Triandis, H.C. (1971). "The culture assimilator: An approach to cross-cultural training". *Journal of Applied Psychology*, **55**(1), 95-102.

Goff, S.J., Mount, M.K., & Jamison, R.L. (1990). "Employer support child-care, work-family conflict, and absenteeism: A field study". *Personnel Psychology*, **43**, 793-809.

Greenglass, E.R., Fiksenbaum, L., & Burke, R.J. (1994). "The relationship between social support and burnout overtime in teachers". *Journal of Social Behavior and Personality*, **9**(2), 219-230.

Greogire, T.K., Propp, J., & Poertner, J. (1998). "The supervisor's role in the transfer of training". *Administration in Social Work*, **22**(1), 1-18.

Hofstede, G. (1980). *Culture's consequences: International differences in work-related values*. Beverly Hills, CA: Sage Publication.

Hofstede, G. (1988). "McGregor in Southeast Asia?" In D. Sinha, and H.S.R. Kao (Eds.), *Social values and development: Asian perspectives* (pp. 304-314). London: Sage Publication.

House, J.S. (1981). *Work stress and social support*. Reading, MA: Addison-Wesley.

Iverson, R.D., & Erwin, P.J. (1997). "Predicting occupational injury: The role of affectivity". *Journal of Occupational and Organizational Psychology*, **70**, 113-128.

Juntasorn, K. (1998). *Psycho-social correlates of resistance to Amphetamine usage in secondary schoolers*. Unpublished Master Thesis. School of Social Development, National Institute of Development Administration, Bangkok, Thailand.

Latham, G.P., & Frayne, C.A. (1989). "Self-management training for increasing job attendance: A follow up and a replication". *Journal of Applied Psychology*, **74**(3), 411-416

Leowarin, U. (1991). *Educational and psychological correlates of health behaviors among workers in Bangkok.* Unpublished doctoral dissertation in Development Education. Srinakharinwirot University, Bangkok, Thailand.

Littrell, P.G., Billingsley, B.S., & Cross, L.H. (1994). "The effects of principal support on special and general educators' stress, job satisfaction, school commitment, health, and intent to stay in teaching". *Remedial and Special Education*, **15**(5), 297-310.

Mai-Dalton, R.R. (1993). "Managing cultural diversity on the individual, group, and organizational levels". In M.M. Chemers, & R. Ayman (Eds.), *Leadership theory and research: Perspectives and directions* (pp. 189-216). San Diego, CA: Academic Press.

Major, D.A., Kozlowski, S.W., Chao, G.T., & Gardner, P.D. (1995). "A longitudinal investigation of newcomer expectation, early socialization outcomes, and the moderating effects of role development factors". *Journal of Applied Psychology*, **80**(3), 418-431.

Ma-Oon, R. (2001). *The effect of psycho-behavioral trainings on AIDS prevention behavior of male university students in Thailand.* Research report. Supported by the National Committee on the Research and Development of Thai Behavioral System, National Research Council of Thailand.

Mayfield, J.R., Mayfield, M.R., & Kopf, J. (1998). "The effects of leader motivating language on subordinate performance and satisfaction". *Human Resource Management*, **37**(3&4), 235-248.

McGregor, D. (1960). *The human side of enterprise.* New York: McGraw Hill.

Meekun, K. (2001). *The effect of moral reasoning ability training on teachers' characteristics and behaviors. Research report.* Supported by the National

Committee on the Research and Development of Thai Behavioral System, National Research Council of Thailand.

Nirunthawee, S. (1989). *Alienation and job performance of teachers in Bangkok metropolis.* Unpublished doctoral dissertation in Development Education, Srinakharinwirot University, Bangkok, Thailand.

Pinpradit, N. (2001). *Psychosocial indicators as predictors of polices' work behaviors.* Research report. Supported by the Research and Development of Thai Behavioral System, National Research Council of Thailand.

Punnitamai, W. (1996). "A competency-based model of the Thai new wave leaders: Strategies for identification and development of management talent." *Thai Journal of Psychology,* 3(2), 61-67.

Putti, J.M., Aryee, S., & Liang, T.K. (1989). "Work values and organizational commitment: A study in the Asian context". *Human Relations,* 42(3), 275-288.

Rauktis, M.E., & Koeske, G.E. (1994). "Maintaining social worker morale: When supportive supervision is not enough". *Administration in Social Work,* 18(1), 39-60.

Ronen, S., & Shenkar, O. (1985). "Clustering countries on attitudinal dimensions: A review and synthesis". *Academy of management Review,* 10(3), 435-454.

Saetang, D. (1999). *Conceptualization of transformational and transactional leadership: A cross-cultural study.* Unpublished master's thesis in Psychology, Portland State University, Portland, Oregon, USA.

Sherry, S. (1991). "Person-environment fit and accident prediction". *Journal of Business and Psychology,* 5(3), 411-416.

Sodmanee, O. (1993). *The effect of Psycho-Buddhist training on work effectiveness of Thai teachers.* Unpublished doctoral dissertation in Development Education, Srinakharinwirot University, Bangkok, Thailand

Soonthornvipart, J. (1992). *Important characteristics and leadership effectiveness of department heads in School of Education in Thai universities.* Doctoral dissertation in Educational Administration, Srinakharinwirot University (Prasarnmitr), Bangkok, Thailand.

Soonthornvipart, L. (1989). *Leadership and group characteristics relating to the effectiveness of the Public Agency in Charge of Countering Corruption.* Unpublished Master Thesis. School of Criminology and Criminal Justice, Mahidol University, Bangkok, Thailand.

Sorod, B. (1991). *The influence of national and organizational cultures on managerial values, attitudes, and performance.* Unpublished doctoral dissertation, University of Utah, Utah,

Sorod, B. (2001). *Cross-cultural study of the psychosocial predictors of leadership effectiveness in American and Thai banks.* Research report supported by the National Committee on the Research and Development of the Thai Behavioral System, National Research Council of Thailand, Bangkok, Thailand.

Sorod, B., & Wongwattanamongkol, A. (1996). *A study of job stress of the Thai government executive officers: An analysis of the antecedence and consequence of the stress.* Research report, National Institute of Development Administration, Bangkok, Thailand.

Sukhanon, P. (2001). *Personal and situational correlates of happiness, suicidal ideation, and behavior of high school students.* Unpublished Master Thesis. School of Social Development, National Institute of Development Administration, Bangkok, Thailand.

Sukmanee, B. (1988). *The effect of future orientation and self-control training on work behavior of Thai civil service officials.* Unpublished doctoral dissertation in Development Education, Srinakharinwirot University, Bangkok, Thailand.

Supapol, N. (1990). *Effect of subcultural training on the practicum performance of police cadets in rural Thailand.* Unpublished doctoral dissertation in Development Education, Srinakharinwirot University, Bangkok, Thailand.

Surakitbowon, S. (1989). *Leadership effectiveness of the Deans of Teachers' Colleges.* Unpublished doctoral dissertation in Education Administration, Srinakharinwirot University, Bangkok, Thailand.

Tamawong, S. (2001). *Psycho-social correlates of human right adhering behavior in IPD nurses.* Unpublished Master Thesis. School of Social Development, National Institute of Development Administration, Bangkok, Thailand.

Thacker, J.W., Fiedls, M.W., & Braclay, L.A. (1990). "Union commitment: An examination of antecedent and outcome factors". *Journal of Occupational Psychology*, **63**, 33-48.

The Chinese Culture Connection. (1987). "Chinese values and the search for culture-free dimensions of culture". *Journal of Cross-Cultural Psychology*, **18**(2), 143-164.

Thomas, L.T., & Ganster, D.C. (1992). "Impact of family-support work variable on work-family conflict and strain: A control perspective". *Journal of Applied Psychology*, **80**(1), 6-15.

Tjosvold, D. (1984). "Effects of leader warmth and directiveness on a subsequent task". *Journal of Applied Psychology*, **69**(3), 422-427.

Triandis, H. (1993). "The Contingency Model in cross-cultural perspective". In M.M. Chemers, & R. Ayman (Eds.), *Leadership theory and research: Perspectives and directions* (pp. 167-188). San Diego, CA: Academic Press.

Turner, N., Barling, J., Epitropaki, O., Butcher, V., & Milner, C. (2002). "Transformational leadership and moral reasoning". *Journal of Applied Psychology*, **87**(2), 304-311.

Vanintananda, N. (1993). *Relationship between Buddhist religious characteristics, behavioral science factors of parents and child rearing practices.* Research report number 50, Behavioral Science Research Institute, Srinakharinwirot University, Bangkok, Thailand.

Wannachart, W. (1998). *Psycho-social correlates of AIDS risk behaviors in peer group of male university students in Bangkok.* Unpublished Master Thesis. School of Social Development, National Institute of Development Administration, Bangkok, Thailand.

Wexley, K.N., & Latham, G.P.(2002). *Developing and training human resources in organizations.* New Jersey: Prentice Hall.

Xiaodong, K. (1992). *Effect of social support on job stress and organizational commitment among pharmaceutical scientists.* Doctoral dissertation, Philadelphia College of Pharmacy and Science. Dissertation Abstracts International, **53**(6), 2806B

*Chapter 8*

# Leadership in Indonesia: A Case for Managing Relationship within Organizations

Darwis Suharman Gani
Communication Science and Graduate School,
Sahid University, Indonesia

## Introduction

In the era of globalization it is impossible for a nation to refuse to participate in regional and international cooperation in the fields of science, politics, economy, social affairs, technology, information and culture. Human cooperation in organizations depend on the leadership and the communication management that includes managing relationships among members within the organization.

Indonesia has been known as a multiethnic and multicultural nation, and its 213 million people in 2003, the fourth most populous nation in the world after China, India, and the United States, are spread in 14,000 islands under a warm tropical climate, fertile soils, and the rich and abundant natural resources ( Nirwan Idrus, 2003, Sofia Rangkuti-Hasibuan, 2002, Lee Khoon Choy, 1999 ). It occupies lands of 1.904.549 square kilometers, one third of the entire territory, while the rest are waters. According to Suwarsih Warnaen, (2002), more than 200 ethnic groups are scattered in the island of Indonesia, i.e. 42 ethnic groups in Sumatera, 8 ethnic groups in Java and Madura, 3 ethnic groups in Bali and Lombok, 25 ethnic groups in Kalimantan or Borneo, 37 ethnic groups in Sulawesi or Celebes, and 37 ethnic groups in Papua.

Oppression by colonialists such as the Spanish, the Portuguese, the British, the Dutch and the Japanese, the arrival of their merchants, the missionaries, and other nations i.e. the Arabs, the Indian, the Chinese, and the independence struggle, has caused the Indonesian people according to Koentjaraningrat (1985), Koentjaraningrat (1992), Lee Khoon Choy (1999), Suhartono W. Pranoto (2001), Nirwan Idrus (2003), to have culture and traits. Some of these traits are having no orientation to achievement, escaping from reality and going back to the mystic world, oriented to the past, depending on fate and destiny, being compromisers, being comformists, being well-mannered only to the superior or the ruler, not believing in quality, having a breakthrough or cross cut mentality, confused and uncertain of themselves, undisciplined and likely to neglect responsibilities. The Indonesian culture has all kinds of ethnic aspects consisting of the traditional-agricultural elements (Kwik Kian Gie, 1991), Thomas W. Bratawijaya (1997), the modern industrial parts and the multicultural organization. In their development the elements of the religions also influence the values and cultures of the Indonesians and their ethics (Soerjono Soekanto, 1983, Koentjaraningrat, 2002 ).

The purpose of this paper is to examine how the manager or leader can manage relationships within the organization in the context of the leadership in Indonesia. It will look at what will happen and how the leaders, managers, as well as expatriates face, choose and make decisions to solve their problems. It must be done according to the culture in the multiethnic, multicultural, and multinational organizations or corporations, emphasizing the best relationships within organizations. Hopefully the activities would be useful for leaders, managers or expatriates who come and work in Indonesia.

## Leadership

According to Hardiyanti Rukmana(1990), Thomas W. Bratawijaya (1997), Hans Anlov and Sven Cederroth (2001), the basic leadership in Indonesia are the Eight Behaviour - Hasta Brata, the Leadership Trilogy - Trilogi Kepemimpinan and the Three Obligations - Tri Dharma with the paternalistic and authoritative organization style. James M. Kouzes and Barry Z. Posner (1993), explained that leadership is based on relationships, the heart of leadership is communication, and the heart of organization is communication.

The interesting aspects of changes due to globalization and the era of technology and information to Indonesia are the awareness of employees, who are demanding their rights (Diana Pujiningsih ( 2002). According to Niels Mulder in Hans Antlov and Sven Cederroth (2001), good Indonesian citizens should favour duties rather than rights. New approaches in relationships and also commitment between the leader or manager and the employees, are the making of new industrial relations. These new relations include the return of the employees' rights and giving the change to the leader or manager and the employees to be committed to be partners working together as a team (Johnson Dongoran, 2001). Iman Taufik (2001), believe that in Indonesia, the commitment of the organization to the employees and the employees to the organization - which begin to emerge as a necessity in the arrangement of valuing human dignity and basic human rights - is to have good cooperation and partnership in the management process in the organization or corporation.

In Indonesia, it is difficult to convince the employees that the organization belongs to them - despite the fact that the first couplet of Tri Dharma (The Three Obligations) states "to feel to participate in ownership" or "to have the sense of belonging" (Hardiyanti Rukmana, 1990), (Thomas W. Bratawijaya, 1997) - because they always think and feel that the organization belongs to the management or the ruler. Suhartono W. Pranoto (2001) stated that they must behave as good subordinates, that they are not permitted to make themselves as a partner or feeling that they are part of the management. The employees think that the industrial relations between the employees and the corporate is more than a business contract. It is a personal relationship and the employees involve all of their personality and emotions (Bob Widyahartono, 1999).

As subordinates they appreciate the manager not only as a successful businessman, but he also has to be a protector, a mentor, a father, and must be responsible for them and their extended family (Bob Widyahartono, 1999). For a simple example, there is a tradition for employees in Indonesia go back to their hometowns - mudik - ( Makhfudin Wirya Atmaja, 2003) every year to celebrate religious holidays - such as Idulfitri for Muslims, and Christmas or

New Year for Christians - bringing their families to meet relatives at their hometown and spend the holiday for about two weeks. From the view of the management it is a waste of time, money, and disturbs the work schedule and timetable, but according to the employees it is a tradition of their ethnic cultures and values, which they must hold on to. This habit demonstrates that Indonesians do not value time, are unscrupulous on budget, do not rely on the system and do the jobs for making friends and relationships (Farid Elashmawi, 2002).

The leader in organizations in Indonesia has a role as a father - "wise and honest", and according to Thomas W. Bratawijaya (1997), also as a commander - "firm and brave", a mother - "receiving aspirations for decision making process, a "friend" - closely related, tolerant, willing to have dialogue and discussions, a "knight" - ashamed to carry out corruption, collusion and nepotism, an "educator" - always learning, patient, has objectives, a "priest" - having moral, values and norms, and a "pioneer" - creative, intelligent, a good strategist, besides he or she is benevolent, beneficial, obedient and persistent. The leader, who is described as a knight must be orientated to *Tri Dharma* - the Three Obligations - which consist of behaviors such as sharing, being responsible, and introspective.

In Indonesia several bureaucratic and centralistic organizations, use the basic characteristic of leadership which is called Hasta Brata or Asta Brata (Arifin Abdulrachman,1962), (Selo Soemardjan, 1967), (Soerjono Soekanto, 1990) - Eight Behaviours of Leaders or the Eight Leadership Paths, consisting of the characteristic of the "star" - giving inspiration, the "sun" - honest, motivated and having spirit, "the moon" - having ambition, giving guidance and direction, the "wind" - thrifty, accurate, like working together and having a pleasant atmosphere, the "fire" - strong and determined, the "overcast" - honest, fair and open, the "ocean" - vast and having broad insight, and the "earth" - firm and reliable. There is also the Leadership Trilogy - as explained by Abdurachman Surjomihardjo (1986), Soerjono Soekanto (1990), Hans Antlov and Sven Cederroth (2002) - which consist of being good examples - "the front leader", encouraging motivation and creativity - "the social leader", delegating authorities, developing initiation and having responsibility - "the rear leader".

All of those characteristics are the combination of style, traits and behaviour, emphasizing rationalities without leaving subjectivities, having the power and being equipped with authority, the hierarchy, the status - ascribed, achieved and assigned status -, and the rights (Soejono Soekanto, 1990, Hans Antlov and Sven Cederroth, 2002). Therefore, being a leader in Indonesia is hard. The leaders are reluctant because it is difficult to make decisions and solve problems justly and properly.

The Indonesian people are known as people who like organizations (Hans Antlov and Sven Cederroth, 2002). This describes the characteristics of Indonesians who like family gatherings - as the saying goes "eat or not eat, gather" (Umar Kayam, 1991). They are open, friendly, tolerant and polite (Thomas W. Bratawijaya, 1997, Suwarsih Warnaen, 2002). According to Hans Antlov and Sven Cederroth (2001) and Suwarsih Warnaen (2002), Indonesians have characteristics which could make the organizations work effectively such as being cooperative, having tight family relations, good natured behaviour, being trustworthy and honest.

Indonesia has experienced and accepted organizations with the authoritarian rule and gentle hints (Hans Antlov and Cederroth, 2002), describing the attitude of the people who work for the superior with the spirit of the patron-clientele relations system. Organizations in Indonesia tend to have a centralistic structure with bureaucratic configuration, and a paternalistic and autocratic leadership style (Frans Magnis Suseno, 1993, Thomas Wiyasa Bratawijaya, 1997, Lee Khoon Choy, 1999, Hans Antlov and Sven Cederroth, 2001). It is supported by Fritz Rieger and Durhane Wong-Rieger in Terence Jackson (1995), that Indonesian autocracies have low authority distance or low degree of separation between the superior and the subordinate in the hierarchical structure. It affects the flow of information to the key decision makers and the centralization of decision-making activities. The autocracy with its high power, low group orientation and high intuition, as opposed to analytical and cognitive orientation, describes that the system of the leadership does not work effectively.

## Relationships

The concept of relationships is the real and obvious characteristic of the organizational communication (R. Wayne Pace and Don F. Faules, 1993). According to Gerald M. Goldhaber (1979) the organization is an interdependent relationship network, which means the interdependency affects and influences each other: the organization, the communication and the relationship. Anita Taylor et al. (1977) said that the effective communication is indicated by a good interpersonal relationship and according to Jalaludin Rakhmat (2002) communication distortion causes little damage if there is a good and smooth relationship between the communicants. The most clear, firm, and accurate messages could not prevent failure, if bad relationships occur. G.R. Miller and H.W. Simmons (1976) stated that understanding the interpersonal communication process demands an understanding of the symbiotic relationship between communication and relationship development: communication influences relationship development. In turn, relationship development influences the nature of communication between parties to establish the relationship.

Communication and organization in management science is an art, knowledge, science, and skill, and in several occasions they are called "twins" especially in the process of management functions activities. According to J.W.Carey (1975) and James A.F. Stoner et al (1995) the organization is present not only by the communication, but the communication is in the organization. According to Daniel Katz and Robert L. Kahn (1966), communication is a social affairs process, which has the broadest relevance in activating the function of the group, organization and community, and without communication, decisions can not influence every member of the organization.

The most intimate relationship we share with another person at the individual level, between friends, and of the same age is usually called the personal relationship or interpersonal communication and with them we feel the resonating vibration, and suitable perception, that we feel and care for them (R. Wayne Pace and Don F. Faules, 1993). Positional relationships are determined by the authority structure and functional position of the members of an organization, and as Jay M. Jackson (1959) stated, the communication flow depends on an agreement on the job, authority, pride, and job relationship, and it is important to clear the positional relationship up. The superior and subordinate relationship or top-down relationship - in Indonesia is popular as the patron and clientele or father and son relationship -, is the positional relationship which is the most general and important for the organization to operate (Fredric M. Jablin, 1979).

## Discussion

Indonesia as a multiethnic and multicultural or crosscultural society and nation, faces serious problems in making its multicultures work for the benefit of its people and expatriates. The expatriates bring their own cultures to the organization or multicultural and multinational corporates and the conflict or cultural clash could happen without being noticed. This would be a hindrance to the cooperation and togetherness in work, especially in personal and positional relationships. A lot of characteristics in Indonesian ethnic cultures have positive aspects on supporting the process of modernization, the industrial period and the era of technology and information.

Not valuing and appreciating time is not the monopoly of Indonesians only, some other nations also have the habit, and it gradually becomes a bad habit, such as ignoring the time-table for work or in some cases giving excuses for being late on several occasions. This could give an impact on the activities and the process of management, waste funds and budget, and create undisciplined people. Indonesia has many public holidays. In 2003 there are 13 official holidays, and every year some of the dates change. Besides, Indonesia also has 5 or 6 workdays depending on the firms, corporations and organizations themselves. This situation becomes annoying for planning, since operational and production managers must construct an exact time-table for scheduling work without harming the employees' rights for holidays. It becomes more severe because there is a saying - it is said that it comes from the late Indonesian Vice President Adam Malik - that "everything can be arranged" (Suhartono W.Pranoto, 2001). It reflects the mentality of the "short cut" actions - (Koentjaraningrat, 1985), by avoiding the law, rules, values and norms, provided that in the end they could get what they want without feeling guilty. It also gives chances to establish and create a society with the mentality of Korupsi, Kolusi, Nepotisme (KKN) - Corruption, Collusion, Nepotism.

The organizations in Indonesia are the bureaucratic and autocratic types with the patron-clientele and superior-subordinate leadership styles, and tend to be a centralized structure. Indonesian employees are good people in their jobs but they depend on the leader who must guide, be a father, give attention and advice, give fair rewards, protect and serve them. The important issues are that the knowledge and skill of the leaders is based most on intuition and not the system, which means that the management is rarely realized and understood as a continuous activity. The relationship among the employees is close, but the relationship between the leader or manager and the employees is blocked by the values of hierarchy, position and status.

Among other factors that cause cultural clash and organizational conflict are the differences in values that the managers hold (Herbert J. Davis and S. Anvaar Rasool, 1995). In general, literature on cross-cultural management of multinational firms cites a number of instances where this incongruity has caused expatriate managers to be both perplexed and sometimes paranoid about the outcome of imposing their traditional or home-country management styles upon indigenous personnel (Gellerman, Saul W., 1967, Pezeshkpur, C., 1975, and Badar, Hamed A., Edmund R. Gray and Ben l.Kedia, 1982).

Terence Jackson (1995) stated that increasingly, however, people working in business and management are directly in contact with other cultures. Increasingly, they are in face-to-face contact with foreign managers, colleagues or partners, and misunderstandings could happen, such as what might motivate staff in one country may demotivate staff in another. As a multicultural and multiethnic nation, Indonesia has experiences in managing across cultures and cross-cultural behaviour - including leadership styles, how to manage the cultural differences, to design the organization which will fit the multiethnic management styles and to motivate the employees working in different culture organizations. The cultures of some ethnics seem to be more difficult to adapt to than do the cultures of other ethnics, as do the cultures of some countries.

I. Torbiorn (1982) found that expatriates expressed high levels of dissatisfaction in their overseas assignment for Indonesia - as a part of Southeast Asia - in the areas of job satisfaction, levels of stress and pressure, health care, housing standards, entertainment, food, and skill of co-workers, and greater cultural barriers were reported for Indonesia than for other world regions. The Indonesian human resource described by the DGHE (2003) is low productivity, low creativity, bureaucratic mentality, low competitiveness, not self starter, and low self confidence, with the quality of : 40% below the poverty line, 70% elementary school graduates only, and 1.25% university graduates with 14% in technology, 19% in other sciences and 67% in social sciences.

To interact effectively between people of two cultures there are two factors which should be possessed, namely the relationship development and willingness to communicate. M.R. Hammer et al.(1978) reported :

> Sojourners who are able to establish meaningful relationships with people from the host culture are more likely, it would appear, to integrate themselves into the social fabric of the host culture and to more effectively satisfy their own basic needs and concern of friendship, intimacy, and social interaction.

In Indonesia, the Bahasa Indonesia - Indonesian language - is one of the best to be bestowed upon Indonesians, which could make communication activities - including relationships -, among all ethnic groups done effectively. It comes from the Melayu ethnic, a small ethnic group in Sumatera and the Riau islands and does not come from the Javanese ethnic group which forms about 49% of the population of Indonesia. The language is one of the most important and necessary tools to be used as a means to create and foster interpersonal relationship, such as by using it in conversation to show other ethnic groups that they were "one-of-the-guys": anecdotes, jokes, poems, proverbs, talking about movie and sports stars, history and statistics, and so on (M. Brein and K.H. David, 1976, H. Abe and R.L. Weisman, 1983). M.R. Hammer et al.(1978) found that the ability to communicate with other ethnics is important to cross-cultural adjustment and R.T. Major, Jr. (1965) reported that willingness to use the other ethnic language had a greater influence on successful adjustment than did actual level of fluency in the foreign language, and made the relationship become more intimate.

Personal characteristic, according to Terence Jackson (1995) is one of the factors associated with the performance of who likes to be accepted and appreciated by other ethnics, which contain the technical ability, stress tolerance, flexibility, communication skills, and cultural empathy. Generally, Indonesian employees could and would counterbalance expatriates who have those performances, because - as Suwarsih Warnaen(2002) stated - the Indonesian has unique characteristics, such as diligence, intelligence and science to support the ability of technical aspects. For stress tolerance, Indonesians are good natured, cheerful by nature, calm, religious, and have tight family relations, which would be the stronghold for preventing the influence and effect of the stress, supported by rukun - the basic principle of harmonious life - by avoiding the conflicts (Franz M. Suseno, 1993).

The aspects of flexibility are indicated by the characteristics such as enjoying gatherings, being open, artistic, humourous, and practical, while communication skills are indicated by being honest, trustworthy, good in relationships, polite, orderly, pleased to give, and have warm hospitality, and as Franz M. Suseno(1993) stated also by respect, one of the two basic principles of life - rukun - "in harmony" and hormat -"respect" -, realizing that the relationships between people in the society is arranged by the hierarchy and is closely attached to everyone. The cultural empathy for Indonesians leans on tepa selira, the understanding for other people's feeling (Thomas W. Bratawijaya, 1997), and the ability to understand why other ethnics behave the way they do and the importance in adjusting to a new cultural environment in the organization (Terence Jackson, 1995).

Another problem in the process of relationships in Indonesia, which often makes one confused, even bewildered, is that whenever an Indonesian says "yes", he means he has heard what you said. "Yes" does not mean he agrees with your views - or questions, remarks, orders, and requests (Lee Khoon Choy, 1999). Especially with the traditional attitude of reluctance, as Hildred Geertz (1961) stated also the attitudes of fear, shame and unwillingness, which have been learned since childhood, all describe why the Indonesian is so slow in answering "yes" for having heard and agreed spontaneously and simultaneously. It is hard to interpret the "yes" from the Indonesian, whether the answer is "yes for truly yes", "yes for no", "yes for yes or no". Especially along with the unique characteristics of Indonesian politeness and friendliness (Suwarsih Warnaen, 2002), which is often accompanied by a radiant smile all over the face and alas, presumably the answer is always "yes" or "no" ?

## Conclusion

In Indonesia relationships within organizations should be managed carefully by a harmonious leadership style, especially in multiethnic, multicultural and multinational organizations or corporations, avoiding cultural clashes or ethnic conflicts that causefailure to achieve the organizations' objectives. Relationships are important to Indonesians and in some cases are not properly executed, such as doing it at/with a wrong time, occasion, person, culture, and ethnic. Managing relationships in Indonesia must be done by TEAM - **T**rust, **E**go Identity, **A**ction Skill, and **M**ethod and as a leader, the manager must hold on to the core of leadership: Identity, Information, and Relationships (Hesselbein, F., M. Goldsmith and R. Beckhard, 1998). For Suwarsih Warnaen(2002) their "sensitivity" and "trustworthiness", and Franz M. Suseno (1993) emphasized that the "in harmony" and "respect" of the Indonesians are a unique attitude and behaviour which could support the process of interpersonal relationships, communication and relationships within the organization.

## Reference

Abdurrachman Surjomihardjo (1986). *Ki Hajar Dewantara dan Taman Siswa Dalam Sejarah Indonesia Modern.* Jakarta : Penerbit Sinar Harapan.

Abe, H. and R.L. Weisman (1983). *A Cross-cultural Confirmation of the Dimensions of International Effectiveness.* International Journal of Intercultural Relations,7, 53-68.

Alois A. Nugroho dan Ati Cahayani (2003). *Multikulturisme DalamBisnis.* Jakarta : PT Gramedia Widiasarana Indonesia.

Antlov, Hans and Sven Cederroth. Editors. (2001). *Leadership on Java: Gentle Hints, Authoritarian Rule.* Translator: P.Soemitro, Jakarta : Yayasan Obor Indonesia.

Arief Budiman (1987. "Kebudayaan Kekuasaan atau Sosiologi Kekuasaan." *PRISMA*, No. 3 Tahun XVI, Maret 1987, 61-72.

Arifin Abdulrachman (1962). *Asta Brata Dalam Rangka Manajemen.* Jakarta : Lembaga Administrasi.

Badar, Hamed A., Edmund R. Gray and Ben L. Kedia (1982). "Personal Values and Managerial Decision Making : Evidence from Two Cultures". *Management National Review*, **22**, 3, 65-73.

Bob Widyahartono (1999). "Mengagas Manajemen ala Indonesia". *Majalah Master* **01**, Tahun 1, Agustus 1999, Jakarta.

Buddy Prasadja (1986). *Pembangunan Desa dan Masalah Kepemimpinannya.* Jakarta : CV Rajawali.

Carey, J.W. (1975). "A Cultural Approach to Communication". *Communication*, **2**, 1 - 21.

David, Fred R. (1997). *Strategic Management.* Upper Saddle River, N.J. : Prentice-Hall, Inc.

Davis, Herbert J. and S. Anvaar Rasool in Terence Jackson. Ed.(1995) *Values Research and Managerial Behavior: Implications for Devising Culturally Consistent Managerial Styles.* Oxford : Butterworth-Heinemann Ltd.

Devito, Joseph A.(1986). *The Communication Handbook.* New York : Harper & Row.

Diana Pujiningsih (2002). "Pembangunan Hukum di Indonesia : Cita-cita, Tuntutan dan Tantangan". *Jurnal Penelitian Hukum,* **4**, 253-270.

Directorat General of Higher Education - DGHE (2003). *DGHE Policy on Higher Professional Education in Indonesia.* Paper for OneDay Seminar HBO-Raad and CINCOP. Jakarta.

Farid Elashmawi (2002). "Saya lebih Percaya pada Multiculture". *Manajemen.* No. 161. 32-35.

Fasli Jalal dan Bachrudin Musthafa (2001).Editors. *Education Reform.* Jakarta : The Ministry of National Education and the World Bank.

Frans Magnis-Suseno (1993). *Etika Jawa.* Jakarta : PT Gramedia Pustaka Utama.

Geertz, Hilderd (1961). *The Javanese Fasmily. A Study of Kinship and Socialization.* The Free Press of Glencoe.

Gellerman, Saul W.(1967). "Passivity, Paranoia and Pakikisama." *Columbia Journal of World Business.* **9**,10. 59-66.

Goldhaber, Gerald M. (1979). *Organizational Communication.* Dubu que, Iowa : Wm.C. Brown.

Goffee, Rob and Gareth Jones (1998). *The Character of A Corporation.* London : Harper Collins Business.

Hammer, M.R. et.al (1978). "Dimensions of intercultural effectiveness : An exploratory study." *International Journal of Intercultural Relations.* **1**, 99-110.

Hardiyanti Rukmana (1990). *Butir-butir Budaya Jawa.* Jakarta : Yayasan Purna Bhakti Pertiwi.

Hesselbein, F., M. Goldsmith and R. Beckhard (1998). Editors. *The Organization of the Future.* Translator : Achmad Kemal. Jakarta : PT Elex Media Kompetindo.

Hofstede, G. (1991). *Cultures and Organizations : Software of the Mind.* London : McGraw Hill.

Iman Taufik (2001). "Kita harus Kompetitif secara Global." *Transformasi.* Vol.2.No.1,38-41,62.

Jablin, Fredric (1979). "Superior-subordinate Communication : The State of the Art." *Psychological Bulletin*, **86**, 1201-1222.

Jablin, Fredric M. et al. (1987), Editors. *Handbook of Organizational Communication.* London : Sage Publication.

Jackson, Jay M (1959). "The Organization and Its Communication Problem." *Advanced Management*, **2**, 17-20.

Jackson, Terence (1995). Editor. *Cross - Cultural Management.* Oxford : Butterworth-Heinemann Ltd.

Jalaluddin Rakhmat (2002). *Psikologi Komunikasi.* Bandung : PT Pustaka Remaja Rosdakarya.

Johnson Dongoran (2001). "Komitmen Organisasi : Dua Sisi Sebuah Koin." Dian Ekonomi , *Jurnal Ekonomi dan Bisnis*, VII, No. 1, Maret 2001, 35-56.

Katz, Daniel and Robert L. Kahn (1966). *The social Psychology of Organization.* New York : McGraw-Hill.

Kouzes, James M. and Barry Z. Posner (1993). *Credibility.* San Francisco : Josey-Bass Publishers.

Kouzes, James M. and Barry Z. Posner (1997). *The Leadership Challenge.* San Francisco : Jossey-Bass Publishers.

Koentjaraningrat (1985). *Persepsi Tentang Kebudayaan Nasional.* Jakarta : PT Gramedia.

Koentjaraningrat (1992). *Kebudayaan, Mentalitas dan Pembangunan.* Jakarta : PT Gramedia Pustaka Utama.

Koentjaraningrat (1993). *Masalah Kesukubangsaan dan Integrasi Nasional.* Jakarta : Penerbir UI.

Koentjaraningrat (2002). *Manusia dan Kebudayaan di Indonesia.* Jakarta : Penerbit Djambatan.

Kuntowijoyo (1994). *Demokrasi & Budaya Birokrasi.* Yogyakarta : Bentang Budaya.

Lee Khoon Choy (1999). *A Fragile Nation - The Indonesian Crisis.* Singapore : World Scientific Publishing Co. Pte. Ltd.

Major, R.T., Jr. (1965). *A Review of Research on International Exchange.* Unpublished manuscript. The Experiment on International Living, Putney, VT.

Makhfudin Wirya Atmaja (2003). "Mudik : Perjalanan Spiritual untuk Intraspeksi." *Manajemen*, No. 173, 48-50.

Maurits Simatupang (2002). *Budaya Indonesia yang Supraetnis.* Jakarta : Papas Sinar Sinanti.

McVey, Ruth T. (1967). *(Ed.) Indonesia.* New Haven, Conn. : Human Relations Area Files.

Miller, G.R. and H.W. Simmons (1976). *Explorations in Interpersonal Communication.* Beverly Hills : Sage Publications

Muhadjir Effendy (2002). *Masyarakat Equilibrium.* Yogyakarta : Ben-tang Budaya.

Nirwan Idrus (2003). *Indonesia - A Blueprint for Strategic Survival.* Jakarta : Centre for strategic and International Studies.

Ong Hok Ham (2002). *Dari Soal Priyayi sampai Nyi Blorong.* Jakarta: Buku Kompas.

Pace, R. Wayne and Don F. Faules (2000). *Komunikasi Organisasi -Strategi Meningkatkan Kinerja Perusahaan. Editor/ Translator : Deddy Mulyana.* Bandung : PT Remaja Rosdakarya.

Pezeshkpur, C. (1975). *The Effects of Personal Value Structure on Decision Making : A Study of Relationship between Values and Decisions of University Business Administration Students.* Unpublished Ph.D. Dissertation, Louisiana State University.

Rieger, Fritz and Durhane Wong-Rieger in Terence Jackson. Ed. (1995*). Model Building in Organizational/cross Cultural Research : The Need for Multiple Methods,Indices and Cultures.* Oxford : Butterworth-Heinemann Ltd.

Robbins, Stephen P. (1990). *Organization Theory: StructureDesigns and Applications.* Englewood Cliffs, N.J.: Prentice-Hall, Inc.

Rukmana Handiyanti (1990). *Butir-Butir Budaya Jawa.*Jakarta :Yaya-san Purna Bhakti Pertiwi.

Samodra Wibawa (2001). *Negara-Negara di Nusantara.* Yogyakarta : Gadjah Mada University Press.

Selo Sumardjan (1967). *Pola-pola Kepemimpinan dalam Pemerintahan.* Jakarta : Lembaga Pertahanan Nasional.

Soerjono Soekanto (1983). *Beberapa Teori Sosiologi tentang Struktur Masyarakat.* Jakarta : CV Rajawali.

Sofia Rangkuti-Hasibuan (2002). *Manusia dan Kebudayaan Indo̲nesia. Teori dan Konsep.* Jakarta : Dian Rakyat.

Stoner, James A.F., R. Edward Freeman and Daniel R. Gilbert, Jr. (1995). *Management.* Englewood Cliffs, N.J.: Prentice-Hall, Inc.

Suhartono W. Pranoto (2001). *Serpihan Budaya Feodal.* Yogyakarta : Agastya Media.

Sukamdani S. Gitosardjono (1999). *Wawasan, Pandangan dan Harapan tentang Pendidikan.* Jakarta : Harian Ekonomi Bisnis Indonesia.

Suwarsih Warnaen (2002). *Stereotip Etnis dalam Masyarakat Multietnis.* Yogyakarta : Matabangsa.

Tardjan Hadidjaja dan Kamajaya (1978). *Serat Centhini.* Yogya : U.P. Indonesia.

Taylor, Anita (1977). *Communicating.* Eaglewood Cliffs, N.J. : Pren-tice-Hall,Inc.

Thomas Wiyasa Bratawijaya (1997). *Mengungkap dan Mengenal Bu-daya Jawa.* Jakarta : PT Pradnya Paramita

Torbiorn, I. (1982). *Living abroad : Personal Adjusment and Personal Policy in the Overseas Setting.* New York : Willey.

Umar Kayam (1987). "Keselarasan dan Kebersamaan : Suatu Penjelajahan Awal." *Prisma* No. 3, Tahun XVI, Maret 1987, 18-32.

Umar Kayam (1991). *Mangan Ora Mangan Kumpul.* Jakarta : PT Temprint.

*Chapter 9*

# Culturally Sensitive Leadership in the

# Philippine Setting

Benito L. Teehankee
Graduate School of Business, De La Salle University
Manila, Philippines

The increasing globalization of business has put more managers in cross-cultural leadership situations. In the Philippines, expatriate executives with no prior management experience in the country are put in positions which make them responsible for the performance of hundreds of Filipinos. To a Western executive, managing in the Philippines appears to be a familiar experience at first glance. The country is known for its wide use of English, having been occupied by the Americans for almost 50 years before the second world war. The educational system has been largely patterned after the American system, and most college students studied using reprinted American textbooks. Mass media -- including television, movies and newspapers – are replete with American material. Given this backdrop, the Western manager could understandably assume that Filipinos think and work like Americans; and can thus be led like Americans. Is this a reasonable assumption? Or will this lead to crossed expectations and disappointments for the Western manager? This chapter attempts to shed light on these general questions by drawing on the work of social scientists and management writers who have analyzed how Filipinos think and behave.

In particular, the chapter focuses on the following questions:

1.  What are some characteristics of the value structure of the Filipino and how does it differ from Westerners?
2.  How does the Filipino's value structure relate with how he or she carries out work in an organization and how can managers lead given such a value structure?

This chapter is, therefore, addressed to managers who need to appreciate the nuances of Filipino culture in order to bring out the best among the Filipinos they work with.


## A Conception of Leadership

The conceptions of leadership, which have been developed by theorists and researchers, are too many to summarize here.   Nevertheless, it would be a useful preliminary to clarify the conceptual perspective of leadership that this chapter takes.   Leadership here refers to the acts of a manager intended to induce willing commitment and initiative from subordinates towards the accomplishment of important organizational goals.   Clearly, the emphasis of leadership goes beyond achieving mere compliance from people.   Moreover, the consistent application of appropriate leadership by managers enables an organization to achieve ever-increasing levels of performance and a general sense of excellence among all its members.


## Recognizing the Importance of National Culture in Organizational Leadership

The experience of Filipinos under almost 400 years of Spanish colonization and subsequent American occupation has influenced their thoughts and attitudes about work, relationships and organizations.   The result is a way of thinking, which combines deeply held Filipino values (often with a regional flavor) with

Spanish-inspired practices and overlaid with American-influenced education. The manager who leads in a Filipino setting needs to understand this delicate interplay of influences on the Filipino worker's psyche.

Much of the popular literature on organizational leadership and motivation are Western in origin. In fact, a Filipino textbook on organizational behavior (Martires, 1992) described close to a dozen leadership theories and models from McGregor to Bennis while mentioning only one Filipino author, Lupdag (1984), as having attempted to empirically develop a Filipino conception of leadership. Despite the prodigious output of Western authors in leadership model building, the pioneering work of Geert Hofstede (1983) has shown that such theories must be applied with caution in non-Western settings and always in a way that takes into account the national culture of the people involved. In support of his contention, Hofstede performed an international survey covering 50 countries that served to profile national cultures along the four dimensions of power distance, uncertainty avoidance, individualism and masculinity.

Hofstede's findings provide a comparison of the Philippines with a few selected Western countries.

**Table 1:  Profile of Philippine National Culture versus Selected Western Countries**

| National Culture Dimension | | | | |
|---|---|---|---|---|
| **Country** | Power distance | Uncertainty avoidance | Individualism | Masculinity |
| Philippines | High | Low | Low | High |
| United States | Low | Low | High | High |
| Canada | Low | Low | High | High |
| Great Britain | Low | Low | High | High |
| Germany | Low | High | High | High |

Source:  Hofstede (1983)

As Table 1 shows, the Philippines can be characterized as high in power distance and masculinity while being low in uncertainty avoidance and individualism. The Philippines shares similarly low uncertainty avoidance and high masculinity ratings with the United States, Great Britain and Canada. Managers from these countries would, therefore, feel right at home with the

Filipino's relative openness to ambiguous situations and interest in material success.[1]

The differences are more instructive, however. In contrast to the Philippines, these three countries have lower power distance and higher individualism. With respect to power distance, managers coming from these three countries need to adjust to the greater acceptance of hierarchy among Filipinos. For example, Filipinos find it surprising that American executives expect to be called by their first names. Most Filipinos will take a while to adjust to this practice since they are accustomed to addressing seniors as "Sir" or "Ma'am". As far as individualism is concerned, Filipinos are known to be quite collectivist in orientation, often showing partiality and care for members of the family (both nuclear and extended) and the in-group of friends (called the "barkada") over organizational goals.

Another contrast can be noted with respect to Germany. German managers, by virtue of their country's higher uncertainty avoidance rating, may find the Filipino indifference about rules quite unsettling. For example, the mere issuance of a policy memorandum by a manager would not carry too great a weight among Filipinos if unsupported by other leadership strategies, such as collective consultation and a clear explanation of the policy's benefits to the individual. In fact, even the existence of long-standing rules does not prevent Filipinos from considering themselves justifiably "exempted" from such rules because of personal exigencies.[2] For example, Westerners driving in Manila will immediately notice the flagrantly selective observance of traffic rules.

The need for Westerners to better understand Filipino culture in support of their leadership goals is affirmed by Filipino social scientists. Jocano (1990), a noted Filipino anthropologist, put it this way:

> ...many expatriates find it difficult to sustain good interpersonal relationships with their Filipino managers, employees and workers. Even their social interactions with Filipinos outside of business are often fraught

---

[1] The low relative importance supposedly given by Filipinos to relationships versus material success implied by the high masculinity rating is not borne out by local social science research. In fact, Filipinos value smooth interpersonal relations very highly.

[2] Gonzalez (1987) thinks that this tendency is a carry-over from Filipino colonial experience, when colonial authorities would create rules that would be broken when expedient.

*with miscommunication, misunderstanding and frustration.    ...only a few foreigners seem to have transcended the cultural barriers and are able to interact with Filipinos without much difficulties.   These few are the ones who ... go out of their way to learn the nuances of the local culture, including the language.  They are also the most successful businessmen who enjoy their stay in the country.  (p. 10)*

Jocano saw the potential conflict between workers and managers schooled in Western leadership approaches (whether expatriate or Filipino) along three dimensions, namely (1) objectivity – subjectivity, (2) self-reliance – reciprocity and (3) individuality – collectivity.    Figure 1 depicts the dimensions and their polarities.

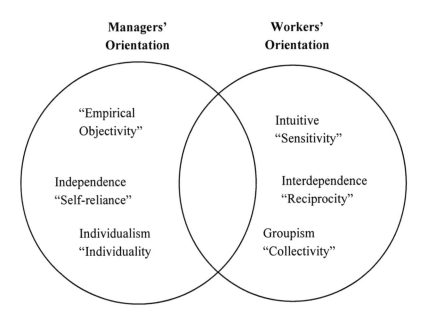

**Figure 1:  Diagram showing the contrasts in orientation of Western-educated managers and Filipino workers Source: Jocano (1990, p. 10)**

Jocano's empirical objectivity and individualism dimensions may be related to Hofstede's uncertainty avoidance and individualism dimensions, respectively. It must be pointed out, however, that Hoftstede was referring to inter-cultural dimensions (i.e., dimensions on which national cultures can be compared) while Jocano is referring to intra-cultural dimensions (i.e., dimensions on which subcultures within the Philippines may be compared such as that of managers vs. subordinates).    High uncertainty avoidance cultures favor clear rules and demand compliance to these rules, irrespective of personal circumstance.    Similarly, Jocano's schema shows that Western-educated managers favor objectivity and facts as a basis for decision-making and action. In contrast, Filipino subordinates tend to value their subjective experience and personal circumstances as a basis for decision-making.    For example, while Filipino workers would agree with the importance of minimizing absenteeism in fairness to the company, they would fully expect that their own absenteeism, when caused by domestic or other personal emergencies, would be understood by the manager.

Jocano's self reliance-reciprocity dimension is related to but conceptually distinct from Hofstede's individualism-collectivism dimension.  Reciprocity, in particular, highlights the Filipino concern for interdependence or being part of a network of social obligations characterized by debts of gratitude ("utang na loob").    This goes beyond being part of a group.  It focuses on the mutual obligations that arise because one has received help from another member of a group.  For example, a Western manager may expect Filipino Worker A to voice out a concern about a flaw in a colleague's (Worker B) presentation during a meeting.    Worker A may hesitate to do so because Worker B may have also refrained from publicly pointing out a flaw in Worker A's presentation – although Worker B may have pointed this out in private.  Thus, what might appear to the manager as collusive behavior which condones mediocre performance may be simply "looking out for each other" in the eyes of the workers.    It is also important to note that such reciprocal obligations are not easily extinguished by returning favors.  They tend to persist in time for the individuals involved.

In practical terms, the challenge for the leader is to find the common ground represented by the overlap of the circles in Figure 1 and not to simply insist on the "one right way" of doing things from the manager's perspective.    This means that a manager will need to be concerned with both the objective facts of a situation as well as the subjective world of subordinates. For example, a Filipino may object to the hiring of a new employee but not be able to provide solid justification when pressed by the manager. Later developments may show the basis for the objections to the hiring decision such as the poor fit with the team or related issues. Thus, in such cases, the manager would do well to take subjective concerns into account even as facts are being gathered to support a final decision.

The need to reconcile apparent dilemmas and contradictions is a recurrent theme in Philippine leadership situations and could be an example of the "low uncertainty avoidance" phenomenon noted by Hofstede (1983). As a result, managers would do well to exercise flexibility and adaptability when dealing with Filipinos, a practice called "pakikibagay", without necessarily losing sight of organizational imperatives.

Flexibility and adaptability based on sensitivity to the needs of a situation will be appreciated in a manager because Filipinos pride themselves as having these same traits. Jocano (1990) explained that:

> *Some ... have described Filipino sensitivity as a weakness. But ... this trait is also the major source of Filipino psychological strength. It makes them flexible. ... They have endured centuries of colonization without psychological breakdowns ... They were able to modify much of the colonial influences to suit their traditional ways of thinking, believing, and acting (pp. 28-29).*

## Filipino Value Orientations and Their Implications for Managerial Leadership

The previous discussions broadly outlined key dimensions where Filipinos differ in value orientations as compared to Westerners. This section delves into these and related specific value orientations in more detail.

Filipino values have been analyzed by both foreign and local social scientists. Some of the early work was done by Americans (Lynch 1981; Hollnsteiner, 1981) and have been refined by Filipino social scientists. These findings have served as basic knowledge regarding how Filipinos think and behave. We will discuss clusters of related value orientations below with their implications for effective managerial leadership.

*Social Acceptance and Smooth Interpersonal Relations*

Frank Lynch (1981), an American Jesuit and social scientist, codified Filipino values extensively and his analysis still holds considerable weight today. He argued that "social acceptance, economic security and social mobility ... are basic aims that motivate and control an immense amount of Filipino behavior" (p. 111). Lynch further argued that these aims and basic values are in order of importance, with social acceptance being the most important of all.

In clarifying the concept of social acceptance, Lynch referred to the situation where a Filipino "is taken by [his] fellows for what he is, or believes he is, and is treated in accordance with his status" (p. 111). Furthermore, and perhaps more importantly, social acceptance exists when "one is not rejected or improperly criticized by others" (p. 111). In support of this point, Guthrie (1981) uses the important Filipino concept of "amor propio" or self-esteem: "... the need of the Filipino to be treated as a person, not as an object." Because of this need, the Filipino guards against losing face ("kahihiyan") as much as possible.

The need for social acceptance among Filipinos gives rise to a related concern for smooth interpersonal relations (SIR). Lynch (1981) explained SIR and the related practice of "pakikisama" or "getting along" in these terms:

*SIR or smooth interpersonal relations may be defined as a facility at getting along with others in a way as to avoid outward signs of conflict: glum or sour looks, harsh words, open disagreement, or physical violence. ... It means being agreeable, even under difficult circumstances, and of keeping quiet or out of sight when discretion passes the word. It means sensitivity to what other people feel at any given moment, and a willingness and ability to change tack to catch the lightest favoring breeze.*

*...Pakikisama ... means "giving in", "following the lead or suggestion of another"; in a word, concession ... especially to the lauded practice of yielding to the will of the leader or majority so as to make the group decision unanimous. [This often requires the practice of ] euphemism... the stating of an unpleasant truth, opinion, or request as pleasantly as possible... (p. 112-113).*

SIR has been noted in other Asian countries like Thailand (Komin, 1999) and has been traced to training in kinship relations during formative years. Filipinos are encouraged to learn to "get along" with relatives in order to cultivate long-term goodwill and cooperation. Such a psychological investment can yield valuable support from kinsmen in the future (Jocano, 1990). This perspective tends to transfer naturally to the work setting, where workmates can be seen as members of a new "family" of in-group members whose cooperation is very important for getting things done.

Martires (1992) synthesized this particular social orientation of Filipinos:

> ... the Filipino has retained the basic values and institutions which existed in pre-Spanish setting. ... His Eastern moral and social conscience continue to prevail. He strives very much for economic and social mobility but insists on attaining this with dignity and fair play. He wants to go up financially but in a setting where smooth interpersonal relationship prevails, and he is treated as a human being and not a machine. He wants to work with a superior who is friendly, just, fair, understanding, good, kind and considerate (p. 50).

The value for self-esteem and smooth relations among Filipinos has important implications for managerial leadership.

1. An important requirement for any manager to be perceived as a good leader by a Filipino is to be have genuine regard for a worker. Filipinos look for caring leaders. By this we mean managers who will make time to interact with subordinates, listen and understand their concerns, and value their contribution to the organization, especially by consulting the worker on matters where he or she is knowledgeable. Interestingly, the "caring" can also be shown in less formal ways such as birthday greetings, small gifts from trips (called "pasalubongs") or treats. Managers who are more comfortable with arms-length relationships may find these behaviors dangerous invitations to very personal and unproductive relationships with subordinates and in fact this can be the result. The manager, however, can remain faithful to professional objectives for peak performance while acknowledging the human needs of subordinates. The aspirations of the organization can be better communicated through the improved relations that a caring approach usually brings about.

2.  Giving critical or corrective feedback to a subordinate is best done in private. This will not only be considered a sign of sensitivity on the part of the manager but also make the feedback more acceptable. A highly confrontational approach would be ineffective in gaining commitment to performance – although it could achieve surface compliance. In the worst case, it would engender resentment towards the manager which would be difficult to heal. A public loss of face is considered a major indignity.

3.  Praise for performance should be generally targeted at groups. Affirmation of an individual's performance can be done in public but with care to avoid making someone else suffer by comparison since this other party will lose face as a result. This situation can lead to strain between the affirmed person and the one who loses face. Even worse, it can alienate the performer's work group, who may have contributed substantially to the achievement being recognized.

4.  The manager needs to establish the workgroup as a large in-group where mutual acceptance and positive regard among co-workers is achieved. On the surface, this is very similar to standard teambuilding strategies with concrete productivity objectives. For Filipinos, however, the development of smooth relations in the workplace can tap into a deep cultural vein, which can release a deeper form of commitment with productivity only as a by-product. Specific strategies for establishing an in-group sentiment is related to the next value orientation to be discussed – the mingling of work and leisure.

### Work and Leisure

While "duty before pleasure" is an often quoted Western slogan, the tendency to harmonize work with leisure has been noted by social scientists among Filipinos (Mercado,1981). Filipinos do not see work as separate from fun. Work is closely tied up with other social practices and the climatic conditions in the country. Rural folk, for example, traditionally made hard farm work under the sun more bearable by combining it with singing, drinking and eating. This phenomenon is less pronounced in the urban centers but is still fairly noticeable. Office workers derive much satisfaction from office camaraderie and every birthday occasion is marked by merriment and the expected treat or "blowout" by the celebrant.    This does not mean that Filipinos do not consider work a serious matter.    They simply do not consider it separate from their social needs.    Western observers found the festive atmosphere during the EDSA People Power II street protests, which led to the ouster of former president Estrada, difficult to comprehend.    To those who participated in the protests, the matter was grimly serious, but the merriment and entertainment reinforced the group's solidarity and made the long hot waits more tolerable.

What are some implications in these examples for managerial leadership? Managers can enhance their leadership effectiveness by tapping into the Filipino penchant for a festive atmosphere, at least when occasions allow for it. Some examples:

1.   A work group's progress towards tough milestones, for example, can be marked by small celebrations with light snacks.    This sends a message of appreciation and by allowing pause to collectively rejoice in progress, the group strengthens its commitment for the next milestone.
2.   New members to the work group can be welcomed with some ritual fanfare by an assigned or volunteer group of old members.    Such an "icebreaker" reduces the tensions that normally accompany the entry experience for a new employee.    It also shows regard to the original members who feel that they are welcoming the new member to their "family".

*Professionalism with Personalism*

Filipinos are collectivists by nature.    In fact, most of their aspirations and interests are significantly affected by their group memberships, namely in the family, the extended family or kin and in the in-group of close friends ("barkada").    Because of such group loyalties, it can be a challenge to develop loyalty for an organization as a whole, and in fact, this should not be assumed to automatically arise among members of an organization.    One mistake that can be made is to insist that purely professional concerns – meaning organizational and not family or in-group concerns -- dominate a worker's priorities.    It must be realized that a Filipino's very identity and sense of meaning is significantly tied to his group membership.    To ask him to ignore this membership is to ask him to give up his identity.  It would be wiser to link the interests of the organization with the interests of the family and in-group.

As professionals, Filipinos are generally committed to the improvement of services for all organizational clients.   Cultural norms, however, specify a simultaneous preferential consideration for in-group and family members (Hollnsteiner, 1981).  The challenge to contemporary management leadership, therefore, is not only to integrate each unit objective into a unified corporate goal, as argued by orthodox management theory, but also to link such goals to personal and group goals and sentiments (Jocano, 1990).

To the Filipino, the professional and the personal cannot be completely separated.  Aquino (1988) narrates events surrounding a major reorganization of the market research department in a steel company.  The department was transferred into the marketing department and renamed as the market services unit.  The new unit's function was limited to providing research services to marketing for the weekly reports to top management.  This was a major change from its previous function of conducting long term studies with strategic importance for the whole company.   The resulting loss of status among members of the unit led to demoralization and the eventual resignation of staff members.   Aside from the perceived "demotion" among the unit's members, the work had become routine and regimented.  This arrangement no longer met the need for creative work of the unit members.  This change effort made sense from a task structure point of view but failed to consider personal sentiments. The result was lost productivity and staff expertise due to resignations.

Some implications for managerial leadership are the following:

1.  Managers need to spend time getting to know the personal backgrounds and aspirations of subordinates, at least in the areas which the subordinate is willing to disclose.   For example, married Filipinos take pride in the accomplishments of their children as well as the efforts they make as parents to do well for their children.   Occasionally discussing family concerns can give valuable clues to a manager on the motivations of the Filipino worker.  This empathetic practice is already gaining recognition as an effective management practice even in the West (Goleman, 1995).

2.  Policies and working conditions need to be reviewed in terms of its sensitivity to the needs of employees and their families.   This is akin to

the recent trend in "family-friendly" companies in the United States because of the growing need to retain talent in a competitive job market (Levering and Moskowitz, 2001). While a fairly recent Western phenomenon, this personalistic concern for employee welfare has been appreciated by Filipinos all along.


## Preparing to Manage in the Philippines

Jocano (1999) reports a study conducted with a multinational microprocessor manufacturing company based in Metro Manila. The study sought to discover, among other things, managerial traits that are liked ("nagugustuhan") and disliked ("hindi nagugustuhan") by Filipino workers. The traits identified by 250 respondents of the study are shown in the tables below listed in vernacular Filipino with rough translations in parentheses.

**Table 2: Traits of managers that are liked ("nagugustuhan") by Filipino workers (Jocano, 1999: 127)**

| TRAITS | NO. OF RESPONSES | % |
|---|---|---|
| Mabait (kind) | 125 | 50% |
| Madaling lapitan (approachable) | 119 | 47.6% |
| Matulungin (helpful) | 110 | 44% |
| Maunawain (understanding) | 95 | 38% |
| Masayahin (joyful) | 90 | 36% |
| Marunong makisama (cooperative) | 62 | 24.8% |
| Marunong mag-utos (knows how to give orders properly) | 50 | 20% |
| Maaasahan (dependable) | 46 | 18.4% |
| Masipag (industrious) | 30 | 12% |
| May pasensya (patient) | 15 | 6% |

The relational bias of the Filipino is apparent from the traits listed as most expected from managers. Interestingly, traits such as kindness, approachability and helpfulness are more associated with managers fulfilling roles as mentors and coaches rather than as more directive "bosses". Thus, these less traditional roles for managers may actually provide a better fit for

Filipino workers.    While Filipino workers acknowledge and respect rank (recalling the high power distance Filipino culture noted by Hofstede above), they appreciate managers who behave in ways that make rank virtually unobtrusive.

Table 3 shows managerial traits that are not liked by Filipino workers.    In contrast to the likable traits discussed above, the most disliked traits of managers are those that make authority and rank obtrusive. For example, being boastful, haughty and rude shows insensitivity to the worker's feelings and reminds him or her of not being quite as important as the manager.

**Table 3:  Traits of managers which Filipino workers do not like ("hindi nagugustuhan")[1] (Jocano, 1999: 128)**

| TRAITS | NO. OF RESPONSES | % |
|---|---|---|
| Mayabang (boastful) | 107 | 42.8% |
| Mapagmataas (haughty) | 101 | 40.4% |
| Mataray (rude)[2] | 90 | 36% |
| May kinikilingan (having favorites) | 79 | 31.6% |
| Palautos (demanding)[3] | 68 | 27.2% |
| Ayaw tumanggap ng pagkakamali (proud)[4] | 46 | 18.4% |
| Makasarili (selfish) | 30 | 12% |
| Mahirap lapitan (unapproachable) | 25 | 10% |
| Walang malasakit sa tao (uncaring) | 15 | 6% |
| Makulit (annoying)[5] | 10 | 4% |

[1] I provide additional clarificatory footnotes to explain nuances of the traits.

[2] Blunt.

[3] Gives orders too frequently.

[4] Too proud to admit mistakes.

[5] Annoyingly persistent.

The above discussion of managerial traits suggests some strategies for preparing foreign managers to lead in the Philippine setting.    Firstly, managers can enhance their capacity to lead in the Philippine setting if they can build their competencies as mentors and coaches.    This can improve their being perceived as helpful, kind and approachable while also achieving business goals.    Secondly, managers can have themselves assessed with respect to interpersonal impact. How they come across when giving directions or performance feedback is particularly critical.

Naturally, rapport with Filipino workers is not instantly achieved, even by acculturated expatriates. Social interaction with Filipinos proceeds through a relatively predictable path of deeper levels of rapport (Lapeña, 2002). The stages are shown in Figure 2.

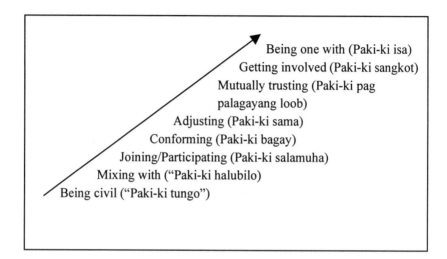

**Figure 2: Levels of Filipino Social Interaction with Increasing Rapport (Lapeña, 2002)**

Managers who want to achieve high levels of commitment from Filipino workers can gradually move up various levels of social interaction. A gradual approach will not only be seen as more sincere, it will also allow both sides of the interaction to assess whether they are ready to move to the next level. At the lowest level of civility, managers may acknowledge the presence of the Filipino through greetings of "hello", a wave of a hand or a smile while slightly nodding the head. To be greeted by name is viewed very positively.

The level of "mixing" may involve chatting in the work area, cafeteria or corridor. It may be one-on-one or with a group. Light non-work topics may be slowly introduced at this stage such as the latest basketball game or vacation spots.

The level of "joining" may involve doing things with the Filipino such as putting materials together, working on a computer file together, or preparing a meeting room together.

The level of "conforming" may involve using words in the vernacular such as "kumusta" for hello, etc., or sampling local food such as "adobo".

The level of "adjusting" may involve modifying personally preferred behaviors (not involving a sacrifice of personal principle) to be more Filipino-like such as having snack breaks ("merienda") with Filipinos (even if this is not one's usual practice) or being more tolerant of late-comers in meetings.

The level of "mutually trusting" may involve discussing work issues more in-depth with the aim of actively listening and suspending judgment. If this level is successfully achieved, Filipino subordinates will freely share their viewpoints even if these may diverge from that of the manager.

The level of "getting involved" may involve electing to work on personal projects with a Filipino such as joining in a civic club. It may also involve supporting and devoting time to a Filipino's work initiative even if the outcome of the initiative is uncertain.

The highest level of "being one with" is achieved when the manager's highest aspirations and that of the Filipino converge into one. At this stage, the Filipino can be counted upon to always go the extra mile to achieve mutually agreed upon goals.

Knowledge of expected managerial traits and social interaction practices is very important for the manager seeking to lead Filipinos effectively.


## Conclusion:   Leading the Filipino for Good Relations and Teamwork

A review of traditional Filipino values and their seeming conflict with Western professional values present many dilemmas to a manager. However, the attention given by some management writers in the last two decades (Lee, 1997; Kouzes and Posner, 1987) to good relationships as a source of organizational commitment would not surprise Filipinos. They know that they work best with those with whom they have good relations. Thus, the effective leader of Filipinos needs to establish positive relationships with subordinates. Such relations build trust and provide the leader with a communication channel to elevate everyone to a higher purpose, which extends beyond the immediate in-group.

To further build teamwork, the leader will need to establish recognition of a common purpose that benefits all existing in-groups within a company, and that can only be achieved through inter-group cooperation. This can be done through constant informal communication and the display of caring alongside the formal communications commonly used by managers. Both forms of communications should use gentle persuasion and an appeal to common interests. The recognition of the Filipino need for combining work and "play" can also improve results.

The Philippines is a country in transition. While it retains many of the cultural orientations of countries that have not fully developed an industrial order, the forces of urbanization, Western exposure and mass media are continuously diluting and modifying these orientations. The economic pressures wrought by the global slowdown has made even Filipinos less sensitive to the sentiments of those they manage. Corporate restructuring and transfers from one company to another have made Filipinos less collectivist and more individualistic in the workplace. Clearly, however, these are adjustments to exigencies and do not reflect the underlying nature of Filipinos. Therefore, the astute manager of Filipinos has a better chance of achieving commitment and bottom-line results by applying Western management concepts in a culturally sensitive manner. A story about the late Don Andres Soriano, founder of one of the largest Filipino conglomerates, dramatizes this contention. Soriano was said to have been so accessible to the rank and file that they could shake his hands along the corridors and occasionally request for small sums of money for particular needs. When advised by his vice-presidents to keep his distance from the rank and file he would remark: "You have staff and people under you who work hard and well for you. But these lowly employees with whom I mix, they will die for me!" (Franco, 1986: 4)

## References

Aquino, Marlene Anne. (1988). "Cases on leadership and changing behavior". *Philippine Values Digest*, 3(1), 75-78.

Franco, Ernesto A. (1986). *Pinoy Management*. Metro Manila: National Bookstore, Inc.

Goleman, Daniel. (1995). *Emotional Intelligence*. New York: Bantam Books.

Gonzalez, Ricardo L. (1987). *Corporate Culture Modification: A Guide for Managers*. Metro Manila: National Bookstore.

Guthrie, George M. (1981). "The Philippine temperament". In Nestor N. Pilar and Rafael A. Rodriguez, (Eds.), *Readings in Human Behavior in Organizations* (pp. 90-108). Quezon City: JMC Press, Inc.

Hofstede, Geert. (1983). "The cultural relativity of organizational practices and theories". *Journal of International Business Studies*, Fall 1983. 75-89.

Hofstede, Geert. (1985). "The interaction between national and organizational value systems". *Journal of Management Studies*, **22**, 347-357.

Hollnsteiner, Mary R. (1981). "Philippine organizational behavior: Personalism and group solidarity". In Nestor N. Pilar and Rafael A. Rodriguez, (Eds.), *Readings in Human Behavior in Organizations* (pp. 327-331). Quezon City: JMC Press, Inc.

Jocano, F. Landa. (1990). *Management by Culture: Fine-tuning Management to Filipino Culture*. Quezon City: Punlad Research House.

Jocano, F. Landa. (1999). *Management by Culture: Fine-tuning Management to Filipino Culture (Revised edition)*. Quezon City: Punlad Research House.

Komin, Suntaree. (1999). "The Thai concept of effective leadership". In Henry S. R. Kao, Durganand Sinha and Bernhard Wilpert (Eds.), *Management and Cultural Values: The Indigenization of Organizations in Asia* (pp. 265-286). Sage Publications: New Delhi.

Kouzes, James M. and Barry Z. Posner. (1987). *The Leadership Challenge: How to Get Extraordinary Things Done in Organizations*. San Francisco: Jossey-Bass.

Lapeña, Ma. Angeles. (2002). *Sikolohiyang Pilipino*. Unpublished PowerPoint material.

Lee, Blaine. (1997). *The Power Principle: Influence With Honor*. Simon and Schuster: New York.

Levering, Robert and Milton Moskowitz. (2001). "The 100 best companies to work for". *Fortune*, **143**, 64-77.

Lupdag, Anselmo. (1984). *In Search of Filipino Leadership*. Quezon City: New Day.

Lynch, Frank. (1981). "Social acceptance". In Nestor N. Pilar and Rafael A. Rodriguez, (Eds.), *Readings in Human Behavior in Organizations* (pp.109-120). Quezon City: JMC Press, Inc.

Martires, Concepcion R.. (1992). *Human Behavior in Organizations.* Mandaluyong City: National Bookstore, Inc.

Mercado, Leandro N. (1981). "Notes on the Filipino philosophy of work and leisure". In Nestor N. Pilar and Rafael A. Rodriguez, (Eds.), *Readings in Human Behavior in Organizations* (pp. 147-152). Quezon City: JMC Press, Inc.

*Chapter 10*

# The Egalitarian Leader: Leadership in Australia and

# New Zealand

Neal M. Ashkanasy
UQ Business School, University of Queensland, Australia

Edwin Trevor-Roberts
UQ Business School, University of Queensland, Australia

Jeff Kennedy
Nanyang Business School, Nanyang Technological University,
Singapore

The Antipodean nations of Australia and New Zealand lie at the western edge of the South Pacific Ocean, and to the south of Asia's eastern extremity. Colonized in the late Eighteenth Century by the British, Australia and New Zealand are usually categorized as developed Western nations. Indeed, this is so, as both countries are English-speaking, boast high standards of living, and enjoy sophisticated technologically oriented economies. Nonetheless, they are geographically remote from the centers of Western civilization, and are located relatively close to the emerging new economies of East Asia. As such, Australia and New Zealand undisputedly have a close affinity with the nations of South-

East Asia. Consequently, and consistent with the theme of the present volume, managers in this region need to understand the nature of leadership in this part of the world. In this chapter, we endeavor to accomplish this aim by examining the bases of effective leadership in Australia and New Zealand and compare leadership styles between these two nations using data from an international cross-cultural study of leadership, the 61-nation Global Leadership and Organizational Behavior Effectiveness (GLOBE) project (see House et al., 1999).

The overall aim of the GLOBE project was "to develop an empirically based theory to describe, understand, and predict the impact of specific cultural variables on leadership and organizational processes and the effectiveness of these processes" (House et al., 1999, p. 183). This was to be accomplished by examining the relationships between societal culture, organizational culture, and organizational leadership. In this respect, the first and third authors of this chapter were "Country Co-Investigators" (CCI's) in the GLOBE program, representing Australia and New Zealand, respectively. Ashkanasy and Kennedy were thus responsible for the collection of quantitative and qualitative data for their country, and for interpreting the results within the context of their culture. Trevor-Roberts conducted the comparative analysis of Australian and New Zealand leadership styles reported in this chapter. Specifically, this chapter is based on a comparative study of leadership styles between Australia and New Zealand undertaken by Trevor-Roberts, Ashkanasy & Kennedy (2003).

The aim of this chapter therefore is to discuss and to compare leadership in Australia and New Zealand. Cultural similarities and common themes between these two countries will be discussed followed by a treatment of the practical aspects of what constitutes effective leadership in these countries. We conclude that leadership in both countries is characterized by the universal dimensions of leadership identified in the GLOBE project, but that these countries also share an important element of egalitarianism that derives from their historical and cultural development. We also note that there are some important differences in the manifestation of leadership across the two countries that are important for managers to appreciate.

Leadership is defined by the GLOBE project as: "The ability of an individual to influence, motivate, and enable others to contribute toward the effectiveness and success of the organizations of which they are members" (House et al., 1999, p. 184). Within this definition, the GLOBE team set out to ascertain which specific leadership behaviors are universally endorsed across cultures and which are culture-specific. The results of the GLOBE project showed that universal dimensions of leadership that facilitate and impede leadership do exist across cultures, but that the behaviors by which effective leadership is actually manifested differ from country to country (den Hartog et al., 1999). The culture-specific leader behaviors and attributes are derived in turn from implicit *Culturally-endorsed Leadership Theories* (CLT's) that underlie perceptions of what constitutes effective leadership behavior. CLT's are the implicit theories that members of a particular culture have about their society and the nature of relationships and hierarchy within their society. The underlying hypothesis of the GLOBE study is that the perceived effectiveness of organizational leadership in different cultures is dependent on the CLT of organizational members.

Comparing leadership in Australia and New Zealand also reveals a cross-cultural challenge. While these two countries seem to have near-identical cultures, closer inspection reveals subtle, yet important, differences in the makeup of these cultures and how a leader's effectiveness is perceived. In this respect, it is important for managers not to assume that their leadership style will necessarily be immediately effective in another culture. A detailed study of the nuances of each culture will enhance their ability to manage relationships and effectively lead teams.

Finally, we note that the significant impact of Australia and New Zealand on the world economy belies their modest size – a mere combined population of less than 24 million, and representing a tiny fraction of the world's economy. As we commented earlier, Australia and New Zealand are seen to be Western economies, yet they lie closer to the emerging economies of South East Asia. As such, they are at the same time part of both Asia and the developed Western world. Yet it could be argued that they belong to neither domain. Indeed, their remarkable economic resilience during the 1998 Asian financial crisis demonstrates their independence from their geographic neighbours, while similar resilience during the market corrections of 2000-2001 shows that they are not so closely tied to the Western economies either. In the following discussion, we highlight in detail the historical antecedents of culture in Australia and New Zealand, present the results of our leadership research within the framework of the GLOBE project, and outline some recommendations for managers.

## Cultural Background

The importance of the context of leadership has long been known to be crucial in determining the effectiveness of a leader. In this respect, a great deal of attention has been placed on the micro situation; for example, the level of stress, a specific task, and the nature of the organization itself (Yukl, 1989). More recently, there has been an increased recognition of the impact culture has on a leader's perceived effectiveness (Hofstede, 1980, 2001). Increased globalisation and enhanced communication methods now mean that executives of large organizations need the skills to manage a diverse workforce across multiple cultures. Even executives who operate in one country must now take into account international trends on their business and understand the impact of their leadership style on employees from different cultures.

The theory underpinning the GLOBE project is that an effective leadership style is dependent on the culture in which it takes place (House et al., 1999). Each culture has an implicit theory of what constitutes effective leadership referred to as CLT's. To understand how to lead and to manage relationships in different countries we must therefore first understand the culture that exists within each country. The following sections briefly describe the main cultural elements of Australia and New Zealand.[1]

### Australia's Cultural Develpment

Australia is a land of stark contrast that, in the 213 years since the beginning of European settlement, has managed to create a complex history full of contradictions. For example, Australia is the most sparsely populated continent on earth barring Antarctica, yet has one of the most urbanised societies; and it is physically removed from its British heritage, but is still distinct from its Asian neighbours. Just as some Australian mammals, such as the kangaroo and wombat, exist nowhere else in the world, Australians too have evolved a unique culture. The 1998 Asian economic collapse, for example, had a much smaller impact on the Australian economy than commentators around the world expected. More recently, the Australian economy has proved remarkably strong in the face of the economic downturns experienced in the Northern Hemisphere.

The most recurring theme to emerge from Australian culture, and a focus of the present chapter, is that of egalitarianism. Egalitarianism is based upon the belief that all Australians are economically and culturally equal. The upside of egalitarianism is that the country appears particularly friendly because everyone is viewed and treated the same. Egalitarianism, however, has also engendered a striving for mediocrity and a mentality of criticising and cutting down high achievers, also called the "tall poppy syndrome" (Feather, 1994). In a recent example of this attitude, New South Wales Police Commissioner, Peter Ryan, became so frustrated that he exclaimed, "They are so bankrupt in their arguments that they can only tell me that I'm doing it wrong. They never come up with alternatives" (Moodie, 1998).

Another element of egalitarianism is a belief that there should be equality of access for all Australians. This is espoused in the slang term "fair go" – meaning that everyone should be given the same level of opportunity. For example, the belief that anyone can have their own home is very important to Australians. Australia's large welfare system for disadvantaged and unemployed people is also testament to a striving for equality. To understand how these deeply entrenched attitudes arose, it is important to understand Australian history, which is discussed briefly below.

Human habitation of Australia by Aborigines is estimated to have commenced between forty to sixty thousand years ago. Aborigines eventually inhabited almost the entire continent and lived a technologically and economically simple, but socially complex life. It is estimated that, at the time of the first organized European settlement in 1788, there were somewhere between 300,000 and 1 million Aborigines living in Australia.

European settlement of Australia and the start of its modern history began with the arrival of Captain Cook and the First Fleet with its cargo of British and Irish convicts and their gaolers. The expansion of the penal colony's population and the arrival of a wave of free settlers, attracted by the lure of unlimited land, were, sadly, accompanied by a sharp decline in the Aboriginal population through extermination, disease, and loss of traditional land.

Eventually, the population of free settlers outstripped the penal population, as settlers were continually lured to Australia (although transportation of convicts continued until the mid-Nineteenth Century). The settlers and the freed convicts, however, did not always live together easily, especially since the governor at the time was forced to appoint ex-convicts to positions of authority. In this case, it is arguable that the egalitarian and anti-authoritarian values of Australian society can be traced to these early appointments. In essence, an individual's past and family lineage were no longer relevant in the harsh and remote Australian environment. Egalitarianism thus became a necessity for the new arrivals simply to survive. Australia subsequently experienced rapid growth as large scale grazing opened up the country, followed by the gold rush during the second part of the Nineteenth Century and waves of immigrants arriving from other countries, especially Asia. On 1 January 1901, the six colonies became States in the Federated Commonwealth of Australia, although the nature of Australia, as a nation of rugged individualists who needed to rely on one another for survival, was already largely determined .

Despite its early history and periods of restrictive immigration, contemporary Australia is a multicultural and pluralist society. In particular, the White Australia Policy, introduced following the formation of the Federation in 1901, and not officially ended until 1973, encouraged British and other European immigrants to Australia, excluding all non-Europeans. Once this policy was revoked however, Asian and other non-European immigration increased rapidly to form one of the most multicultural societies in the world. The 1996 census showed that 16.2% of Australia's approximate 19 million people were born overseas, and that a further 19% of Australians born in the country had at least one parent born overseas. Australia is, however, still coming to grips with its multicultural society and racial past. For example, Aboriginal land rights were only recognised in the High Court in the mid 1990s.

Nonetheless, despite the early evolution of a distinct national culture, and governmental moves to foster national development, Australians have traditionally tended to relate closely to their colonial identity and to focus on their geographically distant British and Irish heritage. At a referendum in 1999, for example, Australians rejected a republic model that would have cut their last constitutional links with the UK. This has served also to leave Australia culturally detached from its Asian neighbours.

This identity is most evident in respect to Australia's participation in military engagements. Australia entered early into the two world wars because of its British attachment. During World War I Australia suffered one of the highest per capita casualty rates but gained an enduring image of national identity with the perceived heroism of the ANZACs – the Australian and New Zealand Army Corps[2]. World War II was a different matter however, when Britain was forced to look to its own defence, and Australia was left more or less to fend for itself under threat of Japanese invasion in the Pacific. Consequently, Australia established in 1952 an important and necessary alliance with the US, the ANZUS treaty. In particular, WWII marked an end to Australians' perception that their nation was little more than a British colony, although many Australians still maintain their attachment to the Mother Country. Nevertheless, Australia's economic and cultural identity is today more focused on its geographic neighbours and the US. Australia, for example was an ally of the US in the Korean and Vietnam wars.

In recent years however, Australia has finally shown signs of maturing as a nation, and today places less emphasis on its historical relationships with Britain and the US. For example, Australia led the international peace keeping force, Interfet, into East Timor in the late 1990s. Commanded by the Australian Major General Peter Cosgrove, the Interfet force earned international praise.

*Summary* Australia has had an eventful 213 years of European history. Its early origin as a convict settlement combined with the harsh environment began the individualist and egalitarian ethos, and also created an element of anti-authoritarianism that is still prevalent in today's society. In this respect, Australia's culture presents unique challenges for leaders to manage and communicate effectively.

## New Zealand's Cultural Development

The history of New Zealand is entwined with Australia because of their geographic proximity. New Zealand comprises the last two sizeable islands to be occupied by homo sapiens. It lies at the outer edge of the largest ocean in the world, has marked variations in climate and topography, and is populated by 4 million people. In spite of its small size, however, New Zealand has placed itself well and truly on the world stage with notable heroes and achievements in sports, science, and the arts, and a sense of national pride that belies the country's size. New Zealand is a mix of cultures with a brief, yet intense history. The "Kiwi" identity is unique and, while components of this identity may be found in other cultures, it is the particular combination of cultures together with the shared experiences and history of the nation that form its uniqueness.

The earliest inhabitants of New Zealand, the Māori, migrated from Polynesia around 1000AD. The Māori people retained aspects of their Polynesian culture, while adapting to the challenges of a less tropical and more rugged physical environment. Māori society is interdependent and communal in nature with social groupings based on extended families. Further, since the signing of the Treaty of Waitangi in 1840 between the British settlers and the Māori Chieftains, indigenous culture has played a more central role in New Zealand culture than it has in Australia.

European history of New Zealand began with its discovery in 1642 by Abel Tasman although European settlement did not begin until the mid 1770s. The early settlers were freemen who came from the prison colony established in Australia, as well as American and British whalers and sealers who established bases on the New Zealand coast, some of which expanded into larger settlements. This early settlement highlights the first major difference between Australia and New Zealand's early historical development – that free settlers initiated European settlement in New Zealand, in contrast to Australia's European origins as a penal colony.

New Zealand became a British colony in its own right in 1841 and a Central Government was formed in 1876. From its beginning, the central government took a socially progressive stance in running the country. For example, free compulsory education was introduced in 1877; in 1879 universal male suffrage was introduced; and, in 1893, New Zealand became the first country in the world to extend the vote to women.

New Zealand's strong social trait of egalitarianism was first formally seen in The Industrial Conciliation and Arbitration Act of 1894, which was established to share national wealth and protect workers. This Act demonstrated the emphasis that the settlers placed on equality and freedom and their pioneering spirit in an unforgiving land that required them to work together just to survive. This strong sense of egalitarianism continues to be firmly entrenched in the New Zealand psyche. Similar to Australia, egalitarianism in New Zealand extends to the belief that people should be considered equal in all aspects of life. The tall poppy syndrome – a propensity to denigrate high achievers – also permeates through the New Zealand culture.

Together with Australia, New Zealand made substantial contributions to the Twentieth Century wars in Europe and Asia, and high regard for the actions of the ANZACs continues today. The dominant and enduring cultural theme portrays New Zealanders, like their Australian neighbours, to be self-reliant pioneers, brave and heroic, demonstrating initiative under pressure. These characteristics engendered leadership based on example rather than insistence on bureaucratic procedures by officers who were seen to be modest and democratic in their dealings with troops.

Following WWII, and paralleling events in Australia, New Zealand's identification with Britain as the Mother Country declined further. An increased relationship with the US saw the signature of the ANZUS security treaty in 1952 and involvement in the Korean and Vietnam wars. In the 1970s, New Zealand's major export market, the United Kingdom, joined the European Common Market. This had a significant adverse economic impact on New Zealand, and provided increased momentum for the shift towards an Asia-Pacific orientation for economic, political, and cultural affairs.

Another important element of the New Zealand cultural archetype is a practical, problem-solving approach to life. This involves a willingness to tackle problems and take on responsibilities outside one's normal role. Innovative solutions using tools or materials at hand are valued, which stems from the pioneering settler history and dependence on farming. Sir Edmund Hillary, for example, was not only the first person to climb Mt. Everest; he was the first to drive a motorised vehicle overland to the South Pole, where he used converted farm tractors for the expedition.

Today New Zealand is an increasingly multicultural society. In the 1996 census, almost 20% of the population claimed identification with two or more ethnic groups. Around three-quarters of the population are of European descent, and almost 15% are Mäori. Pacific Islanders and Asian ethnic groups comprise 4.8% and 4.4% respectively of the overall population.

*Summary* Despite its small size and isolation from the rest of the world, New Zealand has become a confident and prosperous nation. New Zealanders are exceptionally proud of their country, are open, honest, and adventurous, with a rugged sense of survival. Like Australia, New Zealand has firmly and independently taken its place in the Pacific.

## GLOBE Project - Societal Culture

The GLOBE project undertook a quantitative study of societal cultural values using two forms of assessment: (1) the *values* of a society described in terms of what they "should be", and (2) the *practices* or behaviors of a society expressed in terms of what takes place "as is". Nine dimensions were identified and are used to gain a deeper understanding of societal culture. A brief description of each of these dimensions as well as the score and rank (out of 61 countries who responded) for Australia and New Zealand are shown in Table 1.[3]

The results of the cultural component of the GLOBE study, as expected, reveal the Australian and New Zealand cultures to be characterized by high levels of individualism (low scores on Collectivism II), high levels of performance orientation, and relatively low levels of power distance. These characteristics are consistent with other Anglo cultures such as England and the US. The data, however, also reveal that there are some notable differences in the cultural orientation of Australians and New Zealanders. New Zealand, for example, ranks much higher than Australia in terms of Collectivism I, which is a measure of collective distribution of resources, while Australia ranks much higher in terms of Assertiveness. The low power distance and individualism evident in the cultures of these countries is entirely consistent with their historical and cultural development, as we have detailed earlier in this chapter.

## Leadership

As discussed, cultures can be distinguished based on the leader attributes and behaviors that are most frequently enacted, acceptable, and effective in a particular culture (den Hartog et al., 1999). Based on questionnaire responses, the GLOBE project team identified twenty-one leader attributes. A second-order factor analysis of these attributes subsequently produced the six universal dimensions of leadership listed in Table 2.

These six universal CLT dimensions represent classes of leader behavior rather than specific leader behaviors. Each dimension is discussed briefly below.

*Charismatic/Value Based Leadership* This dimension is universally endorsed as contributing to a leader's effectiveness. This is because a Charismatic/Value Based leader espouses a vision congruent with the values of followers, based in turn on their cultural norms.

**Table 1: GLOBE Culture Scale Scoresa and Ranksb**

| Cultural Dimension | Description | Australia | | | | New Zealand | | | |
|---|---|---|---|---|---|---|---|---|---|
| | | As Is | | Should Be | | As Is | | Should Be | |
| | | Score | Rank | Score | Rank | Score | Rank | Score | Rank |
| Power Distance | The degree to which members of a collective expect power to be distributed equally. | 4.74 | 53 | 2.78 | 25 | 4.89 | 47 | 3.53 | 3 |
| Uncertainty Avoidance | The extent to which a collective relies on social norms, rituals, and procedures to alleviate the unpredictability of future events. | 4.39 | 19 | 3.98 | 51 | 4.75 | 12 | 4.10 | 48 |
| Humane Orientation | The degree to which a collective encourages and rewards individuals for being fair, altruistic, generous, caring and kind to others. | 4.28 | 21 | 5.58 | 20 | 4.32 | 19 | 4.49 | 61 |
| Collectivism I | The degree to which organizational and societal institutional practices encourage and reward collective distribution of resources and collective action. | 4.29 | 29 | 4.40 | 42 | 4.81 | 5 | 4.20 | 51 |
| Collectivism II | The degree to which individuals express pride, loyalty and cohesiveness in their organizations or families. | 4.17 | 52 | 5.75 | 27 | 3.67 | 59 | 6.21 | 3 |
| Assertiveness | The degree to which individuals are assertive, confrontational and aggressive in their relationships with others. | 4.28 | 22 | 3.81 | 25 | 3.42 | 60 | 3.54 | 41 |
| Gender Egalitarianism | The degree to which a collective minimises gender inequality. | 3.40 | 30 | 5.02 | 8 | 3.22 | 38 | 4.23 | 47 |
| Future Orientation | The extent to which individuals engage in future-orientated behaviours such as delaying gratification, planning and investing in the future. | 4.09 | 20 | 5.15 | 49 | 3.47 | 48 | 5.54 | 31 |
| Performance Orientation | The degree to which a collective encourages and rewards group members for performance improvement and excellence. | 4.36 | 16 | 5.89 | 38 | 4.72 | 5 | 5.90 | 34 |

a Scored on a 1-7 scale, where 7 is the highest score.
b Rank in the list of 61 nations included in the GLOBE study.

**Table 2: GLOBE Leadership Scales and Scores**

| Attribute No. | 1. Charismatic/ Value Based | 2. Team Orientated | 3. Self-protective | 4. Participative | 5. Humane | 6. Autonomous |
|---|---|---|---|---|---|---|
| | | | **Second Order Leadership Dimension** | | | |
| 1 | Visionary | Collaborative Team Orientation | Self-centered | Autocratic[b] | Modesty | Individualistic |
| 2 | Inspirational | Team integrator | Status conscious | Non-participative[b] | Humane | |
| 3 | Self-sacrificial | Diplomatic | Conflict inducer | | | |
| 4 | Decisive | Malevolent[b] | Face saver | | | |
| 5 | Integrity | Administratively competent | Procedural | | | |
| 6 | Performance orientated | | | | | |
| Australian Mean[a] | 6.09 | 5.81 | 3.05 | 5.71 | 5.09 | 3.95 |
| NZ Mean[a] | 5.87 | 5.44 | 3.19 | 5.50 | 4.78 | 3.77 |
| GLOBE conclusion | Universally facilitates leadership | Varies between cultures. | Universally impedes leadership | Varies between cultures. | Varies between cultures. | Varies between cultures. |

[a] On a 1-7 scale, where 7 indicates the highest level.
[b] Reverse scored item.

*Team Orientated Leadership* Endorsement of this dimension was found to vary between cultures. These behaviors represent a style of leadership focusing on the team and emphasizing the relationships between the members of that team.

*Self-Protective Leadership* This dimension was found universally to impede a leader's effectiveness. These behaviors represent a bossy yet self-interested and evasive leader, who relies on formalities and procedures.

*Humane Leadership* The endorsement of this dimension was found to vary between cultures. This set of behaviors represents a leader who is generous, compassionate, patient, and modest.

*Participative Leadership* This is another leadership style where endorsement was found to vary from culture to culture. A Participative leader is one who works well with other people and actively participates in the task being undertaken.

*Autonomous Leadership* This dimension was based on the single attribute of individualism, and encompasses an independent and autonomous approach. This was another dimension whose endorsement was found to vary between cultures.

Also shown in Table 1 are the mean scores for the Australian and New Zealand samples. These data reveal that effective leadership in the two cultures is generally similar, with high levels of Charismatic/Value Based and Team Oriented leadership expected, accompanied by low levels of Self-Protective leadership. Leadership in both countries was also characterized by an emphasis on Participative leadership, and moderately high levels of Humane leadership.

Using the Australia and New Zealand data from the GLOBE study, Trevor-Roberts, Ashkanasy and Kennedy (2003), re-analysed the twenty-one leadership attributes using both exploratory and confirmatory factor analysis. The results of these analyses were then compared in order to highlight the differences and similarities in leadership between these two nations, and to understand dimensions of leadership unique to each culture. The specific objective was to see which of the dimensions that emerged in the re-analysis corresponded to the universal GLOBE leadership dimensions, and which were unique to these two cultures.

## Australian Leadership

Four dimensions of leadership emerged in the re-analysis of the Australian data, and are listed in Table 3.

Table 3: Australian Leadership Dimensions

| Attribute No. | Second Order Leadership Dimension | | | |
| --- | --- | --- | --- | --- |
| | 1 Visionary | 2 Narcissistic | 3 Egalitarianism | 4 Bureaucratic |
| 1 | Visionary | Autocratic | Humane | Procedural |
| 2 | Inspirational | Self-centered | Collaborative Team Orientation | Administratively Competent |
| 3 | Team Integrator | Malevolent | Modest | |
| 4 | Decisive | Conflict inducer | Integrity | |
| 5 | Performance orientated | Non-participative | | |
| 6 | Diplomatic | Face saver | | |
| 7 | Self-sacrificial | Status conscious | | |
| 8 | | Autonomous | | |
| Etic/emic [a] | Etic | Etic | Emic | Emic |
| Facilitaes/ Inhibits leadership | Facilitates | Inhibits | Facilitates | Inhibits |

[a] Etic = universal; emic = country-specific.

*Factor 1: Visionary.* This factor corresponds closely to the universal Charismatic/Value Based GLOBE leadership dimension. This suggests that although the universal Charismatic/Value Based leadership is perceived to contribute to a leader's effectiveness, the behaviors that manifest this leadership style in Australia are unique in many ways. This factor represents a style of leadership that provides a vision and inspires followers in a manner that is tactful, diplomatic, and yet decisive.

*Factor 2: Narcissistic.* This factor represents a leadership style that is individualistic and self-centered and is perceived to impede a leader's effectiveness. It is similar to the universal Self-Protective leadership dimension and is seen to inhibit effective leadership.

*Factor 3: Egalitarianism.* This factor is an emic (culture-specific) style of leadership that parallels the "mateship" phenomenon identified by Ashkanasy & Falkus (In Press). In this sense, mateship represents an unselfish and collaborative regard of friends and workmates. It represents a style of leadership that is generous and compassionate, while being group-orientated and focused on building a collaborative team. Such a leader needs to be honest, sincere, and modest. The mateship element is reflected in the emphasis on the team, integrity, and modesty. The importance of the group arguably stems from Australia's penal history and an all-pervasive tall poppy attitude.

*Factor 4: Bureaucratic.* This factor is perceived to impede the effectiveness of Australian leadership and represents a style that emphasizes formality and the need to follow established routines and patterns. Such a leadership style also includes an administrative component, indicating the need to be organized and follow rules and procedures. This ineffective leadership style is consistent with observations about Australian individualism and the lack of respect for authority. Australians prefer their leaders to rely less on rules and bureaucratic procedures, sometimes referred to as a "larrikin" attitude. Bob Hawke, Australia's Prime Minister from 1983 to 1988, is an example of this style. For instance, although he was widely popular, Hawke often forged his own direction while ignoring the sensitivities and formal rules of his own political party.

In summary, our re-analysis of the Australian leadership data reaffirmed the general GLOBE conclusion that visionary (positive) and narcissistic (negative) characteristics play a central role in assessments of effective leadership, but also revealed two emic dimensions, which characterize Australian leadership. These dimensions represent egalitarian (positive) and bureaucratic (negative) leadership, and are entirely consistent with the analysis of the development of Australian culture that we outlined earlier.

## New Zealand Leadership

Four dimensions of leadership also emerged from the re-analysis of the New Zealand data, shown in Table 4.

*Factor 1: Egalitarian Team Leader.* This factor highlights the importance of team leadership in New Zealand. It is similar to the universal GLOBE Team Orientated leadership dimension, but with slightly more decisive, performance orientated and charismatic overtones. This style of leadership appears to encompass personal managerial skills focused on creating and maintaining a working group. A leader in New Zealand must be consultative, collaborative, loyal and group-orientated with excellent communication skills and an ability to coordinate a team. Tied in closely with this team approach is a need for a leader to be decisive while simultaneously being diplomatic and maintaining integrity.

## Table 4: New Zealand Leadership Dimensions

| Attribute No. | Second Order Leadership Dimension | | | |
|---|---|---|---|---|
| | 1 Egalitarian Team Leader | 2. Inspirational | 3. Narcissistic | 4. Bureaucratic |
| 1 | Decisive | Inspirational | Conflict inducer | Procedural |
| 2 | Team Integrator | Face saver | Autocratic | Status conscious |
| 3 | Administrativel y Competent | Visionary | Self-centered | |
| 4 | Integrity | Performance orientated | Malevolent | |
| 5 | Collaborative Team Orientation | | Non-participative | |
| 6 | Diplomatic | | | |
| 7 | Modest | | | |
| 8 | | | | |
| Etic/emic [a] | Emic | Etic | Etic | Emic |
| Facilitaes/ Inhibits leadership | Facilitates | Facilitates | Inhibits | Inhibits. |

[a] Etic = universal; emic = country-specific.

*Factor 2: Inspirational.* The second factor to emerge was an inspirational leadership style, similar to the universal GLOBE Charismatic/ValueBased leadership dimension. This leadership style requires effective leaders in New Zealand to display positiveness, enthusiasm and confidence, and to boost the morale of followers. These leaders must also be performance orientated, must "get things done" and, consistent with the first factor, they must also undertake all of this with a focus on the team. An effective leader in New Zealand leader must be inspirational and performance orientated within the setting of their team.

*Factor 3: Narcissistic.* This factor is similar to the GLOBE Self-Protective dimension and represents an ineffective style of leadership that is self-centered, non-participative, and autocratic. This leadership style is individualistic and disregards the team, contrary to what was identified as effective leadership in the previous two factors. Acting in a self-effacing manner, without overtly displaying power or status, is important for effective leadership in New Zealand, and is consistent with the egalitarian undertones of the culture.

*Factor 4: Bureaucratic.* This factor represents a dimension of leadership unique to the antipodean nations, which is seen to inhibit effective leadership. It is dominated by a procedural approach and encapsulates a ritualistic, formal, cautious leadership style -- a tendency to follow a habitual routine. Congruent with the Narcissistic factor, such a leader is aware of class and status boundaries and acts accordingly. Such a reliance on formal rules and procedures goes against the New Zealand psyche of egalitarianism and the importance of managing the team rather than the process.

To sum up the re-analysis of the New Zealand leadership data, we again affirmed the wider GLOBE findings that inspirational (positive) and narcissistic (negative) behaviors are key determinants of effective leadership. In this analysis, as for the Australian data, a bureaucratic (negative) dimension was found. The positive leadership dimension of egalitarian team leadership was the pre-eminent determinant of effective leadership in New Zealand. Thus reflecting the historical development of the New Zealand culture.

## Summary of Leadership Dimensions

Our analysis has shown that the two universal GLOBE dimensions of Charismatic/Value Based and Self-Protective leadership were evident in both the Australian and New Zealand data. These dimensions were apparent both in the wider analysis of the GLOBE data, and in the re-analysis of the Australian and New Zealand data. Nonetheless, we have also shown how the particular attributes and behaviors that represent these universal dimensions differ in each country. Further, our analysis has highlighted the importance of emic dimensions of leadership that reflect the cultural foundations of leadership within each culture. In the Australian analysis, these factors were labelled Egalitarian (a leadership facilitator) and Bureaucratic (inhibitor). In the New Zealand analysis, the emic dimensions were labelled Egalitarian Team Leader (facilitator), and Bureaucratic (inhibitor). It must also be noted that, while the culture specific dimensions of leadership in Australia and New Zealand share similarities, they are distinctly different in important respects that reflect the different CLTs in each culture. Both cultures place an emphasis on egalitarianism and disdain for authority, and both cultures have a tendency to cut down the tall poppies. The major difference, however, is in the New Zealanders' emphasis on team leadership – a recurrent theme in New Zealand's cultural development.

## Discussion: What Do the GLOBE Results Tell Managers?

As we have already noted, Australia and New Zealand belong geographically to the Asia-Pacific group of countries, and an understanding of leadership within these nations is therefore an intrinsic part of understanding leadership in this region.

Australia and New Zealand also share similar historical and cultural backgrounds, and are often seen by other countries as being indistinguishable. Our analysis, however, has highlighted the fact that, while similar, there are some important differences in each country's approach to leadership. We argue that these differences stem from differences in the cultural developments that have taken place in each country since European settlement began in the Eighteenth Century. Consequently, an understanding of each culture's nuances is a critical step in understanding leadership in a particular culture. Consistent with the theme of this volume, therefore, understanding culture is a key to effectively managing relationships with subordinates, peers and within teams.

A major conclusion of the GLOBE project analysis, as reported by House and his associates (Forthcoming, 2004), is that there are leadership dimensions that are universally applicable, and others that vary between countries. In our analysis of the Australian and New Zealand data, however, we have shown that there are nuances within the universal dimensions of leadership that also reflect the culture of each country, even when the cultures are ostensibly very similar. For example, although a dimension similar to the universal Charismatic/Value Based dimension was found in New Zealand, it differed because of the strong team orientation inherent in the New Zealand culture. In the following paragraphs, we discuss these dimensions in more detail, and draw some implications for management practice in Australia and New Zealand

## The Universal Leadership Dimensions

The Visionary/Inspirational and Narcissistic dimensions that emerged from the analysis of the Australian and New Zealand data were similar, but not identical, to the universal GLOBE dimensions. The New Zealand respondents reported a more inspirational or motivational dimension within a team setting, suggesting that an effective leader in New Zealand needs to focus his or her attention primarily on the needs of the team, including the team members' performance aspirations. The Australian factor, on the other hand, was characterized by a visionary leader who is decisive, performance orientated and, while still ensuring the success of the team, leads as an inspirational individual.

Nevertheless, the Australian inspirational leadership dimension has an added emphasis on diplomacy, suggesting that, while leaders in Australia need to be inspirational to be effective, they must do so in a very tactful manner. This presents a challenge for Australian leaders; they must maintain a balance between achievement and the maintenance of equality; between leading and maintaining his or her role as a "mate". An effective leader in Australia must be perceived as part of the group and not as leading from in front. Leaders who are able to achieve this fine balance and are down to earth and diplomatic in their behaviors may avoid the ubiquitous tall poppy syndrome.

The manifestation of the GLOBE Self-Protective leadership style, which was found universally to impede leadership effectiveness, was also identified in both the Australian and New Zealand data. Interestingly, the manifestation of this dimension in the Australia and New Zealand data corresponded closely to the original GLOBE dimension. The behaviors in this instance describe the major attributes of ineffective leadership: being self-centered, autocratic, and emphasizing status, hierarchy, and procedures. Such a leadership style is arguably the most universal of leadership traits, and leaders in every culture must strive to avoid these kinds of behavior.

## Culture Specific Leadership Dimensions

Two emic, or unique, dimensions of leadership emerged in the Australian and New Zealand data sets. One of these, Bureaucratic, is a dimension that is seen to impede effective leadership and represents a leadership style based on rules and authority. The emergence of this factor supports the notion of individualism in these countries that we noted in our earlier discussion and an inherent dislike of rules and regulations.

The second emic dimension that emerged from the Australian and New Zealand data was seen to enhance leadership, but was specific to each country. The Australian dimension of Egalitarianism represents a leadership style that focuses on the group and the concept of mateship. Such a leader manages the relationships in the team by being "one of the boys", by "sticking with my mates through thick and thin". Such a leader must have a high level of integrity and be trustworthy and honest, while all the time maintaining the egalitarian ethos.

A dimension similar to this Australian Egalitarianism emerged in the New Zealand data called Egalitarian Team Leader. It is similar to the Australian Egalitarianism dimension, but with more emphasis on leading in a team. This reflects the recurring emphasis on teamwork that we have noted earlier as pervading New Zealand culture. An effective leader in New Zealand must focus on the pragmatic issues of getting the job done within a team context. They must be able to bring people together effectively to form a cohesive productive work team focused on the team goal. The attributes of the dimension suggest that New Zealand leaders are most effective when they are simultaneously decisive and consultative.

The New Zealand Egalitarian Team Leader and the Australian Egalitarianism dimensions appear in our analysis to be key dimensions of leadership in these countries, but they also highlight a difference in leadership style between the two nations. Australians seem to have a more social or affiliative approach to leadership as captured by the Egalitarianism dimension. This is contrasted with the New Zealand approach that appears to emphasize a more outcome-orientated team spirit.

## Conclusion

The recurring theme of this volume is that effective leadership is essential for organizational success in the Asia-pacific region. This chapter is based on analysis of data obtained from middle managers in Australia and New Zealand as a part of the 61-nation GLOBE project. A key finding of our study is the importance for managers to understand both universal enhancers and inhibitors of leadership as well as those dimensions of leadership unique to a specific culture. The results reinforce the universal rule that a Charismatic/Value Based leadership style contributes to a leader's effectiveness regardless of the culture, although we also found some important differences across the New Zealand and Australian cultures. Similarly, a Self-Protective leadership style will impede the effectiveness of a leader, irrespective of national culture. Our results also highlight the need for managers to learn about the mores and history of particular cultures in order to understand the CLTs that determine the specific characterisations of effective leadership behavior in particular countries.

In Australia, leaders are expected to be more socially orientated and affiliative, and to place less emphasis on the work task or outcome than their New Zealand counterparts. At the same time, Australian leaders are expected to articulate a vision and to get things done in an egalitarian way. In New Zealand, on the other hand, leaders need to place more emphasis on motivating and inspiring, to be team orientated, and to focus on the work at hand. The most common theme emerging from this research with respect to New Zealand leadership is the emphasis on the team. An effective leader must be able to lead a team to achieve the goals they have set. Furthermore, New Zealand, like Australia, has little tolerance for self-promoters, supporting the notion of team leadership as opposed to individual leadership.

Finally, we note one caveat to our analyses. This concerns the multicultural makeup of each of these countries. As we have already observed, the Australian population currently encompasses a wide range of nationalities from around the world. In the instance of New Zealand, Mäori cultural values (such as the higher emphasis on communal relationships) differ in many respects from the dominant European values surveyed in this study. As such, cultural differences between the different ethnic groups will mean that there is variation in leadership styles within each country, as well as between them. Nonetheless, the themes that have emerged in our data are consistent with the historical development of culture in Australia and New Zealand, and therefore represent an overarching style of effective leadership in the Antipodes.

In conclusion, characterizations of effective leadership in Australia and New Zealand share an underpinning of deeply culturally embedded egalitarianism. Thus, to a large extent, those behaviors that constitute effective leadership in Australia will also be perceived as effective in New Zealand. As such, we label leadership in the Antipodes as Egalitarian Leadership. Within this model, however, styles of effective leadership in Australia and New Zealand also exhibit subtle differences. The best managers will understand and appreciate these differences, and adjust their approaches to leadership accordingly.

## References

Ashkanasy, N.M., & Falkus, S (In Press). "The Australian Enigma." In J. Chhokar, F. C. Brodbeck & R. J. House (Eds.), *Managerial Cultures of The World: A GLOBE Report of In-Depth Studies of the Cultures Of 25 Countries*. Thousand Oaks, CA: Sage.

Chhokar, J., Brodbeck, F.C., & House, R.J. (In press). *Managerial Cultures of the World: A GLOBE Report of In-Depth Studies of the Cultures of 25 Countries*. Thousand Oaks, CA: Sage.

Den Hartog, D.N., House, R.J., Hanges, P.J., Dorfman, P.W., Ruiz-Quintana, A., and GLOBE Associates. (1999). "Culture specific and cross-culturally generalizable implicit leadership theories: Are attributes of charismatic/transformational leadership universally endorsed?" *Leadership Quarterly*, **10**(2), 219-256.

Feather, N.T. (1994). "Attitudes toward high achievers and reactions to their fall: Theory and research concerning tall poppies." In M.P. Zanna (ed.), *Advances in Social Psychology*. New York: Academic Press.

Hofstede, G. (1980). *Culture's consequences: International differences in work-related values*. Thousand Oaks, CA: Sage Publications.

Hofstede, G. (2001). *Culture's consequences, Second Edition: Comparing values, behaviors, institutions, and organizations across nations*. Thousand Oaks, CA: Sage Publications.

House, R. J., Hanges, P. J., Ruiz-Quintanilla, S. A., Dorfman, P. W., Javidan, M., Dickson, M. W., Gupta, V., and GLOBE Associates. (1999). "Cultural influences on leadership and organizations: Project GLOBE." In W. H. Mobley, M. J. Gessner, & V. Arnold (Eds.). *Advances in Global Leadership*, vol. 1(pp, 171-233). Stamford, CN: JAI Press.

House, R. M., Hanges, P.J., Javidan, M., Dorfman, P. W., Gupta, V., and GLOBE Associates. (Forthcoming, 2004). *Leadership, Culture, and Organizations: The GLOBE Study of 61 Societies*. Thousand Oaks, CA: Sage Publishing.

Kennedy, J. C. (In Press). "Leadership and Culture in New Zealand". In J. Chhokar, F. C. Brodbeck & R. J. House (Eds.), *Managerial Cultures of The World: A GLOBE Report of In-Depth Studies of the Cultures Of 25 Countries*. Thousand Oaks, CA: Sage.

McGibbon, I. C., & Goldstone, P. (2000). *The Oxford companion to New Zealand military history*. Auckland, NZ: Oxford University Press.

Moodie, A. (1998). *Local Heroes: Celebration of success and leadership in Australia*. Prentice Hall: Australia.

Trevor-Roberts, E., Ashkanasy, N. M., & Kennedy, J. (2003). "The egalitarian leader: A comparison of leadership in Australia and New Zealand." *Asia-Pacific Journal of Management*, **20**(4), 513-536.
Yukl, G. (1989). "Managerial Leadership: A review of theory and research." *Journal of Management*, **15**(2), 251-289.

# Endnotes

---

[1] The description of Australian history and culture is adapted from *The Australian Enigma* (Ashkanasy & Falkus, 1997) while the New Zealand culture analysis is adapted from *Leadership and Culture in New Zealand* (Kennedy, in press). Both of these articles form part of the GLOBE Anthology (Chhokar, Brodbeck & House, forthcoming 2004).

[2] Although under joint command, ANZAC soldiers served in their own countries' units and uniforms. The term 'Australasian Corps' was originally suggested for this force, but there was a reluctance among both Australians and New Zealanders to lose their separate identities completely (McGibbon and Goldstone, 2000).

[3] Australian respondents comprised 344 middle-level managers in the telecommunications and financial sectors. They were employed in 15 different companies. The New Zealand respondents comprised 184 middle-level managers in the telecommunications, financial, and food-processing industries, employed in 36 companies.

# Index